'32 Ford
THE DEUCE

'32

THE DEUCE

A formal and sporting history of
Ford's first V8 and the Model B

Tony Thacker

OSPREY

DEDICATION
'We did not invent the 8-cylinder car. What we did
was to make it possible for the average family to
own one. As always, we have done the pioneering
work. Motor manufacturing practices will follow
the trail we have blazed.'

Henry Ford

First published in 1984 by Osprey Publishing Limited
12–14 Long Acre, London WC2E 9LP
Member company of the George Philip Group
Reprinted spring 1985

British Library Cataloguing in Publication Data

Thacker, Tony
  The deuce.
  1. Ford automobile
  I. Title
  629.2'222   TL215.F7
ISBN 0–85045–594–4

Editor Tim Parker
Design Joy Fitzsimmons

Filmset by Tameside Filmsetting Ltd
Ashton-under-Lyne, Lancs
Printed & bound by Butler & Tanner Ltd
Frome, Somerset

Contents

Preface

It was dark, the roads were glazed with ice and snow, and the temperature was down around −20 degrees centigrade. Nothing unusual in that, it was after all February in Sweden and my wife and I were heading north from Gothenburg. Nothing unusual in that either. We had made the trip practically every winter for almost a decade. Something, however, was to happen which would change the direction of my life for the next few years.

We eventually arrived at the home of Bengt and Maj Sandin, where we were to spend the night. Bengt is an old friend who, like me, is into motorcycles and old cars, especially old Fords. As we talked Bengt told me about a 1932 Ford Tudor sedan that he had found in a Swedish scrapyard and purchased for a mere £100. A real find in a country whose people have scoured every yard in Scandinavia in the search for vintage tin. I exclaimed how I had always wanted a '32 Tudor, and Bengt's reply was to say that I could have the body from this one. All he wanted was the chassis and grille shell.

I couldn't believe it, a '32 sedan and all I had to do was get it back to England.

It would be another two years before I managed to get the car, or what was left of it, home, but in the meantime I had one of the great disappointments of my life.

Speaking about my 'find' to another Swedish friend, Bo Bertilsson, I was told that the car was mine only because nobody else wanted it. I didn't understand what he was saying until he explained that the English sedans were ugly and nothing like their American counterparts.

I still didn't know exactly what Bo meant, so I got hold of pictures of two hot-rodded English Model B sedans owned by photographer Mike Key and John Wilkinson, and compared them to pictures of American '32s. The most obvious difference was in the doors; the American version had conventional rear-opening doors, but the English car had front-opening, suicide doors. There were other more subtle differences; nothing specific, but they just looked different.

At the time I was working as technical editor of a British publication, *Hot Rod & Custom* magazine, so I decided it would make an interesting feature to chronicle the differences and try to explain why Ford, who didn't usually do things like that, had bothered to make two slightly different versions of the same model.

My search led me initially to Ford's UK head office in Brentwood, Essex, where public affairs officer David Burgess Wise opened up their archives. Unfortunately, there was very little, except back numbers of the *Ford Times* and a production record for Dagenham. The Model Bs were shown on this, but there was no information as to why they should differ from their American counterparts.

When I wrote the article I knew enough to state that the bodies were entirely different, but I could only surmise as to why. The question lodged itself in the back of my mind.

Eventually, I got back to Sweden with a trailer to collect my now less than desirable 'English' sedan. The pile of rusty, battered and torn body panels which greeted me was a sad sight. I'd only previously seen the car, when complete, in the

early winter light of a Swedish morning. What I had here was a true basket case. Stupidly I never took any photographs of my find, but believe me it was bad. So bad that when the UK customs talked about import duty I declined and offered to let them keep the rusty remains. They, too, declined.

Once home, careful inspection revealed that although it was an English sedan in pretty bad shape, the cowl and front screen being separated from the rear portion of the body, it was mostly all there and thankfully, due to Henry's use of heavy-gauge steel, probably repairable – but not by me. I am not the world's best metalworker, I'm not even one of its also rans. Sadly I decided to pass the car on to my old friend Robin Ditcher, who is slowly restoring the car.

The question of the American and English versions continued to puzzle me and I determined to find the answer. After checking several references the realization came to me that there were no books specifically about the 1932 Fords. Sure there was original material like the *Ford Times* and there were excellent restoration guides like Ray Miller's *The V8 Affair*, but nothing relating to the car's development.

I don't really remember when the idea to write my own book came. I only know that it took me about a year to get around to approaching Tim Parker at Osprey with my proposal. To my surprise he was keen to go ahead and immediately had contracts drawn. What surprised me more was the amount of time it would take me to complete the manuscript. I thought a few months, maybe six, would see it finished; instead it has been almost two years, and even now I feel I have a lot to learn.

The problems began when I realized there were so few sources to turn to. Brentwood had revealed little upon my initial inquiry, most of their early records having been thrown away when Ford moved offices.

So I went to Dearborn and the Ford Archives and even there many of the pre-production

photographs had been lost in a library fire in 1971. Was this a conspiracy I wondered? Nevertheless, I persevered, unlocked the door of the archive accessions and have, I believe, got as close as anyone to understanding the development of the 1932 Fords.

In some ways I am thankful to Henry Ford, who kept records of everything, especially on film, but unfortunately he developed his V8 engine in secret and paid scant attention to the appearance of the car it was to power. There is therefore little on file to indicate what happened to whom and when. I am, however, grateful to the Ford Archive Oral History staff, who conducted and transcribed interviews with Ford staff in the early fifties. Without those reminiscences nobody would be able to collate the colourful history of Ford. It was these personal accounts, plus the books written by Harry Bennett and Charles Sorensen, which led me off in a slightly different direction to look at the times, the man and the company. Sometimes the action outside the Rouge was just as interesting as what was going on inside.

I have therefore not set out to write a restorers' guide; there are several of those around already and not without their mistakes, I might add. Instead I have tried to write about Henry Ford, why it was important that he built the 1932 Ford and why it has made such an impact on the motoring world from Indianapolis to Indo-China.

This book is a tribute to those guys who have raced, rallied, rodded and restored what in my opinion was one of Henry's finest. Without their interest there would not be the huge market there is nowadays for reproduction '32 parts, which just about enable you to build a complete car from new components exactly as Henry had it built over fifty years ago.

Tony Thacker
Tunbridge Wells, Kent
June 1984

LEFT *Bengt Sandin loads his find, a rare English bodied '32 Tudor, onto a truck. He kept the chassis but gave the body to me. Sadly this was way beyond my restoration capabilities so I moved it on. Instead I built the hot rod Roadster,* RIGHT. *It is based on an original pair of rails but sports an English made fibreglass body (with detachable hard top), Ford V6 power with a C4 auto box and a Jaguar Mk 2 Powr-Lok rear axle. The car took two years to build at the same time as I was writing this book – both were finished in early 1984*

Foreword by Jeff Beck

The myth is that I bought my first Deuce for £125 in London's Portobello Road, but that's not true. The truth is I swapped a '63 split-window Chevrolet Corvette for it and £800. John Crittall, the car's previous owner, was the one who bought it for the ridiculous sum of £125 from the Portobello Motor Company. My 'Vette was forever laid up in Alain de Cadeney's workshop, so I used to borrow John's car to smoke around in.

I knew a bit about hot rods even then, having devoured every American rodding book and magazine I could find since my teens, so I knew that the car had the right look. It even had a V8, someone having fitted English Ford Pilot running gear complete with the flattie and juice brakes; it was already a hot rod when I bought it. Well, eventually John wanted the car back. I didn't want to part with it, so in the end he took the 'Vette, gave me £800 and I kept the '32.

It was about then that I met Celia Hammond. She'd seen me smokin' the 'Vette around London and decided that she wanted me and the car. When we eventually met she couldn't believe I'd swapped the 'Vette for that old pile of junk – which it was. The suicide doors flew open, it only had half a window in the driver's door and I would cut my arm every time I signalled right; it was a bastard to start and it jumped all over the road and would only run up to 70 mph, but I loved it. *Bonnie and Clyde* had just been released and that old Tudor really caused a stir in Chelsea.

By now I was really getting into '32s, reading all the magazines, and then I remembered that de Cadeney's American mechanic used to talk about an old 'Uncle Henry' parked in their mews. That was rodded too, with a Chrysler Hemi and a Jaguar front axle, but by the time I'd traced the owner the car had gone.

Nevertheless, those were happy times, London was the place to live, my music career was taking off and I earned enough money from a tour to do the sedan up, so I took it back to R. W. Lawrence in Croydon, England, where I'd worked as an apprentice. This time they were going to work for me and I had them strip and repaint the whole car in Rolls-Royce Regal Red, and that cost me £280. Retrimming cost another £400, but the car was still mechanically the same, only getting worse.

In 1965 I made my first solo tour of the USA and saw my first street rods. I even got the chauffeur to stop one day and ask a guy if he would give me a ride in his T bucket. He did and I was hooked. I flew back to England with my first American hot rod, a T bucket called the *Boston Strangler*. I drove that T all summer until the English weather finally drove me back into the sedan. I decided to fix it up and fit a Chevy V8, which was the hot thing then according to the magazines. The guy who sold me the T, Rick Heinrich, said he'd send over all the bits and then fly over himself to help put it together. In due course the bits, a Chevy V8 with a Turbo-Hydro box, a Corvair front end and a Chevelle rear axle and Rick, arrived. Along with an old friend, Les Chester, we then spent the next three months working in a filthy old Nissen hut fitting it all under the sedan and we never took the body off. I learnt a lot that winter, including how to weld, but the steering geometry was all wrong, probably because we tried to adapt the wrong steering box or maybe because of the 13 in wide slicks. They were illegal for England, but I drove the car to London and back. The look was right, it was low in front and had that California rake. Eventually, I narrowed the wheels and painted it myself, but by then my tastes were changing and I knew what I had wasn't quite right.

Two years later I went to the Street Rod Nationals in Memphis, Tennessee. There were 1200 street rods and I was blown away. I was looking for something to buy and had my eye on a five-window coupé, but Celia had spotted this hi-ridin' three-window built for street 'n' strip. The owner-builder, Lynn Pew, worked for GM and that 327 had all the right parts and ran real strong. When I bought the car and told Lynn we were

Rockstar and rodder Jeff Beck hangs onto the windscreen of his steel Roadster recently rebuilt by the driver, Roy Brizio. The Roadster now resides in California with a couple of other of Beck's Bs. There are, however, four more back home in Britain. Jeff's been foolin' with such machines almost 20 years now and still finds time to handle much of his own work

setting out to drive to Chicago to fly it home, he couldn't believe it. It had a 4.56 rear.

After a 700-mile drive and a 4000-mile flight the car was back home and I knew then that this and not the T bucket was my first real hot rod; this was after all a '32 Deuce Coupé. Gradually the English weather got to the straight yellow paint, so I resprayed it pearl yellow and Aztec Gold candy with cobwebbed panels, but I drove it every day.

In the back of my mind I still wanted a five-window, and in 1974 someone told me to go see a movie called *American Graffiti* and, just like so many other kids, I wanted that coupé. I called Pat Ganahl, then editor of *Street Rodder* magazine, and asked if he knew of any five-windows for sale. Within half an hour he rang back with four numbers. The car I eventually bought, unseen, other than Polaroids, from Ron Foreman was shipped to England and turned out not to be the expected rip-off but a great car with a trunk full of spares. I sat in the car, poked my arm through the rolled-down window in that classic Milner pose and loved it. Some time later Pat took me to Universal Studios to meet George Lucas and see the actual car used in the film, but Lucas didn't want to sell it. You know, I think Lucas is Milner; you don't make a film like that and not be part of it, just look at the sequel.

1976 became a high spot in my love affair with the '32 Ford, I bought three of them. By then I had been accepted by the American rodders, so much so that Andy Brizio lent me his roadster and that got me hooked on rag tops. Meanwhile I'd bought another five-window from Roy Fjastad of the Deuce Factory to use as daily transport during an enforced exile from the British Inland Revenue. Then I heard about this '32 Hiboy owned by Dick Rundell. He was desperate to sell and Dan Woods talked me into buying it. It had an Ardun conversion, four pairs of Webers and smoked like hell. While I was out of town I had Pete & Jake's pull the smoker in favour of a small-block Chevy, and it was great to have them pick me up at the airport in it just a few weeks later.

As if that wasn't enough I went to a swap meet that turned out to be disappointingly full of classic cars. Disappointing until I heard the unmistake-able sound of a Chevy V8 and through the lot rumbled a chopped '32 Tudor called *Super Prune*. I'd seen the car in plenty of magazines; it had been an Oakland Show sweepstakes winner in '67 and had been built by Phil Kendrick. The car was for sale and the next day Celia and I bought it for just $6000. Although he'd taken my money the guy tried to back out of the deal and it took me two days to get the car. By the end of 1977 I was the proud owner of six Deuces.

Not content, I went to the 1978 Street Rod Nationals at Columbus and found a chopped Tudor body which, from the hieroglyphics on its door, had seen life as a taxi in San Francisco's Chinatown. Besides four buckets of accumulated sand the body contained a 1938 copy of the *LA Times*. The body was shipped home to England and was to replace the tired old English sedan which had never been quite right.

It is a sad fact that the English climate and street rods don't go together, and trying to keep all the cars in perfect condition is impossible, but gradually they are all coming together. The three-window has a new Deuce Factory chassis, a recent chop and new candy red paint. The *Graffiti* coupé, though slightly impractical for England, is almost complete even down to the one-into-four fuel block, but I still need a Man-A-Free four-carb manifold. The ex-Fjastad five-window has a new Roy Brizio frame, a blown small-block and shiny new black paint. The roadster met a tree late one night, and went back to Roy Brizio for a complete rebuild, and there it stays for the time being. *Super Prune*, well, that sat in the back of the garage, an old Scout hut, and just about survived the weather; it has recently been shipped back to California where it belongs. The Columbus sedan got built but never really got finished because I got sidetracked with a '34 coupé, but I'll get around to it.

The only addition of late is the cherryist three-window coupé that I found right here on my own doorstep in Yorkshire. The car was a four-cylinder right-hand-drive model in almost perfect restored condition. That sits in another corner of the garage complete with a flathead V8 ready for my old age when I want to drive a stock Deuce. You see, I just love 1932 Fords.

That original English Tudor was sold several years ago and I know it went to make the mould for a poor fibreglass replica, but after that it vanished. I often wondered what happened to it until, helping Tony with his research for this book, we traced the car to Birmingham, where it is in the hands of Paul J. Mason and Al Stevens. Al, a restorer by trade who works for Paul, intends to rebuild the car, as a hot rod, which it always was, with a 400 ci Pontiac V8.

Old Fords never die, they just go faster.

Jeff Beck

Acknowledgements

I have read much and talked to thousands of people about '32 Fords. I can only thank them all most sincerely. The list of books will do as a bibliography also.

BOOKS
Allard, the Inside Story by Tom Lush
British Cars of the Early Thirties compiled by Olyslager Organisation
Henry Ford by Cy Caldwell
Henry Ford by William Adams Simonds
Ford: The Times, The Man, and the Company; *Ford: Expansion and Challenge 1915–33*; *Ford: Decline and Rebirth*; all by Allan Nevins and Frank Ernest Hill
Ford by Booton Herndon
Ford: The Dust and The Glory by Leo Levine
Ford V8 Service Bulletins by Post-Era Books
Early V-8 Ford Service Manual by Clymer Publications
Forty Years With Ford by Charles E. Sorensen
Moving Forward by Henry Ford and Samuel Crowther
Mill & Factory 1936 by Conover-Mast Corp.
The Best of Ford by Mary Moline
The Cars That Henry Ford Built by Beverly Rae Kimes
The Big Idea by Dennis Hackett (The story of Ford in Europe)
The Early Ford V8 by Edward P. Francis and George DeAngelis
The Encyclopedia of the American Automobile by Karl Ludvigsen & David Burgess Wise
The Ford Dynasty by James Brough
The Ford Road by Lorin Sorensen
The Triumph of an Idea by Ralph H. Graves
The Wild Wheel; The World of Henry Ford by Garet Garrett
The V8 Affair by Ray Miller
Wildbill to Wildcat by Keith Barber
Showtime by Michael Sheridan and Sam Bushala
1932 Ford Judging & Restoration Standards by David G. Rehor
The Fordiana Series by Lorin Sorensen
We Never Called Him Henry by Harry Bennett
Picture A Ford by IPC Transport Press Ltd.
Various Ford reprints by Polyprints
Ford 1903 to 1984 by David L. Lewis, Mike McCarville and Lorin Sorensen
Skywalking – The Life and Films of George Lucas by Dale Pollock
Legion Ascot Speedway 1920s – 1930s by John R. Lucero

I would also like to thank a host of magazine publishers, editors and journalists .who have provided bits of information, photographs or just leads in this never-ending search.

Business Press International Ltd – *Motor*
Campbell Publishing (NZ) Ltd – *New Zealand Hot Rod*
Challenge Publications Inc. – *Rod Action* magazine
Ford Publishing – *Custom Rodder* magazine
Floyd Clymer – *Veda Orr's Hot Rod Pictorial*
Graffiti Publications – *Australian Street Rodding*
Haymarket Publishing Ltd. – *Classic and Sports Car*
Krause Publications – *Old Cars Wekly*
Link House publications – *Custom Car*
McMullen Publishing – *Street Rodder* magazine

A special thanks go to the Petersen Publishing Company, which has, over the past 20 years, given me hours of pleasure with all of their titles including *Hot Rod* magazine, *The Best of Hot Rod*, *Peterson's History of Drag Racing*, *Ford in the Thirties* by Paul R. Woudenberg and the *Complete Ford Book* series. If Pete Petersen hadn't been there encouraging, supporting and recording those early days, none of this would have been possible.

A special thanks must go to the members of The Early Ford V8 Club of America, who perpetuate the Ford tradition, and to the staff and contributors of the club magazine, *The V8 Times*. This has been a constant source of news, interest and information, and is one of the few things I watch the postman for.

There have also been a bunch of people who have been unquestionably helpful in the research and compilation of this material. Without them none of it would have been possible and I thank you all.

Jeff Beck, Pat Ganahl, Frank Oddo, Mike Key, Dick Scritchfield, Tom Lush, Alan Tiley, Keith Barber, David Burgess Wise, C. J. Prew, Bert Thomas, Tommy Jeakins, Brian Giess, Bengt and Maj Sandin, Roy Fjastad, Claus Espeholt, Hans Thudt, Dave Cole, David Rehor, Tom McMullen, James A. Moore, Steve West, Kent Jaquith, Leif Fredriksson, Tex Smith, Warren Hokinson, Steve Knowles, Chris Nicoll, Nick Orme, Ian Penberthy, Pierre Alexandre, Wally Wheatly, and, of course, Tim Parker, who agreed to publish.

Organizations that supplied photographs include BBC Hulton Picture Library, Henry Austin Clark Jr Collection, The National Motor Museum at Beaulieu, Indianapolis Motor Speedway, United Press International, National Film Archive, and, of course, the 'Henry Ford Museum, The Edison Institute', which is an invaluable source of material for any Ford historian.

Lastly, I would like to thank Henry Ford, his family and all his employees, past and present, for making the whole project possible and purposeful.

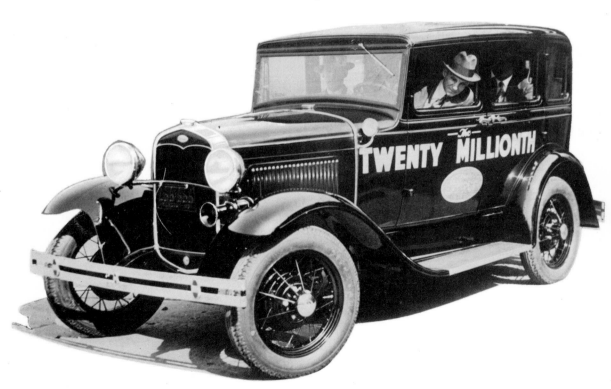

1 Chevy beats Ford?

After a run of 19 years and a production total in excess of 15 million units the Model T, upon which the Ford empire was founded, almost caused its collapse. The car, good though it still was in 1927, had been upstaged by its contemporaries, and the director of this epic, Henry Ford, was not altogether blameless. His dogmatic resistance to change must have pleased the other American automobile manufacturers and their bankers when, for the first time, Chevrolet beat Ford into the number one position.

Competition was springing up all around Ford, adopting his mass-production methods and perhaps, though he would never admit it, turning out better cars. Hardly a stylish car, the T was nevertheless a sturdy stump puller, but technical advancements put its 176 ci four-cylinder engine, producing a mere 20 bhp, way behind the competition. They were already toying with, if not actually producing, stylish cars with six- and eight-cylinder engines.

That first body blow came in a year when new car registrations were down by nearly one million units. For Chevy not only outsold Ford, but they did it to the tune of a quarter of a million more cars. Ford had of course been shut down for most of the year, throwing 60,000 workers out onto the street, trying to get the new Model A into production. It was eventually released on 2 December, but its conception and birth had been slower and costlier than was anticipated. It was almost 18 months from 26 May, when the last T rolled off the line, until the A was in full production, at 6000 units per day, in November 1928. The cost to Ford had been heavy, over one billion dollars (US) and the loss of market leadership in 1927 and again in 1928, when Chevy outsold Ford by another quarter of a million units.

The new product may have seemed advanced for Ford, which it was, but within the automotive world as a whole it was regarded as already obsolete. The four-wheel brakes were new, as was the three-speed selective transmission, but the engine was a primitive door stop.

Initially laid out by Laurence Sheldrick the prototype produced only 20 bhp, no more than the T engine it was supposed to replace. In desperation Harold Hicks was given three weeks to double its output, and double it he did. Enlarged water passages, a Y-type manifold, a Zenith carburettor and matched gaskets increased the output to the desired 40 bhp.

Better than nothing, or even the initial 20 bhp, it was still less than most of the competition. Only Chrysler and Dodge had output figures lower than the Model A and both of their engines were in their final year of production and not their first. Most of the contemporary engines produced in the region of 50 bhp, the A suffering from archaic pressure lubrication, a small-diameter crankshaft lacking counterbalancing, both of which restricted the rev limit, and poor breathing. It can be argued that the A's shortcomings were due to Henry Ford's inflexible engineering principles.

However, what did make the A snappy was its power-to-weight ratio. Weighing in at a mere 2400 lb it was 500 lb lighter than Chrysler's six, which produced 54 bhp, and a whopping 1000 lb lighter than the smallest 63 bhp Buick. The weights of all cars were rising with the exception of Ford, where Henry conducted a relentless search to reduce both the number of parts and their weight, saying, 'The more a car weighs, naturally the more fuel and lubricants are used in propelling it; the less weight, the lighter the expense of operation. Weight has nothing to do with strength.' The A's massive displacement, 200.5 ci, helped to account for its gobs of torque.

ABOVE *Chevrolet took the lead in the sales race for the first time in 1927 and repeated its victory the following year. 1928 would also see the introduction of its first six cylinder engine*

LEFT *The Model A, introduced at the very end of 1927, was a typical Ford product. A sturdy stump puller with a good power to weight ratio but with little attention paid to its appearance. Initial sales might have been better had Ford been ready for full scale production when the car was introduced. Instead it took them almost 18 months to reach full capacity and it would be 1929 before they had Chevrolet licked*

A good turn of speed and plenty of acceleration were qualities which soon endeared the Model A to the public. It had other familiar Ford attributes such as reliability, robustness and cheapness, which soon put Ford back on top. With the slow gestation period over Ford once again licked Chevy in 1929 by over half a million registrations and made a resounding profit of 91 million dollars.

The competition, however, were not standing still, they had tasted victory, had seen that the giant could be toppled and were busy developing chassis, suspensions, engines, transmissions and, perhaps more significantly, styling. Registrations of other marques began to climb, and although this indicated an expanding market which peaked in 1929 it also indicated that Ford was losing its stranglehold on that market. Plymouth almost trebled its share of the market with its now longer, sleeker, more comfortable cars. The comparable Chevys with their six-cylinder engines and six body styles, all priced between $595 and $725, made them the cheapest sixes in the world. Incidentally, Chevrolet's model change-over had taken a mere 120 days, Ford took five months and would not be in full production for almost 18 months.

Luckily for Henry his son Edsel was more a stylist than an engineer and he made a significant contribution to the development of the Ford product during the thirties. Indeed Henry said of him, 'He knows style – how a car ought to look.' The A, styled after the Lincoln, a division of the Ford Motor Company operated by Edsel, premièred annual body changes unprecedented at Ford in the twenties.

Unfortunately the boom time was about to end and although Ford had one of its best years in 1929 with registrations well over $1\frac{1}{4}$ million units, almost as high as the Model T in its heyday, the last week of October would see an end to steady growth for many years to come. The Wall Street crash devastated the industrial world, causing banks and industries to close overnight, throwing millions of workers penniless on to the streets. The automobile industry fared perhaps worst of all, even the giants such as Ford and General Motors were to see a dramatic drop in sales.

As we have experienced with the recession of the eighties, the slump of the thirties was to see no magical quick recovery; it would be a long, hard slog. Henry Ford, mistakenly foreseeing a rapid upturn, tried to compensate for the shortage of money by cutting his prices. This he did by slashing his dealer discounts from 20 to 17.5 per cent. As there was a huge glut of second-hand cars on the market all this did was to put many dealers out of business or cause them to switch to other more profitable makes. He had already been forced to put up some of his Model A prices when it was made clear to him that some body styles actually lost money; on the Tudor it was $300. Nevertheless he battled on in his entrepreneurial way, announcing in November the $7 day and a 60 million dollar building programme. Regardless of his efforts the world market shrank by 40 per cent and world automobile production was halved.

Ford's market share, as a result of 29 million dollars' worth of advertising, rose in 1930 by over five per cent, but sales actually fell by a quarter of a million. 1931 was worse if anything with sales falling by another half a million, and for the third time Ford lost the market leadership to Chevrolet.

In fact Ford's production was down by almost 50 per cent, whereas Chevrolet's drop was negligible. Henry Ford knew that something had to be done, something which would catch the imagination of the buying public just as much as his beloved Model T had.

2 An eight or a four?

Of course, Henry had known all along what was going on, but being a secretive man had told few of his plans or experiments. It is difficult, in these days of shareholders, directors, unions, worker participation and their consequent, endless meetings, to appreciate the way in which Henry Ford, worked. Had that popular term 'the man' been in use then it might have been coined to describe Henry Ford, because in world industry in the thirties he was 'the man'. The massive Rouge River plant at Dearborn, just 15 miles from Detroit, Michigan, now the world's largest manufacturing complex, covering 1200 acres, had been in production since 1920. The Edison Institute, Henry's memorial to his friend Thomas A. Edison, opened in October 1929 and displayed, in both the Henry Ford Museum and Greenfield Village, the history of America. His Village Industries plan, to take work to agricultural areas, was already supplying him with steering wheels and speedometers. His soya bean experiments were progressing and would, within the next few years, provide the raw materials for horn buttons, gear knobs and door handles and, although they were not without their problems, the foreign companies and branches were doing well.

Though time-consuming passions these projects still took second place to Henry's first love, the Ford motor car.

He could often be seen wandering around the Rouge plant, where he would stop and talk to his workers, many of whom he knew by name. By checking with everybody he got first-hand, undistorted information and it was this personal contact which found him the men he liked to work with. If a man showed promise and didn't answer back in the negative, Henry would keep an eye on him or possibly take him away to work on some pet project. Such was the case of German immigrant Emil Zoerlein, who eventually retired from Ford in 1959 as manager of the Engine Experimental Fabricating Department. Mr Ford found him at his bench filing an instrument panel for the *Flivver*

Ship (an experimental Ford monoplane) and was impressed. Pretty soon Ford put him to work on some steam engines and then in July 1930 gave him the job of making the ignition system for the V8.

Though there were 14 research laboratories there was no official research and development programme, indeed none of the employees even had working titles. For Henry Ford it was enough that he was in charge, saying, 'We do nothing at all in what is sometimes ambitiously called research, except as it relates to our single object, which is making motors and putting them on wheels. In our engineering laboratory we are equipped to do almost anything we care to do, but our method is the Edison method of trial and error.'

One employee later commented: 'There was a lack of depth in engineering ability in plant engineering, production engineering and advanced engineering. There was no advanced planning as far as I can understand. When we'd compare it with the engineering department of other automobile plants, we didn't have an engineering department.'

So Henry Ford's way was to try it and see and many times he would arrive with a bundled-up pair of overalls under his arm, ready for work. It was A. R. Smith, later to become Sir Rowland Smith, manager of Dagenham, who was ordered by Mr Ford, who was then 67, to 'move over' as he lay beneath the prototype Model Y adjusting the brakes one Sunday in January 1932.

Drawings were also a rare sight in the Ford plant, Ford being almost unable to read them. Invariably Ford would have an idea and would then get someone, or a team, to develop that idea into a component. Even when there was a desperate panic to get the V8 into production, early in 1932, and Laurence Sheldrick tried to hire draughtsmen to get some drawings done for Charles Sorensen, Henry Ford said, 'Well, just make a sketch on the back of an envelope. He can make all you want just from the sketch on the back of an envelope.' Sorensen had to agree, knowing

The massive River Rouge plant, the world's largest manufacturing complex, covering 1200 acres where iron ore goes in at one end and finished cars come out the other. Its establishment in 1920 reduced the production cycle from 14 to four days

full well that it was impossible. Many decisions, changes and developments therefore took place behind Ford's back, his staff resorting to childish tricks to make progress and attain his agreement. To prove that pressed steel was as strong but lighter than a forging, Joe Galamb had to sit on first one and then the other. When the pressing failed to bend Ford declared, 'That's all right.' Joe subsequently became known throughout the plant as 'Stamping Joe' Galamb.

Even Laurence Sheldrick, untitled chief engineer, when trying to sort out the mess, cautioned his conspirators when showing them the results of his labours by saying, 'Don't let anybody ever see this, because we're not allowed to have an organization chart.'

So when Mr Ford was interested things got done, and as his low-priced V8 neared production, Edsel said, 'My father is never happier than when

he is solving some big mechanical problem. When the new Model A was brought out he left many things to others, but I have never seen him give such attention to detail as he is now.'

Engine development had been in progress, if a little slowly and haphazardly, all through the twenties. Various configurations were tried, including several five- and six-cylinder types, but in the main Henry liked fours, saying, 'I've got no use for a motor that has more spark plugs than a cow has teats.'

There had been an X8, begun in 1922, with four pairs of cylinders in a cross form, which might have been destined for the Model A, but it was abandoned in 1928 when C. J. 'Jimmy' Smith, then working in the experimental division, was set to work on the first V8. He recalls that, 'Henry Ford didn't like the six-cylinder engine because the crank was too long and would wind-up; that's the reason he went to the V8.' Experiments were made but nothing came of them because Ford wanted an engine with no water pumps, employing the thermosyphon system used on Model Ts, 'It wouldn't work – it would get too hot.'

Undaunted, Henry Ford pressed on, and in 1929 decided, 'We're going from a four to an eight, because Chevrolet is going to a six.' He abhorred doing anything after the other manufacturers, which may account for his reluctance to adopt various developments.

Distrusting the tendencies of brake fluid he always insisted on mechanical brakes and advertised the 'safety of steel from toe to wheel.' Consequently hydraulic brakes were not introduced to the Ford range until 1939. He preferred torque tube drive as well, saying that Hotchkiss drive squatted under acceleration and jumped when braking. True, but no driver ever complained.

As he revealed his plans to engineer Fred Thoms he also instructed him to, 'Get all the eight-cylinder engines that you can.'

Thoms did as he was told and assembled the nine scrap-yard engines he had obtained for inspection. These came mainly from upmarket cars, all of which were more expensive than a Ford, the lack of cost-effective engineering showing in their construction. Manufacturers such as Cadillac, LaSalle, Viking, Oakland, Cunningham and even Lincoln all produced V8s, but most were of multiple construction, consisting of cylinder blocks and crankcases bolted together. Two previous V8s had been of monobloc design: the 1929 Oldsmobile Viking and the 1930 Oakland Pontiac, but both cars had been much more expensive than a Ford. Nevertheless these vee engines were seen as the ultimate power plant and it was that kind of prestige that Ford was searching for. Ford, however, wanted a cheap V8. He saw immediately that the other more complicated designs made them too expensive for what he had in mind. He planned to build more than 3000 engines a day, whereas his competitors were, in the main, not even building that number in a whole year. He also planned to sell his V8-engined car for less than $600; the other V8-engined cars on the market were mostly above $1000. His own Lincoln cost $4600. Everybody's comment was that a low-priced, mass-produced V8, cast in one piece, was impossible. Henry's answer was, 'Anything that can be drawn up can be cast.'

Development began in earnest in early 1930, but as usual only a secretive Mr Ford could see the whole picture.

Under the direction of Laurence Sheldrick, engineer Arnold Soth had started work on a V8 in May 1930. This 60 degree V8 of square design had a bore and stroke of 3.625 in, giving a total displacement of 299 ci. Once again Mr Ford's directives gave the engineers problems. He wanted this engine built without an oil pump; instead the flywheel would throw oil into a tank in the valve chamber from where it would run down to the bearings. Needless to say it burnt out on the dynamometer. Attempting to overcome this problem Eugene (Gene) J. Farkas, chassis engineer, took it upon himself to design a simple oil pump. Mr Ford was not impressed and showed his displeasure by saying, 'When I want an oil pump, I know a man who can do it for me.'

This rebuke obviously upset Farkas, as he said later, 'Of course I couldn't make any more suggestions. I just went ahead and did the best I could. I wasn't in a very happy frame of mind doing it.'

At about the same time, and unbeknown to anybody else, even Edsel, Ford had started Carl Shultz and Ray Laird working on his ideas in the old Thomas Edison, Fort Myers laboratory relocated from Florida to Henry's Greenfield Village in 1925.

Henry Ford then asked Ed 'Spider' Huff, who had worked with Ford since the Quadricycle and was now head of the electrical laboratory, to develop the ignition system. Huff's unwelcome reply was that it couldn't be done and there was no use bothering with it. That wasn't the kind of answer Ford wanted and that is when he elected Emil Zoerlein to work out the ignition. Ford wanted a distributor mounted on the front of the engine driven directly from the camshaft and said to Zoerlein, 'You'll probably run into a lot of opposition on that, but that is what I want, and that is what is going to go on this engine.' He also cautioned Zoerlein, as he sent him over to the Fort Myers lab., 'What you see back there I want you to keep to yourself and not say a word to anybody about it. We are designing a V8 engine.' Henry Ford was emphatic about its secrecy, even chief engineer Sheldrick was not to know, Ford saying to Zoerlein, 'Keep Sheldrick out.'

Schultz and Laird were concentrating on transferring Ford's ideas into reality, but there seemed little urgency, probably because business was good in 1930 with Ford selling more than one million cars, almost double Chevrolet's total. Progress was in fact so leisurely that in October Ford asked Zoerlein to build him a one-tenth scale working model of his first car, the Quadricycle, as a Christmas present for Edsel. That was finished at 5 am Christmas morning, all three of the engineers working to get it finished in time. They took the rest of the day off, but were back at work the next morning. There were few holidays in the Depression-torn thirties.

Success for Shultz and Laird had come in November, when two different 90 degree V8 designs were completed. One was of the same square dimensions as the ill-fated 299 ci Soth

LEFT *This picture of the four cylinder Model B engine was taken on 29 January, 1932. Although it had the same 200.5 ci capacity as its predecessor, the Model A, it was both lighter and more powerful. England would have two versions, the 24 hp B and the 14.9 hp BF*

BELOW LEFT *This picture of an experimental automatic clutch mechanism was taken on 20 June, 1932. It never went into production*

RIGHT *This early four cylinder chassis was photographed on 2 October, 1931. Notice there is no sign of that distinctive pressing in the side rail, also that the gearbox crossmember merely supports, rather than encloses, the tail-end of the gearbox*

BELOW RIGHT *This aerial photograph was taken on the same day and one can see the lack of strengthening plates around the central crossmember which were added once the car got into production*

engine, but the other had a bore of 3.375 in and a stroke of 3.25 in, giving a displacement of 232.5 ci. With the help of Herman Reinhold, blocks were secretly cast at the Rouge. By February the first engine was running and by June they had four engines, designated Model 24, installed in revamped Model As for road testing. Howard Salle did most of the test driving, but even Henry Ford and his friend Thomas Edison drove them between Dearborn and Ford's winter house in Macon, Georgia. Supposedly this engine was destined for a proposed 112 in wheelbase car which was never produced.

As many as 16 more Model 24s were produced, and though there was still plenty of development work to do the question in Ford's mind was, an eight or a four? He eventually decided that 'the time wasn't right, the Depression was on, business was bad'. Instead he decided to release an improved Model A, and work started on that late in the summer of 1931.

The Rouge was once again buzzing with activity, but nowhere more so than in the engine laboratory, where it was realized that the new four must show a significant improvement over the Model A engine. While the basic block, with dimensions of 3.875 in bore and $4\frac{1}{4}$ in stroke, giving a displacement of 200.5 ci, was retained, numerous modifications were made to increase the power output. A new crankshaft, 10 lb heavier than its predecessor, had larger-diameter main bearings, resulting in an increase in bearing surface area. To this were matched new connecting rods, also with larger-diameter bearings resulting in another bearing surface increase. This assembly, plus the pistons, flywheel and clutch, was all then carefully balanced.

A new, higher-lift camshaft was designed which incorporated a spiral gear cut into the centre

bearing to drive both the new automatic distributor and a new oil pump. This pump gave the new engine forced-feed lubrication and was a significant improvement over the gravity-and-splash-lubricated A engine.

The top end of the engine was also subject to modification. A redesigned cylinder head increased the compression ratio from 4.2:1 to 4.6:1 and machined intake ports were matched to a larger manifold and a bigger, improved carburettor now fed by a fuel pump, greatly improving the engine's breathing capabilities.

Though there was an increase in crankshaft weight the overall weight of the engine, clutch and gearbox assembly was reduced from 473 lb to 447 lb. Thus the Ford engineers had accomplished two goals; they had reduced the weight and had increased the power output from 40 bhp at 2200 rpm to a maximum of 50 bhp at 2800 rpm. A 25 per cent increase was something to be proud of, and as the engine was put into production on 29 November engineers believed they had the perfect four. It may have been perfect for Ford, but as we have seen a 50 hp engine wouldn't have been outstanding in 1927, when the Model A was introduced, and it certainly wasn't in 1932. Contemporary cars, even those with four-cylinder engines, produced more than this and Chevrolet's new six boasted 60 bhp.

A new synchro-mesh three-speed gearbox with helical-cut constant-mesh intermediate gears had been developed during 1930 and 1931 with the aid of Jack Simpson, chief engineer and general manager in the Warner Gear Division of Borg-Warner. It would be a great improvement over the Model A gearbox.

There was also some research and development going on during 1932 into the possibility of an automatic clutch, but it was never to get into production.

Elsewhere in the Rouge, Gene Farkas, who had designed the Model A but had been rebuked by Henry Ford for his unwanted oil pump, was now at work on what, it had been decided, was to be called the Model B. But it was colleague Joe Galamb who came up with a great idea for eliminating the side aprons and suggested a new full-width frame which was visible between the body and the running boards. The new frame would be of 106 in wheelbase, $2\frac{1}{2}$ in longer than the A, and featured a 'Double Drop'. This was in fact only a kick-up over the rear axle; nevertheless it enabled the body to sit nearer to the ground.

Unfortunately these new U-section frames were not torsionally very rigid and to compensate Farkas designed a rectangular section, tubular central cross-member.

It would have been expensive and difficult to make (it necessitated welding) and Charles Sorensen persuaded Henry Ford that it wasn't necessary. Instead he proposed the stamped cross-member used, which imparted little strength, allowed the chassis to flex and consequently adversely affected the steering. Early pictures of the B show the chassis without the full gearbox cross-member, which went into production, and without that distinctive hiccup in the side rails, which was also added prior to production to improve rigidity.

The problem became more apparent as the cars reached the road, and twice dealers would be instructed to mount special strengthening plates. The problem was inherent and Farkas continued with his cross-member campaign until it was accepted for the 1933 model. Henry Ford as usual laid down a few controlling factors, insisting that all his cars had cross (transverse) springs.

His theory was that the unsprung weight of the axle and the wheel must be as light as possible for a good ride. Therefore the light portion of the spring was attached to the wheel while the thick portion was attached to the frame. The theory was good, but it did present problems because his springs were too narrow, and with transverse springs radius rods are needed to locate the axle. Nevertheless, Ford insisted and his engineers complied, and to improve the ride of the Model B they took the hump out of the rear spring and relocated the spring perches behind the axle. This resulted in a wider but lighter spring, a longer spring base and consequently an improved ride. The double-drop frame and the lower rear spring had both helped to lower the overall appearance of the car's silhouette and to continue this theme Farkas opted for 18 in instead of 19 in wheels. These were Ford's new welded spoke wheels of 18 by $3\frac{1}{4}$ in featuring 32 spokes and were made for Ford by the Kelsey-Hayes Wheel Co. With their wider, 18 by $5\frac{1}{4}$ in, Firestone tyres they were mounted on new, 12 in, ribbed brake drums, Farkas increasing the size over the Model A by 1 in to compensate for this heavier, more powerful car.

Something carried over from the Model A was the double-acting Houdaille hydraulic shock absorbers. Ford had insisted on fitting these to the A after saying, 'Somebody must represent the public' and test driving one across an open field. Upon his return he reported, 'Rides too hard. Put on hydraulic shock absorbers.' Houdaille double-acting shock absorbers were only used on high-priced cars such as the Lincoln, and their fitment to the Model A set a new precedent in low-priced production cars.

Languishing in the knowledge that the other manufacturers would have to follow him, as they did, Ford continued to use them in 1932 and in

ABOVE *The Model Y, codenamed Mercury, photographed in March 1932, was designed by Bob Gregorie and was the forerunner of the 1933 Model 40. It was also a scaled down version of the English models for 1932*

BELOW *Where the Model Y was a Model 18 in minature so the Lincoln was its big daddy. Everything about the Lincoln, from its fluted bumper to its belt mouldings was similar in style to the 1932 Fords*

April would uprate their specification to the fully automatic, thermostatic-controlled type, which adjusted themselves according to temperature.

Henry Ford gave many directives for the mechanical design of his automobiles but paid little attention to their styling. He did, however, take note of public criticism of the Model A's cowl-mounted petrol tank. It is unlikely that anybody died as a result of a fire caused by the position of this tank – more often than not it was the impact that killed motorists, but nevertheless there was resistance from both the public and insurance companies to its position. As a result Ford decided it would go at the back and that a fuel pump would deliver petrol to the engine. During its move the tank increased in size from 10 to 14 gallons, but its simple looks belie a complicated construction. Six or eight operations were necessary to draw the two half-stampings out of a single sheet before the formed flanges could be seam welded.

Edsel was more than happy about the tank move because it gave him and designer Eugene T. (Bob) Gregorie more freedom to work on the overall styling.

Gregorie, a boat designer with an eye for streamlining, had started work in Ford's aircraft division in 1931, designing seats and interiors, but had moved under Edsel's wing after Ford drifted away from aviation as a result of his friend and pilot Roy Manning being killed on a test flight. They were, however, still in the aeroplane business. 1932 would see the construction of the last of the tri-motor series and the completion of the 14-A. This was a truely huge aeroplane, bigger than the B-24 bombers Ford would build during the war at Willow Run. Though designed as a passenger plane the 14-A never actually took off.

By 1935 Gregorie had established Ford's first styling department, reinforcing the argument that the 1932 models were all in-house designs based on the preceding Model As. They also reflected the company's general styling trend, which can be seen in the coeval Model Y and Lincoln. I don't believe that they were the work of Le Baron or for that matter of Briggs and possibly destined for Plymouth, as has been suggested by other historians.

Further evidence to support this theory is the fact that both Briggs and Murray were contracted to build bodies for Ford purely on a quotation basis, i.e. the cheapest quote got the job.

Bob Gregorie, according to Laurence Sheldrick's reminiscences, would create styling sketches that were checked by Joe Galamb and Edsel before being put up as full-size clay models.

Pictures of a clay Fordor taken on 10 October, 1931, show a strange car hardly recognizable as the forthcoming '32 Ford. It had an ugly shovelnose grille, moulded-in lights and a raised louvre panel as fitted to the Model A. Interestingly, this was retained for the British models but not the US ones.

At this point Edsel, who had a good eye for styling, would make any criticisms, especially towards the instrumentation and interior. Joe Galamb remembers, 'He was very particular about cushions.' The designers would then make the various changes to the existing clay model – you can see the marks on the front wings where they were eventually cut away – before Edsel checked back, usually in two or three days. After Edsel had okayed the model, drawings for a sample were made, and once that was completed there were no more changes.

Sorensen recounts that, after lunch, 'Edsel would drop in at the body and styling division.

'The tractor, car or truck went through this stage of making small-scale models; then, when one was finally decided upon, a full-scale model would be made. While this was going on, I would drop in on Edsel and discuss the mechanics of the model.

'Henry Ford spent little time on that. Edsel had proved himself a good stylist and his father would let nothing leave Dearborn until Edsel had passed on it.'

One opinion that the grille was designed by Briggs and intended for Plymouth is discounted by Gene Farkas. He remembered remarking to Henry Ford that he didn't like the new Chevy grille because it looked like chicken mesh and Ford replied, 'I'll tell you something, we don't want any chicken wire on our car.' So the new air-flow grille shell was designed, looking every bit like its Lincoln counterpart.

Other similarities between the 1932 Fords and their big brother Lincolns appear in the interior. The instrument panel was of a similar oval shape, but had only three gauges, speedometer, fuel gauge and ammeter, compared to the Lincoln's six.

Placement of the various engine controls changed several times prior to and even once in production and certainly from country to country. Early Model Bs had a black-painted dash panel with only choke and throttle control knobs. The

This full-size clay model of a Fordor was photographed on 20 October, 1931. Thankfully, it's shovel nosed grille and moulded-in headlights never reached production. In fact it would be five years before that styling was adopted for production. Nevertheless, the car has the general appearance of the 1932 models. Whilst the bumper was retained the raised louvre panel was dropped for US models but retained for English versions and one can see the marks where the front wings were cut away

starter button changed position several times and at one point was a T-handled pull-rod.

When the V8 was introduced it had an engine-turned panel, as did the Lincoln, with the throttle control on the left, choke control in the centre and a dash light switch on the right.

By April the Model B had thorn brown, rather than black, panels with the throttle on the left and the choke on the right. No dash light would be provided until June, a month after the damascened panel was also made standard for all models.

The starter button for all American cars was now on the floor between the clutch and brake pedals, but the British B models had this on the left of the dash panel. There was no dash light, and the throttle control was in the centre and the choke on the right.

The cowl vent handle, both the gear and the handbrake levers and the throttle pedal all underwent various design changes until their ultimate shape, which turned out to be very similar to those found on the Lincoln, was settled. Among Ford's other luxuries for a low-priced car he added for the first time a combination steering/ignition lock, again borrowed from the high-priced Lincoln.

ABOVE *Joe Galamb commented upon how Edsel Ford was very critical of interiors, particularly cushions. This prototype interior was assembled in a wooden framework and photographed on 18 February, 1932*

RIGHT ABOVE *These two pre-production Model B interiors photographed on 30 October, 1931 and 7 December, 1931 respectively, show some of the changes made before the car went into production. Notice on the early photograph the T-handled pull-rod starter, position and shape of the gear lever and the design of the cowl vent handle and the handbrake lever. Notice also the throttle pedal which is not at all like the spoon assembly put into production*

RIGHT *Control layouts were standardized early in production but varied from country to country. The American Tudor (right) layout is somewhat different from that found in other models, for example Danish (left) and English (centre) sedans. The main differences are the deep-set dash board with twin glove pockets and the two-piece steering wheel found in the English cars. There are other minor differences such as the starter button which is on the floor in the American and Danish models but is the left hand dash panel button in the English cars. That button in the other cars is the throttle control. The choke control is the right hand button in English cars but the middle button in the others. That right hand button in American cars is the dash light switch but in English cars they came on with the mandatory side lights*

Though the instrument panel was in fact chrome it was finished with a stainless trim, and although Ford had used rustless steel on previous models the '32 was literally covered with the stuff. It was used for all lamp units, hub caps, door handles, grille trim and among other things the petrol filler cap.

In all ten passenger body styles were designed, along with commercial variants, all of them based

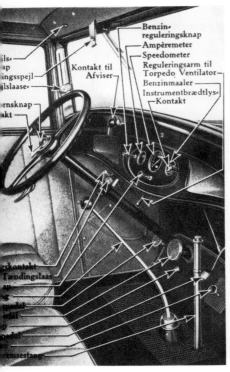

Benzin-
reguleringsknap
Ampèremeter
Speedometer
Reguleringsarm til
Torpedo Ventilator
Benzinmaaler
Instrumentbrædtlys-
Kontakt

Kontakt til
Afviser

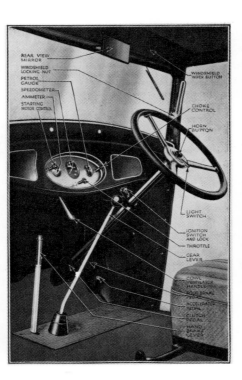

REAR VIEW
MIRROR
WINDSHIELD
LOCKING NUT
PETROL
GAUGE
SPEEDOMETER
AMMETER
STARTING
MOTOR CONTROL

WINDSHIELD
WIPER BUTTON

CHOKE
CONTROL

HORN
BUTTON

LIGHT
SWITCH

IGNITION
SWITCH
AND LOCK
THROTTLE
GEAR
LEVER
COWL
VENTILATOR
HANDLE
COWL BRAKE
PEDAL
ACCELERATOR
PEDAL
CLUTCH
PEDAL
HAND
BRAKE
LEVER

THROTTLE BUTT
AMMETER
CHOKE BUTTON
SPEEDOMETER
COWL VENTILAT
CONTROL
FUEL GAUGE
DASH LIGHT SWI

SUN VISOR
WINDSHIELD
WIPER BUTTON
REAR VIEW
MIRROR
WINDSHIELD
LOCKING NUT
HORN BUTTON
LIGHTING
SWITCH

IGNITION SWITCH
STEERING AND IGNITION LOCK
GEAR SHIFT LEVER
CLUTCH PEDAL
BRAKE PEDAL
STARTER BUTTON
ACCELERATOR PEDAL
FOOT REST
HAND BRAKE LEVER

on previous A models. However, the two-door Phaeton was dropped and in its place came the three-window De Luxe Coupé, which had only been an unreleased prototype in 1931. The 14 beautiful body types eventually advertised included De Luxe versions of the Fordor, Tudor, Phaeton and Roadster. In addition there were two sedans designed especially for the British and European market, a Fordor and a Tudor, both with front-opening, suicide doors.

There was also a third four-door sedan built; it was photographed outside the Ford Engineering building on 2 November, 1931, and in my opinion was an early prototype that never reached production – a strange situation when one considers Joe Galamb's comment that no changes were ever made after the sample was made up.

All of the bodies were publicized as being of one-piece construction, but they were in fact made up of small panels held together in a jig and electrically seam welded before being ground and buffed smooth. Ford had dispensed with wood and hundreds of nuts and bolts, their resultant squeaks and rattles, and can perhaps be forgiven his false one-piece claim.

Bodies built out of the United States and Canada, for instance in England and Australia, still had quite a large wood content, their facilities and equipment not being up to the Rouge standards.

Wood for the Danish-built sedans came from a saw mill at Hov in Jutland, Denmark, where about 100 men were employed. For some strange reason

Cabriolets built in Denmark had their bodies riveted to the chassis.

Ford went welding mad in 1931 and used this new and quite costly process to fabricate not only the petrol tank and bodies but also the rear axle housing and torque tube, exhaust pipe and silencer, radius rods, some cross-members and, of course, his famous welded-spoke wheels.

Although 'Stamping Joe' Galamb was pressing Ford all the time to adopt his stamped steel panels, many parts were still forged. This process was used to form shock absorber arms, rear axle housing ends, torque tube and radius rod ends, spring clips and brake shaft levers.

In a similarly dramatic road test to the one which resulted in the fitting of shock absorbers to the Model A, Ford decided to fit safety glass windscreens to all his cars. Test driver Harold Hicks and a mechanic were thrown through the windshield of an A and were badly cut when a car swerved in front of them. For 1932 Ford not only offered laminated safety glass for the windshield, it was standard throughout on all De Luxe models and was optional at additional cost on everything.

For the first time De Luxe models featured quite prominently in Ford's line-up. Some models such as the three-window coupé, Cabriolet, Convertible Sedan, Victoria and Sport Coupé, though this would become a semi-standard model in mid-April, were available only in de luxe form, and their interiors featured carpets, a choice of upholstery materials, including real leather, arm rests and, surprisingly, because Henry Ford

abhored smoking, ash trays.

Outside, the De Luxe models were adorned with rustless cowl lamps. In Britain, however, side lights were mandatory and these were mounted on top of the wings.

The fluted bumper design was also new for 1932 and was advertised as a safety feature, its double corrugation supposedly preventing another bumper (in collision) from sliding over or under. Interestingly, the same form of bumper was *in situ* on the clay model photographed in October 1931 and scaled-down versions were used on the early Model Ys.

One would think that with all this activity and development going on around him Henry Ford would be a happy man, but he was not. Though, by the end of November, Ford themselves and many of their suppliers were already producing parts for the Model B, Mr Ford wasn't satisfied. As one of his aides quoted, 'His old smile didn't come back as it usually did when things began to hum. Instead, somehow, he seemed to be getting madder and madder. Of course we didn't know what he was thinking – but we knew we weren't yet on the right track.'

By the first week in December Henry had made up his mind. On the morning of 7 December he spent just one hour in consultation with Edsel in his office at Dearborn, where it was decided to cease production of the Model B and for 1932 come out with the world's first low-priced V8. The production lines were stopped, cessation orders went out to the suppliers. In the following days

ABOVE *This odd right-hand drive 4-door was shot outside Engineering as early as 2 November 1931. What it is and why it was built nobody knows. Woudenberg credited it as Spanish. I doubt this, Spanish car bodies would certainly have come from Dagenham or North America, there being no manufacturing in Spain. The Spanish don't drive on the left, either. Experts, David L. Cole and David G. Rehor, suggest that whilst Spain may have built their own bodies this is an American prototype. This too is unlikely because Galamb offers that Edsel never made changes after the sample was made up. If so why did this prototype reach such an advanced stage?*

Note both the similarities and differences between this and production models. Woudenberg describes the wheelbase as 112 in; it certainly looks longer than the standard 106 in. The body is unlike any other production 1932 Fordor; lower over the frame, larger windows, different belt mouldings and no lower moulding. The shape is American around the cowl but English towards the back. The body surrounding the windscreen is American '32 but the chromed windscreen is like that on the late 1931 Model A. The bonnet retains the usual 1932 mouldings but has a raised louvre panel of 22 louvres (a number never stamped into any production side panels). The grille shell appears to be a stamped commercial shell embellished with chrome or stainless trim and fitted with an ornament similar too but not exactly the production version. Lastly, the headlamps appear to be mounted lower and certainly the front wings have a lower leading edge

OPPOSITE ABOVE *In addition Dearborn built a prototype Tudor and Fordor for Europe. Apart from the Model Y these were the first cars Ford had built especially for a foreign market. Although they retained the same American mechanicals the body was entirely different (in fact very similar to the Model Y). Body stamping dies for these bodies were produced at the Rouge, then shipped to England, where Briggs had been encouraged to build a plant at Dagenham. Who saw the need for these models no one knows, sales did not justify the expense of the tooling.*

What is interesting about this photograph is the English style body, complete with right-hand wiper, mounted on a lhd chassis. Incidentally, the Model A raised louvre panel was retained for English production. Note the early crank hole cover and the left side, rear light which should have been on the right for England

Prototype Model B shot on 2 December, 1931 shows the engine with the early type semi-rigid front mount. This was changed in April 1932 with the crossmember, so as to be interchangeable with the V8.

The gearbox crossmember now envelopes the end of the gearbox, unlike the one shown earlier, but that it is not yet a full K-member as released for production. Note the vacuum operated clutch mechanism mounted in front of the starter. In this case on a stamped steel bracket and not the cast bracket with integral water inlet shown on page 155

ABOVE LEFT *Inside, this odd Fordor, from page 27, is an enigma. The dashboard is from a normal sedan but has woodgraining. The dash panel is, however, black as it was on pre-production and early Model Bs but there are only two buttons, the third being removed to the far right side of the dashboard. The steering column is not supported by the usual combination switch*

ABOVE *The 1932 Bodies, built by Ford, Briggs and Murray were advertised as being of one-piece construction. They in fact consisted of stamped sections clamped together and then seam welded and buffed smooth. This Fordor was photographed whilst being assembled on 28 December 1931*

most of the 50,000 workers became busily engaged in ripping out the old equipment and installing hastily designed and manufactured machinery for building the V8.

Few of the staff, and certainly none of the public, knew exactly what was going on. The press were buzzing around Dearborn trying to get a story and the surrounding roads were thronged with photographers and reporters. *Automotive Industries* magazine of 19 December was the first to speculate correctly with an article titled 'Make an Eight, says Ford'. They correctly surmised that Ford was indeed tooling up for a new engine; what they didn't realize, when they said it would go into a 117 in wheelbase intermediate-sized car, was that Ford would merely drop it into his improved Model A.

Of course, some changes would have to be made to accommodate the new engine, especially to the floor pan.

Engine vibration had always been a problem with early four-cylinder engines and was especially so in Ford automobiles. Unfortunately, Henry Ford was slow to accept the possibilities of rubber and Sorensen recounts the arrival of Walter P. Chrysler at Dearborn in his new Plymouth complete with 'Patented Floating Power'. 'He brought his Plymouth car to Mr Ford and me and asked for our opinion of it. The most radical feature of his car was the novel suspension of its six-cylinder engine so as to cut down vibration. The engine was supported at three points and rested on rubber mounts. . . . Henry Ford did not like it. For no given reason, he just didn't like it, and that was that. I told Walter that I felt it was a step in the right direction, that it would smooth out all noises and would adapt itself to axles and springs and steering-gear mounts, which would stop the transfer of road noises into the body.'

So, Mr Ford did not like rubber engine mounts, and sure enough they were not fitted to the Model B even when it went into production. He had, however, taken note of them, as they were fitted to the V8 and would be specified for all models after April.

These mounts had been developed for Ford by Firestone engineers because Ford only had about 200 engineers and, therefore, outside suppliers were often called in to help with development.

Rubber was, for the first time, used extensively by Ford to insulate the passengers from the transmission of noise and vibration. The body was mounted on rubber blocks and an asphaltum-treated fabric placed on the chassis rails. Another first was the use of rubber bushes in both the spring shackles and the shock absorbers. Many other parts were also mounted on rubber pads, including the dashboard and the petrol tank. In all there were over 100 points where rubber was used as either bushings, insulators or anti-rattlers.

Vibration would, however, continue to be a problem, especially with the four-cylinder engine, and to help locate them two $\frac{7}{16}$ in diameter steel rods ran forward from the central cross-member to either side of the engine. There would also be a friction-type shock absorber, mounted to the firewall and bolted to the bellhousing.

Meanwhile, all of this conjecture in the press had caused some concern among Henry's faithful motoring masses. Letters poured into Ford's offices urging that the four type be continued. While this was good news, indicating that the potential market was greater than expected and that some buyers would continue to want fours, Henry found it disconcerting and quickly replied, 'We shall continue to make the four-cylinder model. The eight is only two fours, you know.'

Luckily for him, because of the subsequent production problems, Henry decided to put half his workforce back onto B production while the others and himself concentrated on changing over the plant to get out the V8.

Although Gene Farkas remembers Charlie Sorensen saying at one point, 'Well, we've got to wait until we get through with this eight-cylinder mess.' It was in fact Sorensen, the real originator of the production line, who was responsible for bringing the fledgling into the world. Sorensen

and Herman Reinhold conquered the complex casting techniques needed to produce the blocks and already had pilot production lines ready to roll. It is easy to dismiss these developments in a few words, but those short winter months must have seen an unbelievable amount of feverish work in and around the Rouge plant.

While everything was going in to Dearborn, little, except speculation, was coming out. In early January there were further orders to suppliers for Model B parts, confirming that the B was still on the production schedule, but as yet there had been no word from Ford about what was going on. He was content to let publicity generate itself, that is until early in February, when he and his wife Clara went up to Washington for another one of many meetings with US President Herbert Hoover and other leading industrialists, including Walter P. Chrysler. For some time Hoover had mistakenly thought that things would merely get better, but Henry believed otherwise.

The next morning he announced, 'We're going into production on the V8. We are going to stimulate the economy by the introduction of the V8.' He also announced that he would continue to pay $6 a day, but that wouldn't last for long. To make the announcement of the V8 official he granted a rare, exclusive interview to a respected journalist of the *Detroit News*, James Sweinhart. The interview appeared on 11 February, outlined Ford plans for the coming year and was syndicated across the country, indeed around the world. It even appeared in its entirety in the March 1932 edition of *Ford News*, as

Country Learns of Lord Plans for 1932,

by James Sweinhart.

'What's Henry Ford going to do?'

The whole automobile world has been asking that question since the Spring of 1930, when the industrial paralysis of the world's greatest depression first began to be felt.

And here's the answer:

1 As his major offering for the season now opening he is building a new model, with a new eight-cylinder V-shaped motor.

2 He will continue building four-cylinder cars – an improved Model A.

3 Both the 'V-8s' and the 'Model As' will have roomier bodies of wholly new design, longer wheelbase, lower hung chassis and heavier frame than have yet appeared in any Ford models.

4 The price range of the 10 different models will continue in the low price field.

5 The chassis is so built that the 'eight' and 'four' engines may be interchanged at will.

6 Production will start some time this month with the first public showing early in March.

The question is no longer what Ford is 'going to do' – he's doing it, now, on a mighty and rapidly increasing scale.

A new pulse beats through the vast Ford organization today – it's everywhere evident in the laboratories, the works and the shops.

Henry Ford has again become the direct driving, supervising and creative force behind the engineering undertakings of the Ford Motor Company.

He, personally, is making the supreme effort of his career 'to produce', as he expressed it today, 'what these new times require' – the most advanced form of transportation, at the lowest cost ever known, for the greatest number of buyers ever encompassed by the plans of any one motor manufacturer.

This sudden, tense atmosphere of big things afoot – I asked Ford about it.

He had come into one of the laboratory offices, to sit, for a moment, while something or other was got ready for his eye or hand in the workshops beyond. He was smiling, alertly active, mentally and physically, looking 'fit as a fiddle'. He disposed of my question with a wave of his hand:

'Oh! – That's nothing', he said. 'I've just got back my old determination. That's all.'

'To do what?' I asked.

'To get the price of an automobile down to the mark where the public can buy it. The public will always come half-way to meet a man who does his part to meet the public's demands – I've always found it so.'

Ford moved his chair around, tilted it against the wall and, resting one foot on the edge of the desk, went on.

'You know,' he said, 'the public has suffered a lot. Everything we do now must take into account the people's pocket-book. We developed a corking good "four" and were all ready to let it go, but, we found, it was not the new effort which the public is expecting. That's why we're bringing out the "eight" now.

'You see, the public has its part in these matters. Somehow it instinctively knows when the time is ripe for something new. And even after the industry has produced its best design and developed its best manufacturing method, it only amounts to about 90 per cent of the completed job. The public contributes the other 10 per cent out of its actual use of the car in road experience. Now the public has suffered a lot and has been very patient. It deserves a lot from the manufacturer. From now on the public's pocket-book sits in at every conference.

'And here's something I wish you'd make pretty strong. It's for the raw material supply men. If American manufacturers do their utmost to start the wheels of industry and the material men begin to raise prices, the whole effort may be throttled. In times like these everyone has to take some risk, make some sacrifice and even be willing, for a time, to do business without profit in order to start the normal processes of industry and business again.'

That was Ford's way of disposing of a titanic situation. The first engines Ford ever made had but two cylinders. Then he made a 'four'. The foundation of his whole, world-wide industry was the success of the old Model T 'four'. And the evolution of his 'V-type Eight', now, is not to Ford the epochal event it seems to others. To him it's just another form of his old ideal.

It occurred to me he might have a bit of regret at abandoning the 'four' model. I said as much.

'But we're not abandoning the "four",' Ford answered, 'either in principle or in production. We're going right on making "fours" for all who want them – and the "eight", why, that's just two "fours" put together.'

The idea of building an 'eight' has been in the back of Ford's mind a long time – but it must have been an epochal event throughout the plants of the company the day Ford, personally and alone, decided to bring out an 'eight'.

In the summer of 1921 I remember seeing an 'eight' working on the testing block in the experimental room of the old tractor plant. On the floor nearby, idle, was a 'twelve'. On a pedestal not far away was an X-shaped 'twenty-four'. All multiples of the basic 'four'. And when, in 1927, the Model T was abandoned and the new Model A brought out, it too was a 'four'. But it did not appear until after the results of renewed and extensive experimentation and testing with an 'eight' had been laid aside.

During the latter part of 1930 and the early months of 1931, experimentation with the 'eight' again went forward. The work was done in the Edison laboratory, which Thomas A. Edison used for 40 years at Fort Myers, Florida, and which is now in 'Greenfield', the Ford old American village in Dearborn. Twenty 'eights' were built. Thomas A. Edison rode around in one of them a year ago. Thought was given to bringing the 'eight' model out then – but the depression was on, business was bad, the 'time wasn't right'.

But that didn't dispose of the question. 'An "eight" or a "four"' – in the late summer of 1931 it was again pressing for an answer. It was decided to get out an improved Model A. The engineering laboratories worked long and feverishly at tests and experiments to develop improvements. Ford began to appear daily in the shops, the drafting rooms, the plants, watching the development of each part, watching every detail of design and production – yes, and thinking, deeply, too, those about him say.

Came a day in late autumn when, as one of the Ford lieutenants said, 'we believed we had a perfect "four"'. The improved Model A was put into production. Suppliers all over the country were given orders. Trainloads of raw materials began rolling in. The powerplants started up toward peaks not reached in months. The foundry began working day and night. And the endless carriers of parts started a 24-hour run. Down the assembly lines the improved Model A started rolling in a steady stream.

'But Mr Ford wasn't satisfied', the lieutenant went on. 'His old smile didn't come back, as it usually did when things began to hum. Instead, somehow he seemed to be getting madder and madder. Of course we didn't know what he was thinking – but we knew he felt we weren't yet on the right track.'

Then came the morning of December 7. It was a Monday. Edsel Ford came over from the Rouge Plant and went to his office in the Dearborn laboratories. Henry Ford came over. Father and son were together, alone, for an hour or so. Then suddenly, things began to happen.

Orders went out to the plants to stop production – to

stop production when 35,000 of the new improved 'Model A's', were already manufactured and on their way to the West for early January showing – with 50,000 more of them 'in float'; that is, coming through the plant in finished parts and bodies ready for assembly!

The whole productive organization was suddenly thrown back on its haunches. The carriers slowed down. The trains of raw materials dumped, went out empty and came no more. The assembly line again was empty. Everyone was set to work on something else.

What had happened?

The Ford 'eight' had been born.

Henry Ford had decided to put it into production as his chief offering for the coming year.

That same morning he ordered the laid-away plans to be brought out and prepared for large-scale production.

From that moment Henry Ford personally became the dynamo of the works. He was here, there, everywhere, ordering, directing, changing. A task immeasurable by words confronted him. The whole works had to be changed. Building of the 'eight' would require certain finished parts which Ford did not make – these had to be designed, contracted for, put into production elsewhere. A vast amount of machinery had to be taken out – new machinery, not yet in existence, had to be designed, built elsewhere, brought in and installed. Somehow a rumor got around that Ford had discontinued making the 'fours'. Came a flood of letters urging that the 'four' type be continued. That was good

in itself – it showed something of the market; a lot of buyers would continue to want 'fours'. The volume was much greater than he had planned. For the time, so far as it affected the building of the 'eight', this unexpected demand was rather disconcerting. Ford then had approximately 50,000 men working. He put half of them to work making the improved Model A and with the other half he flung himself into the job of changing over the plant to get out the 'V-Eight'.

Meantime the plans for the 'eight' were coming through. Ford was again about the plant as he was 25 years ago.

'My father is never happier than when he is solving some big mechanical problem,' said Edsel Ford. 'When the Model A was brought out he left many things to others, but I have never seen him give such attention to detail as he is now. He works for hours at a time trying to eliminate a single part. He figures that, the fewer parts in a car the less the risk of trouble. In the Model A this was carried so far that repair bills were cut in two. Our business in parts for the old Model T used to run from $10,000,000 to $12,000,000 a month. On the Model A this fell off to from $3,000,000 to $4,000,000 a month.

It is impossible that 1000s of Model Bs were on their way west for an early showing, as was suggested by Sweinhart. However, this four cylinder Standard Coupé was certainly assembled before the end of November 1931 to have been photographed on 1 December. Details worth noting are the firewall, the starter pull-rod and the crank hole cover

The Model A didn't require as much service.'

Asked as to when the new 'eight' will be ready to show, Edsel Ford said:

'We can't tell, yet. We'll first have to make enough cars to supply our dealers.'

'How certain are you that you have a market for your new cars?' Henry Ford was asked.

'We're not certain,' he replied. 'But we're going to risk it. Someone has to risk something to get things started. And, you know, faith is catching; if we have confidence, others will, too. The chief thing is to meet the public's demand for something new and better at a price the average man can pay. We're doing everything in our power to give the public that kind of a car. It will be the first low-priced automobile in America considering quality and price. And we believe the public will come half way – it always has before.'

'Though you're not certain of your market, you are certain you've got the car?'

'That's it exactly.'

No one would say anything definite, as yet, as to how much the cars will retail for.

—From *Detroit News*, 11 Feb 1932

The automotive world's best-kept secret was out and Ford was to produce the key which would hopefully unlock the mattresses, chests and cookie jars of America, releasing an estimated 1½ billion dollars hoarded by a public who no longer had trust in the banks. James Sweinhart got most of it right except for the part about 35,000 cars on their way west for an early January showing with 50,000 more of them 'in float'. Although there is photographic evidence that some Bs were produced towards the end of 1931, it is unlikely that production was in the tens let alone in the thousands. Remember, there had been only one week's rolling time before Henry decided, on 7 December, to stop and bring out the V8. Ford production records show no Bs being produced until April 1932 and none were shown to the public on that memorable day at the end of March 1932.

Edsel's prophecy that the public would come half-way was proving correct as the whole of America began the gradual journey back to work. Henry Ford had indeed started something; by the second week in February he announced the re-employment of 30,000 men, confidence was gaining, and if the press had been interested in Ford before it was nothing compared to the coverage they gave him in the first quarter of 1932.

There was still much speculation about what the new Fords would look like, how much they would cost and when they would appear. Predictions were made almost daily and in the 16 February edition of the *Automotive Daily News* writer Chris Sinsabaugh declared that the Improved A would sell for $388, or $100 down and $12 a month for 24 months, while the V8 would retail for $588 on about the same terms. Mr Sinsabaugh later went

WHAT FORD ANNOUNCES HE WILL SPEND IN 1932

In Detroit and Michigan, for raw materials, manufactured parts and supplies, freight and shipping rates and labor	$300,000,000
Purchases of raw materials and manufactured parts and supplies throughout the United States, average, per month	52,000,000
In addition to bodies made with his own plants, for bodies from outside makers, mostly in Detroit	140,000,000
To railroads and shipping companies of the country as freight rates	86,000,000
In addition to steel made in his own mills, steel in open market	47,000,000
For Tires	20,000,000
For monthly payroll for 100,000 employes in the Detroit district	18,000,000
For upholstery cloth, carpet, leather and other body trimming materials	48,000,000
For Glass	10,100,000
For additional machinery	6,375,000
For malleable castings	5,044,000
For paint and lacquer	4,854,000
For crude rubber	4,800,000
For gray iron	4,680,000
For hard lumber	4,000,000
For copper	3,500,000
For lead	1,500,000

Handling 236,000 inbound and 228,000 outbound freight cars will require larger railroad working forces.

5,500 suppliers, scattered all over the United States, will employ 300,000 men in addition to those directly employed by Ford.

1,200 of these suppliers are in Detroit and 300 in Michigan, outside Detroit.

on to predict, in the *New York Times*, that a six would replace the four – he was wrong then, too, but I guess it made good copy.

Meanwhile, Mr Ford made himself busy about his factory and kept his own counsel until the end of February, when he announced his intention to spend more than $300 million in Detroit and Michigan alone in 1932. Unfortunately, he could expect little return in the forthcoming year, when he planned to 'risk all' to produce 1½ million cars. Sadly, the total production figure hardly topped the 300,000 mark, but as the V8 engine continued in production almost unchanged for 21 years some return must have been seen.

With production of the first V8-engined cars in sight Ford invited, in the first week of March, selected members of the press to Dearborn to view the new models, six of which stood behind a screen in the corner of a laboratory. The subsequent editorials contained plenty of details about the all-new, long, low, wide, streamlined Ford, but there were still no photographs.

The first picture to appear was of a standard Model B Fordor and it filled half of page 1 of the 9 March edition of the *Automotive Daily News* under the headline, 'The First Picture of the New Ford'. Even though the car pictured was a prototype Improved A it is interesting to note that the V8 engine actually went into production on the same day and 38 were produced.

The following day the *Automotive Daily News* correctly reported that the first completed car had left the assembly line. That first car was a Victoria, and before its body was lowered on to the chassis, principals of the Ford Motor Company looked on as Henry stamped the bellhousing with the figures 18-1. Even wearing his glasses Ford managed to

stamp the figure eight upside down; it was nevertheless an important moment as the one and eight signified his first eight-cylinder engine and the 1 the first one off the line. That first engine, or possibly another one stamped 18-1, now resides in the Henry Ford Museum.

A similar ceremony took place in Walkerville, Ontario, Canada, in March, when W. R. Campbell, President of Ford-Canada, stamped the first V8 to be produced there. The Walkerville plant went on to produce a total of 29 V8-engined cars in March. Production increased steadily over the next few months, but at nowhere near the pace of the Rouge. Meanwhile, Ford's other domestic plants, 33 in all, began to report ready for production, though none would go on-line until April, when the Rouge was able to ship engines.

Total domestic production for March was 1102 V8 passenger cars, two V8 passenger chassis, various A, AA, B and BB comercials in both built-up and K.D. form, plus 1000 four-cylinder passenger vehicles also in K.D. form for export.

Ford claimed an overwhelming 75,000 firm orders for the new V8 by 5 March, sight unseen. Only a few photographs had as yet been published and then only in the trade press, such as the one seen in the *Automotive Daily News* – the general public still had little or no idea what the new cars

ABOVE *A photograph similar to this one, taken on the 6 February, 1932, appeared in the 9 March edition of* Automotive Daily News. *Although this Fordor, registration number 326-017, was adorned with a V8 emblem and V8 hub caps it is unlikely that it was a V8. The first production engine was not ready for assembly until 10 March*

RIGHT ABOVE *On 10 March 1932, Henry Ford took a hammer and punch to the first V8 engined car to leave the assembly line. He punched the figures 18-1. One and eight for his first eight cylinder car and another one for the first of such. Even with his glasses on Henry managed to stamp the eight upside down. This engine, or one similarily stamped 18-1, now resides in the Henry Ford Museum.*
On that auspicious day Henry was flanked by the team of engineers which had brought his dream to reality. Third from the left is Laurence Sheldrick, chief engineer. Next to him stands Joe Galamb, chassis engineer. Pete Martin, stands with his hand on the wing and Henry is to the far right. On the extreme left is W. C. Cowling, Ford sales chief

RIGHT *Another photograph taken on the same day shows the Victoria body being lowered from the mezzanine floor onto the V8 chassis. Standing to the left of the car is Pete Martin. Next to him are Charles Sorenson and Albert Wibel from purchasing and W. C. Cowling. Edsel and Henry are standing in front of the pillar to the left of the photograph*

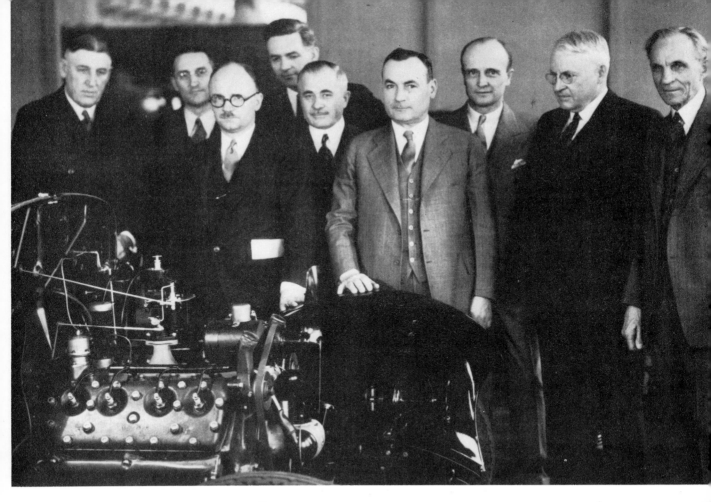

ANNOUNCING THE NEW FORD
V-8 Cylinder

THE NEW FORD EIGHT De Luxe Tudor Sedan

Eight-cylinder, 90-degree V-type, 65-horse-power Engine • Vibrationless

Roomy, Beautiful Bodies • Low Center of Gravity • Silent Second Gear

Synchronized Silent Gear Shift • Seventy-five Miles per Hour • Comfortable

Riding Springs • Rapid Acceleration • Low Gasoline Consumption • Reliability

New self-adjusting Houdaille double-acting hydraulic shock absorbers with thermostatic control . . . New rear spring construction . . . Automatic spark control . . . Downdraft carburetor . . . Carburetor silencer . . . Bore, 3 1/16 inches. Stroke, 3 3/4 inches . . . Piston displacement, 221 cubic inches . . .

90-degree counterbalanced crankshaft . . . Large, effective fully enclosed four-wheel brakes . . . Distinctive steel-spoke wheels with large hub caps . . . Handsome V-type radiator . . . Graceful new roof line and slanting windshield of clear polished plate safety glass . . . Single-bar bumpers, chromium plated . . . Low, drop

center frame . . . Mechanically operated pump drawing fuel from fourteen-gallon gasoline tank in rear . . . Choke on instrument panel . . . Individual inside sun visors . . . Cowl ventilation . . . Adjustable driver's seat . . . Choice of Mohair, Broadcloth or Bedford Cord upholstery in all de luxe closed types.

THE NEW FORD FOUR-CYLINDER CAR

An improved Ford four-cylinder, 50-horse-power engine, operating with new smoothness, is available in the fourteen body types listed below.

A GREAT NEW CAR AT AN UNUSUALLY LOW PRICE •• FOURTEEN BODY TYPES

Roadster	Tudor Sedan	Sport Coupe	De Luxe Tudor	De Luxe Tudor	Cabriolet	Victoria
Phaeton	Coupe	Fordor Sedan	De Luxe Phaeton	De Luxe Coupe	De Luxe Fordor	Convertible Sedan

Ford

GET COMPLETE INFORMATION AND PRICES THURSDAY, MARCH 31, AT ALL FORD DEALERS

This full page advertisement appeared in the Tuesday 29 March 1932 edition of the Virginian-Pilot *and* The Norfolk Landmark. *It also appeared in almost 3000 other newspapers nationwide.*
Notice the four cylinder merits only four lines in the right hand column

looked like. One enterprising movie-maker managed to shoot 40 feet of film of the new Ford being road tested in Dearborn. Wishing only to enlighten the public he sold the film to the Hollywood Theatre of Detroit, who threatened to sell it to the newsreel companies. Ford quickly announced that it would match or better any offer and soon became the owner of the film. In return they agreed to allow the theatre the privilege of exhibiting a new Ford V8 on introduction day. One speculates on how this transaction went down, and what part Ford's tough security boss, Harry Bennett, played.

Nevertheless, the press continued to cogitate on the new Ford and its imminent release. At one point there were even rumours that the V8 project had been scrapped, but Ford were quick to explain that they had only been breaking up experimental

or scrap engines — there had been quite a few between laboratory and line. However, by the third week in March the *Automotive Daily News* were able to report confidently that the next week would see the introduction of the new Ford. Ford themselves as usual had nothing to say, but dealers indicated that Monday, 28 March, would be the day for them and their bankers to see the cars. Tuesday would be for the fleet owners, Wednesday for salesmen and superintendents and Thursday, 31 March, would be the first public showing. In fact Detroit dealers saw the cars on the 28th, while the other dealers had to wait until the 29th, when they were to insert an advertisement, previously sent to them from headquarters, in 2900 newspapers around the country.

The full-page advertisement announced the new Ford V8 Cylinder, showed the Tudor sedan

On Display Today
The New Ford V-8 Cylinder

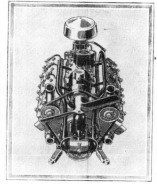

THE INTRODUCTION of the New Ford Eight marks one of the most important events in the history of the automobile. To millions of motorists it brings a wholly new standard of value in a low-price car.

When you see the New Ford Eight and drive it, you will realize that it is the complete answer to your motoring needs. Here are beauty and safety and comfort. Here are exceptional speed and acceleration, the smooth-flowing power of an eight-cylinder engine, reliability and economy. Here are silent second speed and silent synchronized gear shifting. Here, in a word, is all you desire in a motor car at an unusually low price.

The beautiful New Ford V-8 is now on display in this city. There is also an improved Ford four-cylinder 50-horse-power engine operating with new smoothness. It is available in the same fourteen body types as the V-8.

NEW FORD PRICES

FOURTEEN BODY TYPES	EIGHT Cylinder	FOUR Cylinder
Roadster	$460	$410
Phaeton	$495	$445
Tudor Sedan	$500	$450
Coupe	$490	$440
Sport Coupe	$535	$485
Fordor Sedan	$590	$540
De Luxe Roadster	$500	$450
De Luxe Phaeton	$545	$495
De Luxe Tudor Sedan	$550	$500
De Luxe Coupe	$575	$525
Cabriolet	$610	$560
De Luxe Fordor Sedan	$645	$595
Victoria	$600	$550
Convertible Sedan	$650	$600

(All prices F. O. B. Detroit, plus freight and delivery. Bumpers and spare tire extra. Economical terms through Authorized Ford Finance Plans of the Universal Credit Company.)

NEW FORD EIGHT VICTORIA

Eight-cylinder, 90-degree V-type, 65-horse-power Engine • Vibrationless • Roomy, Beautiful Bodies • Low Center of Gravity
Silent Second Gear • Synchronized Silent Gear Shift • Seventy-five Miles per Hour • New Self-adjusting Houdaille
Double-acting Hydraulic Shock Absorbers with Thermostatic Control • Comfortable Riding Springs • Rapid Acceleration
Low Gasoline Consumption • Reliability • Automatic Spark Control • Down-draft Carburetor • Bore, 3 1/16 • Stroke, 3 3/4
Piston Displacement, 221 Cubic Inches • 90-degree Counterbalanced Crankshaft

Two days later this advertisement, here taken from the Galveston Daily News, *also appeared nationwide. It contained the first pictures of the new V8 and for the first time prices of the 14 models. Again the four cylinder received only four lines of copy*

and listed the cars' main features and body styles. No prices were given. Instead the bottom line said, 'Get complete information and prices Thursday, March 31, at all Ford dealers.'

Two days later another full-page advertisement appeared in the daily press. This time it depicted a Victoria, and for the first time a picture of the revolutionary V8 engine and prices for the new cars. Mr Sinsabaugh had been almost right with his $588 predicted price for the V8; it was indeed around the $600 mark, but the new four was in every case $50 less and not $388 as he had supposed.

In fact the four-cylinder Model B was hardly mentioned. In the 29 March advertisement it warranted four lines in the lower right-hand corner. Four lines of similar copy were repeated in the 31 March advertisement, along with a list of prices, but as we have seen no Bs were available for viewing by the public. Nevertheless, they came to view. In all 5,501,952 turned out to see the new Fords. Within the next few days Ford claimed the order books had more than doubled from their pre-introduction figure to 200,000. The question now was, could Ford meet the demand?

3 'Make an eight,' says Ford

Although Henry Ford had engineer Fred Thoms assemble nine of the V8 engines available in 1932 it is unlikely that they provided anything more than reference. They were all too complex in design, most being of multiple construction with separately cast barrels bolted to a crankcase. For Henry there were just too many parts; he wanted something much more simple and his V8 would look nothing like the nine assembled.

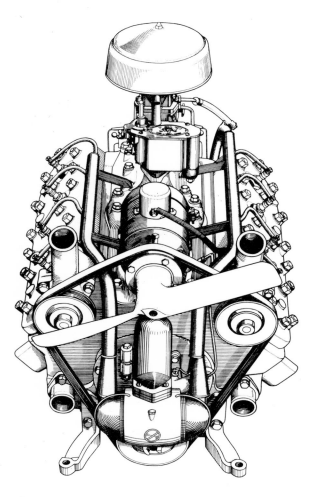

The position of the camshaft between the two banks of cylinders was the cause of the complexity. In previous sidevalve designs there was a plumber's nightmare of inlet and exhaust manifolding along the central valley. To overcome these complications some manufacturers, such as Cadillac, had gone to overhead valves, enabling the exhaust manifolds to be bolted on the outside of the cylinder heads. Unfortunately, this was no answer for Henry, ohv engines were too complicated, had too many parts and could not draw on previous Ford engine development.

Instead he wanted the economy of side valve design but the simplicity of outside exhausts. No one had done this before and no one had made V8 engines on the scale and in the numbers that Ford intended. Nevertheless he would accomplish the impossible, using the vast resources of the Ford Motor Company – the massive Rouge River plant with, in 1932, the world's largest foundry, covering 30 acres, more than $750,000,000 of investment capital, almost 30 years of experience and 'Cast Iron Charlie' Sorensen.

Sorensen was a tall, blond Danish immigrant who had joined Ford as a $3-a-day pattern maker in 1905. He worked his way through the company with a relentless drive, which he expected everybody below him to emulate, until he ruled the Rouge and was possibly the second most powerful man in Fords. Sorensen had pioneered the production lines which made Henry Ford both rich and famous and, perhaps more significantly, had developed a way to cast the Model T engine *en bloc*. Previous and contemporary engines had their cylinders and crankcases cast separately. So what Henry proposed next, in mono casting his V8, was really the next logical step.

As we have seen Ford had installed two engineers, Carl Schultz and Ray Laird, in the old Thomas Edison, Fort Myers laboratory now erected in Greenfield Village and he put them to work developing his ideas for a V8 engine. Ford could hardly read a blueprint and he would drop in

Bob Black on dyno. Six dynamometers were located in the northeast corner of the north end of the Engineering building. The first V8 was sent there in June 1931 but this photograph was taken on 13 May, 1932

two or three times a day checking on progress and dictating the kind of engine he wanted. Schultz had come to Fords under Harold Hicks during the Model A engine development, and Hicks re-membered later, 'I can truthfully say that Carl Schultz knew practically nothing about engines when he came to work for me. He did the layout and detail work under my direction, because I didn't have time to do it myself. That way he learned a lot.' But that was Henry Ford's way.

When he became interested in vanadium steel he was advised to bring in a metallurgist. Ford immediately pointed to a sweeper and said, 'There's a good man, make him a metallurgist.'

It was a similar occurrence which brough Emil Zoerlein into the trio. Ed Huff, head of the electrical laboratory, had said that the type of ignition Ford wanted on the V8 couldn't be made, so Ford gave the job to Zoerlein, who commented many years after the job that, 'It was difficult but I couldn't say it couldn't be done until I'd tried it.'

Ford later told Zoerlein that he had wanted an ignition that would be guaranteed for 50,000 miles and could then be rebuilt. This would create a pool

of jobs for reconditioners and an endless supply of parts that would keep the V8 running for many years. As it happened the ignition system cost the public, who were unwittingly used as the testing crew, millions in maintenance bills. Laurence Sheldrick attributed this to the coils breaking down and the public not knowing how to service the ignition. It required an entirely different service routine to any other distributor before it. You couldn't even adjust the points on the car; the distributor had to be removed and put on a test rig or it had to be replaced.

Again, according to Laurence Sheldrick, Ford dictates for an off-set crankshaft and floating big-end bearings caused problems for the engineers because they were difficult and expensive to make with no tangible benefits. Henry also decided, very prudently, to use existing reliable designs such as the water pumps and the fixed distributor used on

39

the Model A, Zoerlein saying, 'When you make a major change like this on an engine, you're talking millions of dollars. The tooling for the existing pumps was already bought and in operation.'

Although the use of existing water pumps saved money on development and tooling costs the engine was to suffer from overheating problems until a new pump system was fitted in 1937. Henry wanted them mounted at the top of the engine, where they sucked hot water out, rather than at the bottom to push cold water in. Sheldrick reckoned that it was an engineering axiom that you put pressure on the cold side not depression on the hot side. Their position resulted in low pressure and a consequently lower boiling point. Once the water did turn to steam it further reduced the efficiency of the pumps. The overheating problems were, however, not to be fully realized until the car went into production, when many changes would be made, but to no avail. There were to be no thermostats either, Henry deciding that they were unreliable after riding in a new Lincoln with thermostatically controlled blinds in front of the radiator. During his test ride the thermostat failed, closed the blinds and almost caused the engine to boil. Commanding the chauffeur to stop, Henry climbed into a nearby cornfield, returned with a corn cob and instructed the driver to, 'Wedge it open with this.' Upon his return to Dearborn Henry stated, 'Thermostats are crummy.'

Had Henry not insisted on outside exhausts the subsequent overheating problem may not have occurred, but insist he did. Zoerlein remembers, 'To Mr Ford, there was a purpose behind running the exhaust passages through the block. Mr Ford lived in Detroit, and in Detroit winters are cold, and when temperatures get down to zero and sub-zero, it's nice to get a warm engine – right quick. If you passed the exhaust ports through the water jacket, and then on, you got a quick warm-up.' This directive was to cost Henry, rather than the public, hundreds of thousands of dollars in development costs for scrap engine castings.

Though he would have to relent before the engine went into production, at this stage there were to be no fuel or oil pumps either.

Henry was already responding to pressure to move the fuel tank from its cowl position in the Model A to the rear of the car, so some type of fuel feed system was therefore necessary. Initially, a self-feeding carburettor was designed by Mr Otis Funderburke in which the vacuum created in the venturi caused fuel to be sucked out of the tank. It was tried on the V8 and was found to work, but only under test conditions; changes in atmospheric pressure rendered the device useless. Ford subsequently ordered his engineers to explore the possibilities of a pressurized fuel tank, but

manufacturing difficulties and questions of safety negated further development.

The engine would have to employ a fuel pump, especially when the carburettor was to be mounted on top of the engine, where it was difficult to feed by gravity. Unfortunately, the pump which went into production sucked more than it pushed and subsequently suffered from vapour locks. Another problem occurred when water vapour was forced up into the pump from the crankcase. This vapour either condensed and caused the pump mechanism to corrode or, in cold weather, it froze and stopped the pump.

Various remedies were sought, but the vapour lock problem remained throughout the engine's life.

Finally, as we have seen, Henry insisted on total secrecy from the three engineers; they could turn to nobody else for assistance. Zoerlein recalls that Sheldrick, Sorensen nor even Edsel knew what was going on and nobody dropped in at the beginning. Obviously though, as blocks had to be cast and machined, so Ford's chief engineers came to learn of the project. This is how Sorensen managed to have pilot production lines ready so soon.

Emil Zoerlein had begun his difficult task of designing the ignition system. Henry, as usual, posed some limitations. He wanted to eliminate the gears used to drive the distributor from the camshaft and their resultant play; instead the distributor would bolt to the front of the cylinder block and would be driven directly by the camshaft. The distributor would also have to be fixed as it was on the Model A. Ignition timing would be adjusted by rotation of the breaker plate. Lastly, he wanted the distributor and coil built as one unit. In an effort to conceal their experiments and possibly reduce costs Ford directed Zoerlein to adapt a Model A coil.

A two-piece Bakelite cover was designed to slip over a standard Mallory Model A coil with inside primary and two outside secondary windings. The base of the coil was sealed with oakum and it was bolted on top of the distributor.

The idea worked well, but the V8 imposed greater loads and was a higher-revving engine than the Model A had been, causing the outside windings to fail at high speed because they could not react fast enough.

Pre-production and engines up to number 18-4250 had no vacuum advance mechanism, but this was added to all engines, either on the production line or by dealers to their existing stocks, during April 1932.

Ford also instructed Zoerlein to try another concept used on the Model A, namely high-tension wires moulded into plastic with terminals

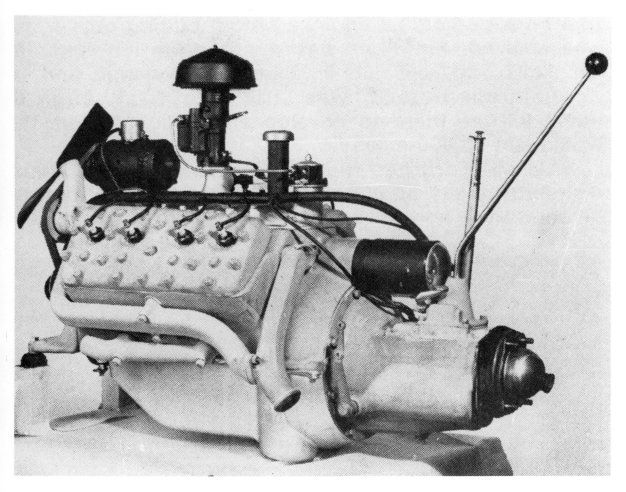

Early prototype V8 engines had the front and rear ports exiting high up on the sides of the cylinder block. Below the exhaust manifold one can see detachable water inlet pipes which were eventually made integral with the block. This engine also has the starter motor mounted high, on top of the gearbox. It was of course removed to the lower left hand side for production

coming out of the end so that Model A spring clips could be used between the nut terminal and the spark plug. Zoerlein tried it, but thirties plastics did not have enough dialectric strength to prevent repeated electrical breakdowns and subsequent misfiring. Eventually the idea was abandoned and conventional high-tension wires were routed through Bakelite tubes. When the engine reached the production stage the Bakelite was discarded in favour of metal conduit.

Zoerlein's other problem, the first being Ford himself, was that he had no test equipment. Greenfield Village and the Fort Myers laboratory were powered by DC current generated by steam engine. When Zoerlein asked if he could set up an electric motor, necessitating AC power, Ford said, 'No, build a steam engine to run at the speed you want for the calibrating fixture.'

The next month was therefore spent making a tiny steam engine, 20 in long with a bore of 2 in and a stroke of $2\frac{1}{4}$ in. To build a steam engine with a rev range between 200 and 2000 rpm is difficult enough, but Zoerlein, proving how versatile he was, managed to build one which ran between 200 and 2400 rpm. It did, however, run erratically in the upper rev range. Zoerlein asked Henry's advice as to how to control it. Ford suggested a Wright-type flywheel governor and it worked. Zoerlein was then able to calibrate his distributor and complete the first of several ignition systems.

By November 1930 Schultz and Laird had two designs ready, one of 299 ci and the other, which Henry would choose, was of 232 ci and was designated Model 24. Nothing more was done in that year; it was almost Christmas and Ford put Zoerlein to work on the one-tenth scale working model of his Quadricycle. Eventually all three engineers would work on Edsel's Christmas present.

That first engine ran at the beginning of 1931. The engineers set it up on a wooden stand and used a steam engine, connected by a belt and pulley bolted to the back of the engine, to fire it up. When it ran the whole building shook, Ford forbidding them to hammer any nails into his precious shed. After that Henry decided to build a garage in the back of the Fort Myers laboratory to test it in. The garage had two stalls for cars and a partitioned area for the test stand. Zoerlein recalls, 'The engine was set up in there and connected to an air brake [dynamometer]. That way we could calculate, versus speed, how much power the engine put out.'

Several more versions of the Model 24 were produced and installed in revamped Model As for road testing. Howard Salle, Pete Petersen, Eddy Halen, Ray Dahlinger and Jimmy Smith and others all drove, as did Henry Ford and his friend Thomas Edison, but there was no way of measuring how much power they had.

According to Sheldrick, road test reports were sketchy at most, 'They would give us test reports, but not the kind I'm accustomed to nowadays. Their reports amounted to 'Damn Good' or 'Damn Poor' and how much gasoline was consumed and how much oil. As far as getting any intelligible mileage figures at different speeds, we couldn't.'

Eventually, in June 1931 it was decided to send an engine over to the engineering building and mount it onto one of six dynamometers, operated by Bob Black, and located in the north-east corner of the north end of the building. By that time Sorensen, Sheldrick and everybody else was in on it, but Henry still insisted on strict secrecy. Harry Bennett, Ford's security boss, recounted in his book, *We Never Called Him Henry*, 'While Mr Ford was developing the V8, he was extremely sensitive about it. He heard a rumour that sales manager Fred Rockelman, who later became President of Plymouth, had discussed the engines with Walter Chrysler and threatened to fire Rockelman if the rumour was true. He had almost everyone in the plant afraid for his job (or was that Bennett?) and got everyone so tense over the whole thing that he achieved the opposite result. Employees were discussing the engine much more than they would have under more relaxed circumstances.

'Mr Ford had me working my head off to find out if there were any leaks. Things came to such a pass I actually refused to look at the engines myself. A dozen times he tried to get me to look at them, and I said, 'No, I don't want to go in there. I don't want to know anything about the things.

'Then one day Alfred Sloan, President of General Motors, and another GM executive came out to the plant to pay a visit to Mr Ford. After a short chat, Mr Ford led Sloan and his companion out into the plant and, to the everlasting confusion of every man in the Ford plant, calmly showed them the two engines. Why Mr Ford did things like that I don't know, he just did them.'

William (Bill) F. Pioch remembers, 'he was one of the few people who was allowed to enter the secret place. Mr Ford didn't tell me not to tell anybody: he just took it for granted. It was a hard place to get into and then keep your mouth shut.'

Zoerlein remembers that though the power wasn't right, once the engine got on to the dyno that was where the development work started.

Fred Thoms had by now been recruited into the group, and said in his reminiscences, 'I was working with Carl Schultz then, and he would draw up an engine and give me the blueprints. The first thing I would have to do was get my motor mounting. The next thing would be to work on the tools. The tools had to come along just about the same time as the cylinder block did – pistons, rods, and everything. I didn't order the casting myself from the Rouge – Carl Schultz usually did that. The casting would be machined right in the Engineering Laboratory machine shop. When the block was all machined and the other parts machined, I had to put it together. We tested these blocks for leaks over in the tin shop and repaired them there. Any little leaks can all be fixed. They would probably throw them out nowadays, but those cylinder blocks cost as much as $20,000!'

With no oil pump these engines tended to burn out, as had their predecessors. Using dippers one bank of cylinders got oil while the other went dry. Eventually Ford relented and a conventional gear pump driven off the camshaft was used, eliminating a major problem.

Nevertheless, the engine continued to run rough. At the time though the engine was a one-piece casting, it had its front-mounted distributor and the engineers had adapted a single-throat Detroit Lubricator-type carburettor, which Ford liked because of its air-valve control. Zoerlein recalls that it 'had two of what we called barn doors. That was quite an accomplishment then to make this carburettor for eight cylinders.' It was a combination of this carburettor, its manifolding and the valve and ignition timing that was causing the problems. With no experience to draw on and no test equipment it was very difficult to get these essentials right. Zoerlein first had to make a manually adjustable distributor so that he could adjust the ignition timing to suit the engine and its compression ratio. From that they could calibrate an automatic curve.

During this period the engine underwent many redesigns. Schultz down-sized it to its eventual and familiar 221 ci capacity. He increased the stroke from 3.25 in to 3.75 in and reduced the bore from 3.875 in to 3.0625 in, presumably to give a

Here then is the result of the labours as it went into production on 9 March, 1932, the day this photograph was taken. It was a monoblock V8 with the distributor driven directly from the end of the camshaft and it was exactly what Henry Ford had wanted

little more clearance between the cylinders as the exhaust passages now ran between them. Earlier experimental engines had the front and rear ports emerging high up on the ends of the block. The two middle cylinders were siamesed and emerged from the centre of each side of the block. The eventual design brought both the front and rear ports out through the side of the block with the siamesed middle ports. This presented the production engineers with even more problems, as all three ports now ran clear across the block right between the bores and through the water jacket. A new cast crankshaft was 1.75 in shorter than the Model A's, but had larger, 2 in diameter, main bearings. These were, however, slightly narrower than the four-cylinder B mains, acceptable because of the less destructive firing overlap, forced-feed lubrication, smaller pistons and the

fact that the crankshaft would be fully counterbalanced. Schultz also continued to work on the cam profile and the valve train, while Detroit Lubricator came in to try to improve carburation by changing the mixture ratio.

With the engine still far from perfect the experimental engine group, called the 'Blue Room' and situated in the Engineering Laboratory, under the watchful eye of Laurence Sheldrick, did some work and Zoerlein continued his efforts to smooth out the rough spots. Eventually he developed an entirely new automatic ignition advance, of which he says, 'That way you retarded the ignition by applying a brake to the disc on which the ignition cam was carried.' He continued, 'We tried various camshafts and carburettor adjustments and we finally smoothed the engine out, and the first reading we got was 65 bhp maximum.'

4 A production man's dream come true

The troublesome details of engine refinement were nothing compared to the problems 'Cast Iron Charlie' was having over at the Rouge foundry. Though the biggest in the world, covering more than 30 acres, with enough capacity to turn out 2900 tons of castings per day, they still had little experience of casting such a complicated shape as the one-piece V8.

This engine, however, was to be but a chapter in the history of the Rouge plant. This prodigy of Sorensen's was under constant change and development as products and production demanded. With an ability to spawn two million vehicles per year, the Ford Motor Company's biggest problem was the continuous supply of raw materials and parts at steady prices. Sorensen commented, 'When a supplier couldn't keep up with our needs for parts or materials, the alternatives were either to cut production or shut down. . . . So, we were driven into gigantic do-it-yourself programs.'

In the twenties a regular supply of plate glass had been a problem, especially as prices rose from 30 cents per square foot to $1.50. To counteract this untenable situation Ford initially purchased an old plant at Glassmere, Pennsylvania, and then installed a modern plant at the Rouge which revolutionized glassmaking. Industry experts had said it was impossible to produce a continuous strip of plate glass, but Ford's smelting furnace with mechanical charging of the silica sand proved them wrong and produced ten million square feet of glass per year, at the ridiculous price of 20 cents per square foot.

Next came the steel mill. Sorensen told Ford it would cost $35 million. 'What are you waiting for?' replied Ford. The development of their own mill encompassed every aspect of steel manufacture from open hearth to blooming and rolling mills for sheets, bars and rods. This development created such an impact it caused Sorensen to recount, 'Besides assuring a dependable supply, the most noteworthy accomplishment of the steel mill was

to shorten the production cycle. The elapsed time between the receipt of raw materials and the finished products in the hands of the dealers had its effect on cost. Before we moved into the Rouge, the production cycle was 21 days. This came down gradually to 14, but after the Rouge steel mill was in operation this cycle was down to four days.'

Ore was shipped by Great Lakes steamer from Minnesota and from Henry's iron mines in Kentucky by railroad (once this had been Ford's own Detroit, Toledo and Ironton Railroad, but it had been sold in 1929 to the Pennsylvania) direct to the Rouge blast furnaces, where it was smelted, the process taking 16 hours.

Additional material for the furnaces came from the Rouge plant itself, either in the form of machine and sheet metal shop scrap or as complete cars. Dealers were finding it increasingly difficult to move second-hand cars, which were being traded in against new ones for much-needed sales, and consequently Ford did two things; they established reconditioning lines in the Rouge and some other plants and put flat prices on various types of overhauls. They also offered dealers a flat price for junk cars, which were then shipped to the Rouge, where, in the open hearth plant, they were stripped down and crushed into a 30 by 40 in block in the largest baler ever built. Sorensen recalls, 'In cost, we did not come out ahead on this somewhat cannibalistic but spectacular operation, but indirectly it helped us sell more cars.'

From the two blast furnaces molten iron was carried in huge ladles upon flat cars to the foundry and a 1200-ton mixer and four 120-ton cupolas. The iron was then transferred to two smaller, 400-ton, mixers, one of which was for engines, the other for smaller parts, gear cases, etc. Supplementing these were 28 cupolas, which melted a further 2300 tons in just 16 hours. Twenty-five tons from a cupola and 25 tons from one of the two smaller mixers were reheated and taken to the pouring line in a moving two-ton pouring furnace.

At this point practice in the Ford plant differed

from that in the rest of the industry. There, the molten iron was taken to the moulds, making the casting process heavy and slow. Sorensen had, however, developed, for the Model A, a system of conveyors that carried the moulds to the two-ton pouring furnace. That way they could produce as many castings as they could get moulds past the pourer and it was all done automatically. From smelting pot to solid block took just one hour and in that hour they intended casting 300 blocks.

Sorensen says, 'What we proposed to do was cast whole a V8 in a single solid rigid block. So I went back to my old trade of pattern making. I had to get out of the designer, Joe Galamb, a layout that I could adapt to our Rouge foundries. With the study of the casting I tied the plant layout group under Hanson.'

Of course the early V8 blocks were cast by hand; that is to say the moulds were prepared by hand as they had been in Model A days. This was back-breaking work which required some skill in the placement of the pattern and cores. First one half of the mould, containing the pattern, was filled with greensand, which was then tamped with mallets. The top half of the mould then received the same treatment before the patterns were removed and the cores carefully fitted. The molten iron was then poured. In the case of the V8 the pattern and especially the cores, of which there were over forty, were very complicated and the moulders were, more often that not, not skilled

ABOVE *Hydraulic baling presses crushed obsolete cars which had been purchased by dealers to release some public money for the purchase of new cars. When mixed with Ford's own machine shop scrap it gave a supply of steel to alloy with iron ore for new production*

BELOW *More than 40 cores had to be precisely fitted into the moulds. Paste was used to hold some of them in place, gauges and fine tolerances were required for exact alignment*

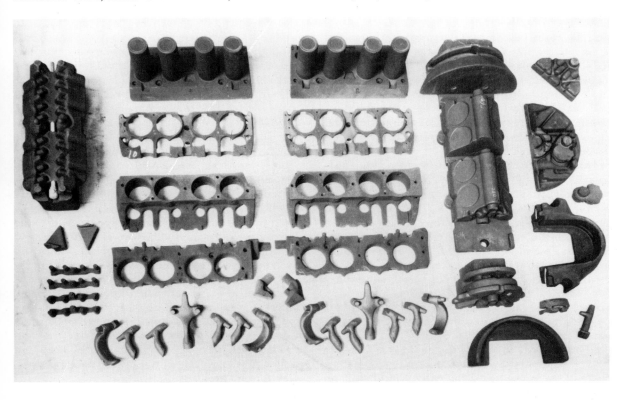

enough to place the cores accurately. If they did get it right then likely as not the cores shifted anyway on the way to the pourer. These problems caused Sorensen to have something like 95 per cent scrappage on the early blocks. It was the exhaust passage cores which were the main problem, as they required precise alignment.

Sorensen now had his work cut out to redeploy the foundry, introducing new techniques, new processes and, for the first time, jigs and gauges to check the fitment of cores in the moulds. Of the period he says, 'With the first hint of building a V8 engine, I sensed that many prior operating notions would have to be set aside. New methods with closer tolerance on dimensions would demand new tools and machines.'

For the first time these men worked to $\frac{1}{64}$ in with GO and NO GO gauges. Sorensen would have to hurry too, because it was already December when Henry decided to come out with his V8 for 1932 and he didn't care what it cost. The engine, though running, was still only an experimental prototype and not only did Henry want it on the market as soon as possible, the whole world was clammering for it.

One of the foundry workers remarked, 'We were scared because of the rush. I worked night and day. We all even forgot to go home, right through the Christmas season. But the really tough part came in the foundry – we had exactly 100 per cent scrap. Everything was wrong. Not one engine came out right.

'Partly it was metal that turned to slag. Partly it was the cores burning up when the hot metal hit them. Partly it was when the cores shifted because they weren't properly anchored.

'Just think of this: there were 54 separate cores in that mould – 54 sand cores that had to stay put just exactly right for the right holes for the valve sections and cylinders and everything in that engine block. Oh, that was a tough one – but we made it.'

In the past skilled production men had been able to assemble a Model A engine mould by eye, but with over 40 cores to fit accurately this was no longer possible. William F. Pioch, head of production engineering, recalls of the period, 'We set up the foundry to make the V8 castings, the same as we had been doing on the four-cylinder job. The result was that our scrap was about 50 per cent. The main reason for that was that we'd get core shifts. The V8 engine had the exhaust ports going through the water jacket of the cylinder block. These cores would shift and, of course, you would get scrap castings.

'This was the problem: the exhaust cores were loose cores, and the production men would just lay them in the mould, and the cores would shift on them. They would have to put them in there and judge proper alignment with their eyes only. Well, that was no good because you get all kinds of people working down there. One good man would get you a good casting, but if your man would be just a little bit careless in placing these cores, you would get a scrap casting.

'So we designed a fixture to place these cores and paste them and get them permanently set. That way you could just take anybody and he couldn't get it wrong, because he had to put these pieces exactly where they were supposed to be. It eliminated all that scrap and problem of repairs. From then on we didn't have any more trouble.'

While the foundry was put onto 'precision workmanship' Harold Hicks took it upon himself to overcome the problem and to design a Cadillac-style engine where the exhaust passages did not go between the cylinders. When Sorensen saw what he had done, he said, 'That's not what Henry Ford wants.' Hicks had to throw the drawings away.

It may not have been what Henry wanted but it wasn't what Sorensen wanted either, as he recounted later, 'None of this could be visualized on the drafting board, and I enjoyed the battles I had with some of the designers in Dearborn. When they found me making changes in design so as to fit the foundry and machine needs, they actually believed I would ruin the engine. But I knew the engine as well as they did because I had lived with it just as closely. They knew nothing about the technique that we were developing in the plant, and I deliberately kept them away from that until we built some engines.'

Of the development Sorensen went on to say, 'We studied every move in the moulding operation and mechanized its handling.' Now, after the patterns were set into their respective halves of the mould, greensand was automatically shot into the flasks from overhead chutes, doing away with all the sand handling by shovel. Instead of being compacted by hand the moulds were mechanically vibrated with a raise-and-drop movement until the sand was compressed. After removal of the pattern the two halves of the mould were mechanically lifted on to a conveyor on which they were transported to the assembly line. Here, the previously fabricated cores were assembled and fitted into the moulds. Again, assembly lines and oven baking of the cores had reduced rejects by 20 per cent over previous methods. From there the completed moulds continued by conveyor to the pouring position, where the two-ton pourer moved above them containing enough of Ford's Grade A iron for three blocks. The iron was alloyed with 3.2 to 3.5 per cent carbon, 1.8 to 2.1 per cent silicon, 0.6 to 0.8 per cent manganese, 0.25 to 0.32 per cent phosphorus, a maximum of

0.1 per cent sulphur and 15 per cent scrap steel.

Checks upon the content of the iron were made every two hours because early castings had suffered badly from the use of the wrong ingredients and had therefore had to be drastically repaired or reworked.

After the pouring the moulds were allowed to cool for five hours before the castings were knocked out. The sand was conveyed away to be sifted and remixed for re-use. Meanwhile, the blocks were conveyed up to the roof to cool further.

Initially, all the engines went over to the Engineering Laboratory for machining before going to the Fort Myers laboratory for assembly. Zoerlein says that the final test work was done there and that the first production cars had their engines built there.

Sorensen and his production engineers had conquered the casting techniques. They were producing around 40 engines per day, scrappage was down to two per cent or less and Sorensen said, 'We produced the finished, machined block for less per pound than our previous four-cylinder cost.'

While the first production engines would continue to be built in the Fort Myers laboratory, Sorensen was busy establishing his production lines. Laurence Sheldrick, who had also been kept right out of the early development of the V8, and was now acting as chief engineer and thus releasing everything for production, said of the period, 'It was really an experimental production set-up which Sorensen had arranged and set up. He must have foreseen what was coming, because he was pretty well ready. He actually had a pilot line ready before the announcement came on production. Between January and March, this thing was whipped into shape.' By the end of March production had more than doubled, with over 100 blocks being completed every day. Production steadily increased until July, when the target figure of 3000 in one day had been reached.

Blocks obviously no longer went to the Engineering Laboratory for machining or to Fort Myers for assembly, instead, after cooling, they were conveyed to the 'White House' for machining. Sorensen recalls, 'Cooling of the casting after pouring was important in order to control hardness and cracking. These controls produced a casting that went through the machine operations with added life to the cutters in the milling machines, drills and reamers. The speed of all operations was stepped up. This, of course, showed the need of new machinery to meet this casting development.

'Improved cutting steels that could handle higher speeds added to the new development. The

Cylinder block 'shake out' at the Rouge foundry. Methods were modern but life was still hard for the foundry workers. The heat was so intense Ford tended to hire black labour for this department as it was supposed that they could stand the temperatures better

solid, rigid, single V8 casting could now stand any load that machines could put on it.'

This statement is confirmed by Bill Pioch's recollection: 'When we went to the V8 engine, it was a different type engine, and from our past experience we really went into high-production machinery, like for instance boring the block. We bored all eight holes at one time. In fact, our machining time on the block wasn't much more than it was on the four-cylinder engine. We had a lot more machining, but it didn't take much more time in labour.'

In the next operation the bores were honed simultaneously. Then one bank of valve seats would be cut before the block was automatically rotated for the other bank to be cut. And so it went on for a mere two hours forty minutes until the block was ready to go to the motor assembly room.

Other cast parts were also conveyed to the motor assembly room and were spray painted and dried while in transit from one building to another.

Once in the assembly room most of the operations were performed by hand but with the extensive use of power tools. It took just another two hours for the jumble of parts to emerge complete and ready for installation.

It had taken the combined resources of Ford's massive manufacturing facility just 94 days, from Ford's December announcement that the V8 was

ABOVE *The overhead bridge between the foundry machine shop and the motor assembly building carries, on a slat conveyor, blocks and other parts for motor assembly. The monorail above carried other parts which were spray painted and dried as they journeyed from one building to the other.*

RIGHT ABOVE *These assembled frames were photographed on 30 June, 1932, prior to being turned over and placed on the final assembly line. At this point both front and rear suspensions, complete with brakes, were in situ as was the exhaust pipe*

RIGHT *This diagram of the V8 Motor assembly line was taken from the 1936 edition of* Mill & Factory. *The layout might have been different in 1932 but I doubt it, though, as many of the photographs used in that publication were in fact taken in 1932. The only department probably not established in 1932 was the motor running-in stands to the right of the diagram*

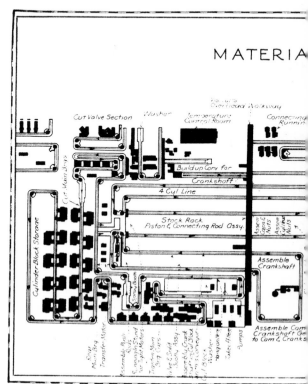

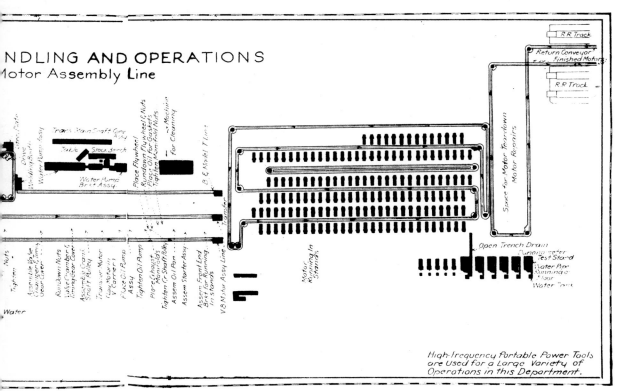

NDLING AND OPERATIONS
Motor Assembly Line

R.R. Track

Return Conveyor
Finished Motors

R.R. Track

Steel Pipe

Drive
Water Pump Assy

Trans. Main Shaft Gear
Assy

Table   Stock Bench

Water Pump
Brkt Assy

Place Flywheel
Rundown Flywheel Nuts
Place Oil Pan Gaskets
Tighten Man-fold Nuts

Machine
For Cleaning

B.E. Motor T Line

Space for Motor Teardown
Motor Repairs

Motor Running In Stands

Open Trench Drain
Running Water
Test Stand
Water Pipe
Running at
Floor
Water Tank

Tighten
Nuts

Assemble Valve
Chamber, Timing
Gear Cover

Run Down Nuts

Valve Chamber,
Timing Gear Cover

Assemble Crank
Shaft Pulley

Trans. or Motor
(Cap Return)
V Carrier

Place Oil Pump
Assy

Tighten Oil Pump

Tighten Oil Pan

Place Exhaust
Manifolds

Tighten Cr. Shaft Bulky

Assem Oil Pan

Assem Starter Assy

Assem Front End
Brkt for Running
In Stands

V-8 Motor Assy Line

Transfer

Water

High-frequency Portable Power Tools
are Used for a Large Variety of
Operations in this Department.

49

back on schedule to 9 March, when the first 38 blocks came off the production line. Although one of those engines would find itself stamped 18-1 the next day and would subsequently roll off the production line in the first assembled V8 car, incidentally a Victoria, Ford could hardly boast that they were ready for mass production. In fact the casting report for 25 March showed that only 39 engine blocks had been made on that day, and of these only 11 were fit to go to the final assembly line. Ford could neither produce nor assemble the millions of parts necessary to manufacture a car. Instead, more than 6000 outside suppliers would contribute parts.

Aluminium castings for sumps, manifolds, pistons, etc., were brought in from the Bohn Aluminum and Brass Company. Bodies were supplied, fully trimmed for around $120–140 each, by both Briggs and Murray. Wheels came from Kelsey-Hayes and tyres from Henry's friend Harvey Firestone as well as Goodyear, B. F. Goodrich and US Tire. Incidentally, Firestone engineers also helped with the design and development of the numerous rubber parts. The one-piece distributor and coil was manufactured by Mallory Electric and Champion supplied the plugs. Carburettors were made for the V8 by Detroit Lubricator and for the four by Zenith.

The gearbox was a Borg-Warner product and radiators were made by both McCord and Long. Door catches came from the Hurd Lock Company and the instrument panel was supplied by Oakes Products. Horns were made by Sparks-Withington, Sparton, GMI and Stewart Warner, while Houdaille made the shock absorbers. Trico made the wiper motor and Schrader made the tyre valves, and all the numerous stainless steel items were formed by Alleghany Ludlum.

Supplementing these thousands of outside suppliers, Ford had his own team of sub-contractors known as the Village Industries. Ford established these small, local factories when he realized what his Model T had done to the cherished American family. It had enabled farm boys, just like himself, to move away from the hard life on the land to big money in the city. To counteract this migration Ford built small factories powered by water to provide the Rouge with much-needed sub-assemblies. This way the farmers could work the land in the summer and then move into the factories for the winter, no longer needing to leave home to earn a living.

Ford's first Village Industry was built at Northville just 15 miles up river from the Rouge. In 1932 the plant employed 180 men and they produced and reconditioned valves. Other plants followed; Nankins Mills, where they made rivets, screws and carburettor parts. Phoenix, which

produced generator cut-outs, voltage regulators and stoplight switches. Plymouth, which produced 95 per cent of all the Ford taps used throughout the world. Flat Rock, where the headlights, taillights and reflectors were made. Waterford, which produced precision gauges, and finally Ypsilanti, which began production, in September 1932, of generators, starters and starter switches.

All of this equipment was shipped to the Rouge, to be stored alongside those parts made on the premises, ready for final assembly. This was to take place in the mammoth B building, which had been initially laid out for the construction of Eagle boats for the US government. It had been designed in such a way that it could ultimately be converted, with the addition of three floors, for the assembly of automobiles.

Once at the Rouge nothing, not the workers nor the parts, was allowed to stand still. Sorensen commented, 'All materials entering the Ford plant went into operation and stayed there. They never came to rest until they had become part of a unit like an engine, an axle or a body. Then they moved on to final assembly or into a freight car for branch assembly.'

Construction began on the frame assembly conveyor, where an upturned frame was fitted with front and rear axle sub-assemblies complete with suspension and brake linkage. The shock absorbers and exhaust pipe were also fitted at this stage.

Ford then employed a special handling device that removed the chassis from the transverse conveyor, turned it over and loaded it onto the final assembly line.

As the chassis journeyed on, groups of men would gradually build up the car, taking parts and sub-assemblies from a moving stock bin called the 'misc. stock conveyor', which ran alongside the assembly line for half the length of the building.

Steering columns and various brackets were added just prior to the engine and gearbox unit being lowered into position from an overhead conveyor.

The petrol tank, frame horn covers and bumpers were attached next, followed by the bulkhead complete with the dash panel.

Wheels, including a tyreless spare, were conveyed overhead and bolted in place prior to the fitment of the grille and headlamp bar assembly.

The bodies, which were themselves sub-assemblies, having already been painted, upholstered and fitted with rear fenders, dashboards and, in the case of De Luxe models, cowl lamps, were then lowered from a mezzanine floor. The bodies were bolted down, the hoods fitted and the car was complete.

Sorensen and his men could be rightly proud of

ABOVE *Engines were conveyed from the motor assembly building to the final assembly line by overhead conveyor. Here, on 6 May, 1932, two employees lower a V8 plus gearbox, into a frame*

BELOW *Bay 34 on the final assembly line in B building (28 June 1932). Men attach parts from the revolving stock bin using overhead power tools. After steering columns and motors, firewalls, complete with dash panels, were fitted. Note overhead wheel conveyor on the extreme left*

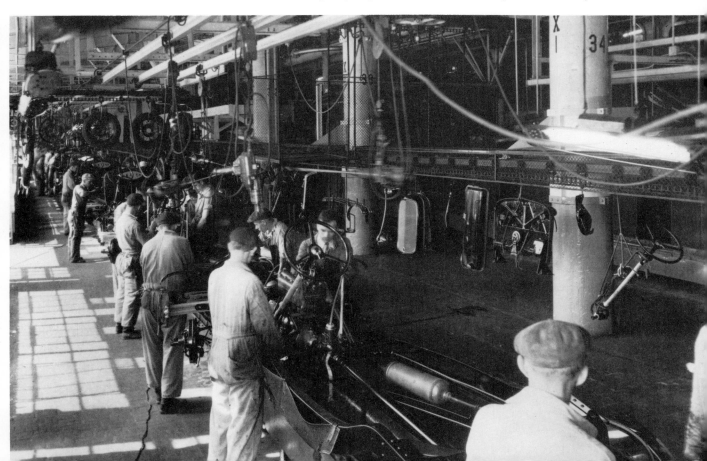

ABOVE *Photographed on 14 November 1932, these are probably some of the last primed bodies to be conveyed into the spray booth.*
From the spray booth bodies continued on to the bake oven.

RIGHT ABOVE *Finished cars receive a final check as they emerge from B building at the end of the assembly line*

LEFT *Bodies were built, trimmed and semi-assembled by Ford, Briggs and Murray. In this photograph taken on 30 June 1932, a Tudor is being lowered onto an almost complete chassis from the mezzanine*

their achievement, the production cycle had been almost halved, from four to just two and a half days. About that period Sorensen said, 'It was a grand feeling to get into something new with such great possibilities. Mr Ford would come to my office for his daily contact. I kept him up to date and always primed him on how the organization was adapting itself to this V8. All his doubts were cleared up. I showed him that to revamp the plant we would spend $50 million in the next two years. Instinctively I knew that would not concern him, but I was amused at one of his remarks about spending money for this new engine.

'"Charlie," he said, "We have too much money in the bank. That doesn't do that bunch in the front office any good. When they look at it they become self-satisfied, and I know they are getting lazy. Let's you and me pull that down. You do that until it hurts. I know this new car will bring in more money than ever, but don't tell them I said so. . . . We have too much money, Charlie, let's you and me get it working."'

Sorensen went on to say, 'The V8 engine showed the way to spend and get it back. It stayed in production longer than the Model T's 19 years. It lasted with no major change for 21 years, and it took that long before it was adopted as a standard type by our closest competitors.' He sums up by saying, 'It was a glorious period; a production man's dream come true.'

5 Driving means buying

As the calendar folded back on 1932 Ford faced many problems. They had already lost many dealers, some closing down, hundreds of others moving to more profitable makes when dealer discounts had been cut to 17.5 per cent in 1930. That had been a good year, with registrations well over one million. In comparison, 1931 was a disaster. Model A production had officially ceased in August and the last American A was produced on 1 November, and although the car would continue to be produced for export from parts on hand until April 1932, nobody particularly wanted to buy it. Registrations of new Fords in 1931 were down by 50 per cent and to compensate dealer discounts were increased first to 20 per cent and then in late 1931 to 22 per cent, but it made little difference. Probably as many as another 1000 dealers went out of business while Ford closed down and readied itself for the new model, and Ford again lost its leadership of the low-priced market. Chevrolet alone sold more cars than Ford, and Plymouth had its best year ever.

Traditionally, the annual selling season started on 1 January with members of the National Automobile Chamber of Commerce, which did not include Ford, announcing their new models towards the end of the year and showing them at the annual New York National Auto Show held during the first weeks of January. This show was followed by similar expositions in Philadelphia, Detroit, Chicago and other major cities across the country. Not being a member Ford usually held his own, simultaneous, show elsewhere in New York. As the public flocked to New York's Grand Central Palace between 9 and 16 January in record numbers there was still no news from Ford and no sign of the new car. Consequently, the public kept their hands in their pockets and waited, much to the chagrin of the other manufacturers, some of whom had released their new offerings early, at the end of 1931, in order to gain some publicity, and much-needed sales. Meanwhile, the news media speculated daily about Ford's plans and heralded

him 'the master of the art of suspense', while his competitors accused him of manipulating the press. Ford was content to let publicity generate itself, saying, 'Our best advertising is free advertising.' Those extravagant days of 1929, when he spent $29 million on advertising, were gone. 1930 saw this figure cut to $8.7 million and in 1932 it was a mere $2.7 million, hardly enough to pay for the two full-page advertisements announcing the new car.

Ford had no choice but to keep quiet, because as yet he had no car to show. It was barely a month since he had taken the decision to reschedule the V8 and his engineers were still trying to refine the engine, get it into production and build the car everybody was eagerly awaiting.

When he eventually revealed his plans to journalist James Sweinhart the whole world soon knew roughly what to expect. The business world rejoiced; if Ford had confidence then everybody had confidence. Resumption of production at Ford meant re-employment for not only thousands of Ford assembly workers but for the hundreds of thousands who supplied them.

Felicitations came from almost every quarter except those loyal Ford owners who lamented the loss of the Ford four and the other auto manufacturers, who now knew what they were up against. In the past Ford had been used as a price sounding board and as Ford had so far mentioned nothing about prices few of them knew what to do. Besides, the market was already depressingly slow and Ford's announcement merely caused prospective buyers to hold back to see exactly what Mr Ford had to offer.

Perhaps most of all it was the Ford dealers who were happiest at the confirmation of a new model. For the past six months they had had nothing to sell but Model As, used cars and spare parts. At long last they had a new car to sell and it was not just any car, it was the world's first low-priced V8.

On 29 March they dutifully trooped along to their nearest assembly plant fully expecting to see the new model. Some of them were lucky, many, unfortunately, had to be content with a 22-minute film accompanied by a recorded message extolling the virtues of the Model 18. After the screening the lucky ones saw a back curtain open in a diamond shape to reveal the new V8. Those who saw it were ecstatic.

On the same day 2900 newspapers nationwide carried a full-page advertisement portraying the new Ford. Two days later another ad. appeared, this time featuring details of the revolutionary engine and, perhaps more important, prices for the 14 models.

Mr Ford's comments on that day were, 'These are the cars and the prices. I think it will be granted that when an eight-cylinder car can be bought for the price of a four, and in some cases less, I am justified in saying that these are low prices. No profit can be expected from them unless we attain a certain volume of production. Naturally, we hope to attain sufficient volume to keep these prices as low as they are now.'

Infinitely more complicated than the Model A it replaced, the Model 18 and its small brother, the Model B, were priced in the same bracket and were in some cases cheaper. Ford had pulled off another engineering coup, but his competitors were not about to lose the foothold they had already gained in the market he had created.

The next day Chevrolet reduced prices on all its models by an average of $50, placing them firmly between the two Ford ranges. The most important section of the market was the two-door sedan and Chevrolet priced theirs at $495, just five dollars cheaper than the V8 Tudor but still $45 dearer than Ford's four.

Walter Chrysler, who had made a tremendous impact on the low-priced market with his Plymouth, was not about to let his market share slide and launched an advertising campaign to publicize his new PB.

It began on 30 March, and full-page advertisements depicted Walter Chrysler leaning on the headlamp of his new car confirming that Plymouth would be fighting for the lowest-priced market with such innovations as Free Wheeling, Floating Power, hydraulic brakes, safety steel body and automatic clutch. The new Fords had none of these gimmicks.

On Ford's big day, 31 March, Walter Chrysler appeared again, this time with his foot on the bumper, clutching the radiator ornament, and demanding that you, 'Look at all three. It is my opinion that any new car without Patented Floating Power is obsolete.' The new PB that Walter Chrysler had kept in the wings awaiting an announcement from Ford was, in many ways, a well-engineered car and a good buy. It had a 6 in

FORD TO MAKE CHICAGO AREA DEBUT MONDAY

Plans for Showing of New Lines Are Elaborate

Chicago, March 24.—The great American game of figuring what Henry Ford will do and when he will do it reached a solution here today when next week was definitely reported as the period for the debut of the next Fords.

As usual officials at the Ford branch and assembly plant are uncommunicative and mysterious but from dealer sources it became known that a schedule has been outlined setting aside Monday as the day for dealers and their bankers to view the new models at the Chicago branch, Tuesday for fleet owners, Wednesday for salesmen and superintendents, and Thursday for the public at the 131st Regiment Armory, Michigan Avenue and 16th Street, and at dealer show rooms.

Visitors at the Ford assembly plant on Torrence Avenue have noted unusual activity in arrival and unloading of box cars. They take this as meaning that the first shipment of the new cars to reach Chicago for exhibit will be completed units built at Dearborn.

With the stage set for the Chicago showing next week, speculation has arisen here as to whether the new models will be launched simultaneously throughout the country. Dealers and distributors of other makes are glad the suspense is soon to be over and they welcome the new four and eight cylinder Ford arrivals.

Chicago newspaper cutting just one week before the new Fords were seen by the public, tells how they were to be presented

	B	V8	Chev.	Ply.
Roadster	449.25	499.25	504	538.50
De Luxe Roadster	489.25	539.25	594	638.50
Phaeton	484.25	534.25	554	
De Luxe Phaeton	534.25	584.25		638.50
Standard Coupe	479.25	529.25	549	608.50
De Luxe Coupe	564.25	614.25	599	
Sport Coupe	524.25	574.25	594	635.50
Tudor Sedan	489.25	539.25	554	538.50*
De Luxe Tudor	539.25	589.25	604	
Victoria	589.25	639.25	634	
Fordor Sedan	579.25	629.25	649	618.50*
De Luxe Fordor	634.25	684.25	704	678.50
Convertible Sedan	639.25	689.25	684	828.50
Cabriolet	599.25	649.25	654	688.50
*Plymouth thrift models				

LEFT *Delivered prices at Detroit, 7 April 1932. FOB prices were, in the case of Ford models $39.25 lower. Source Ford Archives*

RIGHT *A third full page advertisement was sent out by Ford to be placed in local newspapers by dealers. As you can see it was a fairly well detailed appraisal of what was on offer*

longer wheelbase than the Ford, a sturdy X-membered frame, free-wheeling transmission and was very competitively priced. Plymouth were not going to beat Ford, nor for that matter Chevrolet, but they intended hanging on to third slot in the production league, and they in fact had their best year ever with sales of over 111,000.

Chevrolet were also doing rather well and had sold in excess of 100,000 vehicles by the time Ford introduced the V8. With their own 55 city, nationwide show, lasting the week from 2 to 9 April, open 13 hours per day, Chevrolet continued to outsell Ford until the latter reached full production in June. Thereafter sales by both companies began to erode. Chevrolet's dive was much faster and deeper than Ford's.

Notwithstanding these efforts the public turned out in their millions to see the new Ford, 5,501,952 to be exact, and that was on the first day. Incidentally, that figure represented just over half the number of people Ford claimed had turned out four years earlier to see the then new Model A. In New York alone more than double the number of people are reported to have visited the Ford showroom than went to the 1932 National Auto Show.

For those areas where a dealer had no new car to show, Ford had arranged that on 31 March there be a free showing in more than 6000 local theatres of a film entitled, 'Ford Starts Prosperity Drive'. It described first how Ford's introduction of the V8 would help end the Depression and put thousands back to work. This spiel was followed by a detailed look at the car and its revolutionary engine and shots of it in operation on a test track. Originally a silent movie it was later given a sound track by the Metropolitan Motion Picture Company, an RCA licensee, and shown in areas the V8 had still not reached.

They were also given another full-page advertisement to insert in local papers.

Such was the impact the V8 made. This impact was, however, not felt in their pocket books. Perhaps the biggest problem was the fact that there just wasn't much money around. Sure Mr Ford was going to stimulate the economy, but it wouldn't happen overnight and people were either unwilling or unable to answer his call as they had in 1928 and 1929 to buy the Model A.

Important though this fact was it only served to disguise the real problem and that was the fact that Ford just could not deliver. The spectacular interest shown on 31 March was repeated again on Friday and Saturday, and though bad weather reduced the size of the crowds, notably in Philadelphia, Washington, Charlotte and Pittsburgh, it did not dampen enthusiasm. Ford claimed over 13 million people saw his new car over that first weekend in April. Nevertheless, I wonder how many of the proclaimed 200,000 customers who, according to Ford, had placed their orders in the first few hectic days had any idea that they wouldn't receive their cars until August. Even the thousand or so cars which graced the showrooms were to stay where they were, apprehensive dealers being uncertain of when replacements would arrive. It is doubtful that even they had any idea of the problems to follow. In fact the first 4250 V8 cars produced had to be drastically modified by both plants and dealers and then used only as demonstrators. None were to be sold to the public and the dealers, after all the hullabaloo, had little or nothing to actually sell.

The people who had no trouble obtaining a new Ford were those with some clout. The Ford Archives contain many letters requesting preferential treatment for the speedy delivery of a new model and Ford tried to oblige where the request came from either a valued friend or customer or someone of notoriety who could generate some publicity for the Ford Motor Company. Actor Wallace Beery took delivery of two De Luxe Tudors and one Station Wagon, while Buster Keaton and Louis B. Mayer both became proud V8 owners.

Ford obviously did not forsee the production problems which would delay the delivery of his new V8 and cause the other manufacturers,

FORD V-8 HERE

FOR THE NEW AGE—A NEW FORD

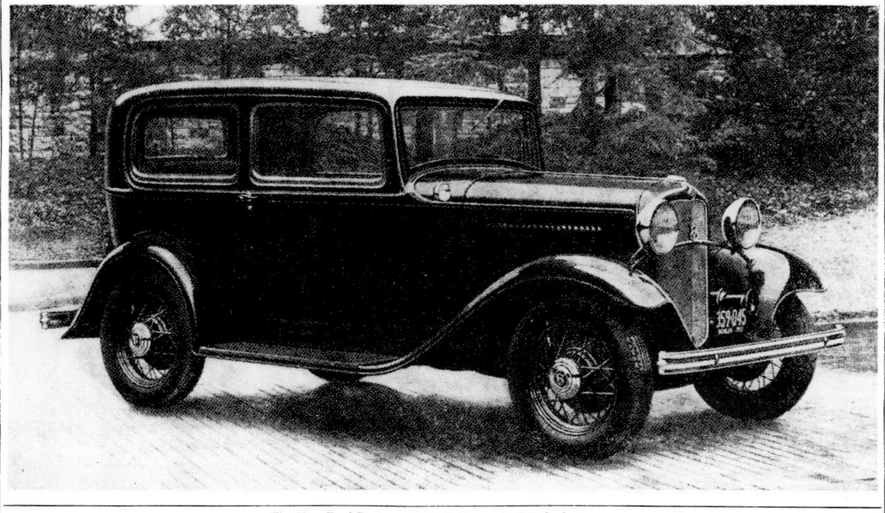

The New Ford De Luxe Tudor Sedan, one of 14 body types.

. H. P. ENGINE, .W BODY LINES RD FEATURES

chronized Gear Shift, Si- it Second Speed Among Other Improvements.

ASSIS IS LONG, LOW

new Ford V-8 represents a le advance in motor car en- ring.

new car is large, long, roomy, powerful and alert. Its eight- ier V-type engine develops 65 power. The car is capable of les an hour.

ie of the mechanical features ubber mounting for engine; draft carburetor; automatic control; fuel pump; rear fuel soft, flexible springs; large anical four-wheel brakes; strong, electrically welded spoke wheels and large tires. frame is cushioned from the ng gear by rubber insulators e spring shackles and shock per links.

14 body types may be ob- 1 also with an improved 50 power, 4-cylinder engine at cost.

INTERIORS ROOMY.

bodies are fresh and mod- from the gracefully rounded iator to rear bumper. Body ors are roomy and richly fin- Seats are of new style, de- for utmost comfort. Driver's in all closed cars are adjust- A large ventilator is provided cowl.

instrument panel is oval, a rustless steel moulding. In- un visors fold out of the way not in use.

ny outstanding features are in the chassis. These include ng, rugged frame; newly de- , soft, flexible transverse can- springs; rubber-cushioned shackles and self-adjusting ilic double-acting shock ab- s and large brakes.

rear spring is mounted on es back of the axle housing s bowed out around the dif- ial housing.

shape of the frame and de- of the springs allow the body mounted close to the road, lowering the car's center of y and improving roadability iding comfort.

E BRAKES EMPLOYED.

large mechanical four-wheel have 186 square inches of ng surface. Brake drums are t alloy iron which tests show not score easily.

steel-spoke wheels are 13 in diameter. Large hubs e the bolts which attach the to the drum. There are 32 -spokes, which are short, y pitched and electrically d to the drop-center rim and shell, forming an unusually unit.

es are 18x5.25 inches. Each tire anced to avoid "tramping" or ion at higher speeds.

INSULATED BY RUBBER.

ber in the spring shackles and absorber links not only in- s the frame and body from shocks but also prevents mech- friction and eliminates the for lubrication at these points. orque-tube drive is used. The transmits the driving thrust point well forward in the car eaves the springs free to per- their function. Radius-rods the axles in alignment.

front axle is of "I" beam sec- of chrome alloy steel for gth and toughness. The axle rply tilted to give great road- and easy steering.

.ND $40,000,000 OR TIRES, RUBBER

RON, Ohio. — Several million besides millions of rubber units, will be required by the Motor Company in its 1932 facturing program, according formation received by rubber anies here. Of the half-billion s being poured by Ford into rial channels, the rubber in- 's share will be approxim ely 0,000, it is estimated. Th be spent for tires, and nder for other rubber acc

ETY FEATURES LISTED

new steel bodies with narrow pillars permit full vision for s. Slanting safety glass wind- s minimize headlight glare four-wheel brakes, newly de- d front and rear radius-rods, stantial front axle tilt, and a enter of gravity all contribute eat comfort and safety.

V-8 FACTS

65 H. P. Engine
Vibrationless
Rapid Acceleration
Low Fuel Consumption
Automatic Spark Control
Downdraft Carburetor
75 Miles an Hour
Silent Second Gear
Synchronized Gear Shift
Large Roomy Bodies
Safety Glass Windshield
Self-adjusting Shock Absorbers and Transverse Cantilever Springs
Comfortable Riding
Low Center of Gravity
Rubber Insulated Chassis
Engine Rubber Mounted

BODIES STRESS STREAMLINES

Low Center of Gravity Adds to Passenger Safety and Roadability.

Modern streamlines characterize the designs of the bodies for the new Ford cars.

From the V-type radiator shell with its grille to the fuel tank in the rear the streamline effect has been carried out. Roof and sill lines are curved and harmonize with the deeply crowned fenders and long wide running-boards. A belt moulding runs back from the radiator.

The windshield, set at a 10-degree slant with narrow front pillars affords excellent driving vision.

An oval instrument panel with controls grouped conveniently materially adds to driving ease. The spark lever has been eliminated through the use of automatic spark control. Choke and throttle are conveniently located on the instrument panel. A coincidental lock on the steering column secures both ignition and steering.

Passenger comfort is insured by ample head room and leg room has been accomplished no by using a double-drop frame. lso by improvements in the

NEW FORD PLANT OPENS

Seattle, Wash.—Recently completed and the third of its kind to be built on the Pacific Coast in two years, the new Seattle assembly plant of the Ford Motor Company has joined other American and Canadian plants in the production of the new Fords.

LOW WEIGHT ECONOMY AID

V-8 but Little Heavier Than Model "A"—Low Operating Costs Are Result.

Long-standing Ford engineering practices governing the relation of weight to safety, speed and economical operation are exemplified in the new V-8, it was pointed out today.

The result of months of tests and research is that the V-8 actually weighs only about 100 pounds more than the Model A and the new four-cylinder Ford weighs even less than its predecessor.

To produce a car with an eight-cylinder V-type engine without materially increasing the weight necessitated a most painstaking study of the design of every part of the car. Wherever possible in the new car, lighter, but equally serviceable and durable materials have been utilized without loss of strength and in some cases substantially increased strength.

Finer steels, rubber replacing metal in numerous parts and aluminum for heavier materials in others to mention only a few of the vital changes, account for the lightness which makes the new Ford V-8 as revolutionary in this regard as the Model T was in its day.

EXCESS WEIGHT WASTE.

Many pounds of excessive weight, which cost in gasoline and performance, have been eliminated in the new Fords by the use of, for instance, a hollow drive-shaft in place of the former solid type which added nothing in strength, safety or durability; by the substitution of rubber for metal in nearly a score of parts including spring shackles, universal joints, engine mountings and shock-absorber mountings; and by the adoption of one-piece construction wherever bolts could be eliminated by the use of welded joints.

It was recalled today that long before the advent of the Model T, Henry Ford pointed out that "the more a motor car weighs, naturally the more fuel and lubricants are used in driving; the lighter the weight, the lighter the expense of operation."

WEIGHT NOT STRENGTH.

"Weight may be desirable in a steam roller but not in an automobile," asserted Mr. Ford. "Strength has little to do with weight. The most beautiful things in the world are those from which all excess weight has been eliminated. Strength is never just weight—either in men or things."

BODY INTERIORS ARE ATTRACTIVE

Many New Features Add to Appearance of Standard And De Luxe Types.

Interiors of the new bodies are fitted attractively. Mohair upholstery is now standard equipment in all closed cars but not in the convertible types. A long-wearing wool cloth is optional in the standard closed cars and either broadcloth or Bedford cord in the de luxe closed bodies. Bedford cord or genuine leather is available in the convertible types. Genuine leather is used for the seat cushions and backs of the de luxe phaeton and in the front seat of the de luxe roadster. The standard roadster and phaeton are upholstered in artificial leather.

Dome lights are furnished in all closed cars. The de luxe closed body types are fitted with cowl lamps, toggle grips, arm rests, ash trays and floor carpets. A robe rail is provided in the de luxe Fordor Sedan.

In both the standard and de luxe coupes the rear window may be lowered for ventilation, or in the latter to permit conversation with persons riding in the rumble seat. For the protection of extra passengers, safety glass is used for the rear windows of all cars having rumble seats as standard equipment.

Hardware is of modern design, exterior hardware being of rustless steel and interior hardware nickel plated. One key controls the door and ignition locks. Unusually wide, deep pockets are recessed in the front doors of all body types.

SHOCK ABSORBERS SELF-REGULATING

New Device Automatically Adjusts Units for Greatest Comfort.

The unusual riding comfort of the new Ford cars is attributable in part to the new Houdaille double-acting hydraulic shock absorbers with which the chassis is equipped.

Two new features have been built into the new shock absorbers. One is a thermostatic control which compensates for varying temperature conditions. The other is an automatic adjustment for sudden road shocks.

Thermostatic coils automatically adjust the shock absorbers to the exact resistance required by varying temperatures so that their ability to cushion road shocks is maintained always at the maximum. Provision for manual adjustment of the shock absorbers is eliminated.

The degree of resistance to sudden road shocks is controlled by a valve operating automatically which regulates the flow of liquid between the chambers. The result is that the shock absorbers always are regulated to give the most comfortable riding under all temperature conditions, on all sorts of roads and at all speeds.

ENGINE OF 90° V-TYPE; INSURES SMOOTHNESS

Cylinders and Crankcase Cast in One Piece. Downdraft Carburetor, Fuel Pump, New Valves Other Features.

The Ford V-8 engine is of the 90-degree type, developing 65 brake horse-power at 3,400 R. P. M. It introduces new mechanical features which simplify construction and minimize wear.

The new engine is remarkably free from vibration. Frequent and overlapping impulses deliver the power in a smooth, constant flow.

The 65-pound crankshaft is of the 90-degree type with its four throws or cranks at right angles to each other. The crankshaft is statically and dynamically balanced. Throws are counterbalanced. There are three large main bearings.

Crankshaft, connecting rods and pistons are in balance and operate with smoothness at all engine speeds. Pistons are of aluminum alloy. Each has three rings. The lower one, being slotted, acts as an oil-control ring.

CAST IN SINGLE PIECE.

Cylinder blocks and crankcase are cast in one piece with the result that cylinders and crankshaft are always perfectly aligned.

New-type one-piece valves which eliminate push rods operate directly off the camshaft. Thus instead of doubling the number of pushrods used in the 4-cylinder engine, they are eliminated altogether.

All connecting rods are of the single-end type and are interchangeable. Those from opposite cylinders are placed side by side on the same crankshaft throw. A new type of floating crank-pin bushing, babbitted inside and out, distributes the pressure load from opposing cylinders over the entire crank-pin bearing surface.

The intake manifold passages are cast integral with an aluminum coverplate between the cylinder blocks. This is a new Ford development.

DOWN-DRAFT CARBURETOR.

The down-draft carburetor is supplied by a fuel pump which is of the diaphragm type operating off an eccentric on the camshaft.

A small opening inside the center of the manifold coverplate runs from the exhaust chamber on one side of the engine block to the exhaust chamber on the other side, allowing a surge of hot gases to pass back and forth and forming a hot spot on the intake manifold, which preheats the gas.

SPARK CONTROL AUTOMATIC.

The distributor is connected directly with the front end of the camshaft and thus operates without any interposed gears. The distributor is fully automatic, spark timing being controlled by vacuum from the intake manifold.

The New Ford V-8 Engine

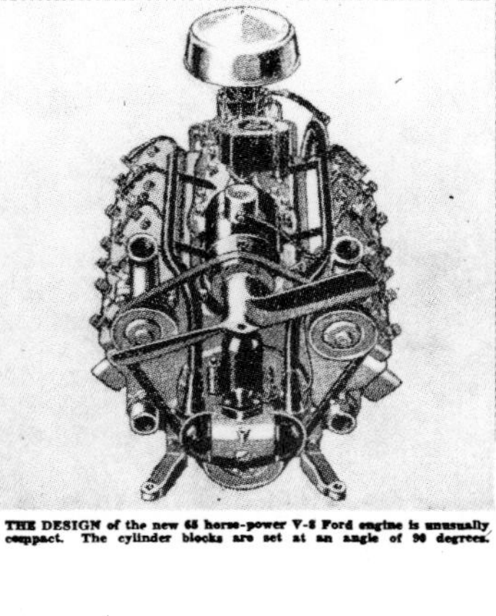

THE DESIGN of the new 65 horse-power V-8 Ford engine is unusually compact. The cylinder blocks are set at an angle of 90 degrees.

NEW 8-CYLINDER CAR; ALSO AN IMPROVED '4'

Represent Ford Faith That Public Will Buy Outstanding Value; Set New Standards In Low-Priced Field.

Once again Ford pioneers the way.

With the introduction of the new V-8 at various points throughout the United States, the Ford Motor Company meets the transportation problem of a new economic era.

Almost a quarter of a century ago Henry Ford gave the world a car that was both low in first cost and in subsequent up-keep, setting a new standard in automobile manufacture for that era. He now gives the public another car which, retaining those essentials, also embodies all the comforts and improvements that modern engineering provides.

By embracing in a low-priced car features heretofore found only in high-priced cars the Ford V-8 has set a new standard for the motor industry.

By the elimination of useless bulk and weight it avoids the prohibitive up-keep charges which the average owner is unable to meet even though he can afford the initial cost of a larger and heavier car. In a word it provides the average individual not only the kind of an automobile he is able to own and maintain but also the kind to which he is entitled in this modern era.

PIONEERS OF A NEW TYPE.

Both the V-8 and the Model T are to be classed as pioneers, but of a vastly different type. They are as different as the problems which each was designed to solve.

The Model T blazed the way for the motor industry. It was almost entirely utilitarian in character. It pioneered in an era when the public was not conscious of its need for motor cars. The V-8 pioneers in an era when that conscious need is universal.

Personal transportation should never be a luxury. It and the latest of its refinements are the rightful heritage of every man, woman and child in America. Modern civilization has given this to them. This heritage is wholly reasonable and the logical outgrowth of higher standards of living.

TO MEET THE PUBLIC DEMAND.

Standards in manufacture and standards of living go hand in hand. One must keep pace with the other. What is even more to the point they should go forward together.

"How certain are you that you will have a market for the new car?" Henry Ford was asked.

"We are not certain," he replied. "But we are going to risk it. Some one has to risk something to get things started. The chief thing to do is to meet the public's demand for something new and better at a price the average man can pay. We have done everything in our power to give the public that kind of a car."

The Ford Motor Company has taken risks in the past, but never at the cost of lowering standards. During the twenty-nine years that it has manufactured automobiles, there have been times when it sold cars at an actual loss. Over a period of years it has realized an average of only a few dollars per unit. Although at times the income ebbed, standards have continuously and consistently risen.

MR. FORD SAYS:—

"Probably most people in speaking of the V-8 will say that we have built another automobile," Henry Ford said. "Well, that is true. But more important is the fact that we have now given the public another standard. No matter by what name an article is called, properly managed business always remembers that primarily it is the manufacturer of standards. That much set, all else follows naturally enough.

"I have said that we are taking a risk. But by that I mean merely a temporary risk. Our experience has taught us that such will be the case. We have faith, and faith you know is catching. If we have confidence others will have confidence too. The public will come half way—it always does. The huge number of advance orders already received demonstrates that point.

"The risk is a good one because it is a risk placed with the people. I know of no better collateral, nor any that is half as good."

V-8 PRICED TO MEET TIMES

Lower Material Costs Reflected in Four and Eight Prices.

For weeks, since it became practically certain that Henry Ford would offer a V-8 and a new four-cylinder car, the universal question has been, "How much will they cost?" Answering that, the price announcement instantly gave rise to another:

"How can he do it?"

It has been known for weeks that the Ford company was bringing out an almost revolutionary eight-cylinder V-type motor that would be interchangeable with a greatly improved four-cylinder motor in any one of fourteen standard and de luxe body types. Likewise it has been known that new cars would have a longer wheelbase, roomier bodies, and a variety of other new features.

LOW PRICES EXPLAINED.

"How can he do it?" Ford Motor Company officials were asked.

Back of the prices, it was explained, is the cardinal Ford policy to produce the best possible automobile priced at a figure and sold in terms within the range of the most modest income to own and maintain. The new cars may be purchased for a small down payment on convenient, economical terms through the authorized Ford finance plans of the Universal Credit Company.

The prices announced, however, would not have been possible two or three years ago. Within the last twenty-four to thirty-six months the economic situation has undergone radical changes.

MATERIAL COSTS DROP.

Steel and iron are lower in price than at any time in the last two decades. Copper is lower than in the last 30 years, while aluminum is cheaper today than at any time since its development. Likewise, rubber, used in one form or another in hundreds of parts of the new Ford, has reached a new low level.

All of these factors, as well as the important fact that the Ford Motor Company owns vast natural resources of the basic materials entering into the manufacture of its cars, contribute to the low production costs which make possible the new prices, and which conform to another Ford principle that "it is better to sell a large number of cars at a reasonably small margin of profit, than to sell fewer cars at a large margin of profit."

14 BODY TYPES ARE AVAILABLE

Fourteen beautiful body types may be obtained with either the V-8 or improved four-cylinder engine. They are:

Roadster.
Phaeton.
Coupe.
Tudor Sedan.
Fordor Sedan.
Sport Coupe.
Cabriolet.
De Luxe Roadster.
De Luxe Phaeton.
De Luxe Coupe.
De Luxe Tudor Sedan.
De Luxe Fordor Sedan.
Victoria.
Convertible Sedan.

These body types may be obtained in a wide variety of color combinations.

LEFT *A four cylinder Panel Delivery was one of the models on permanent display in Ford's Woodwood Avenue showroom at the old Highland Park plant*

RIGHT *With a logical presentation like this who wouldn't buy one of the new Fords*

COURTESY — KNOWLEDGE — ENTHUSIASM
Plus
LOGICAL PRESENTATION
DEVELOP SALES

Beauty	Comfort	Performance	Safety		Value
1. Long low appearance.	1. Roominess.	1. Smoothness	1. Low centre of gravity.	**I D E M O N S T R A T I O N**	1. 8 cylinder smoothness.
					2. Rubber cushioning.
2. Air flow design	2. Comfortable seating.	2. Power.	2. All steel bodies.		3. Self adjusting shock absorbers.
3. New wheels.					4. Silent, synchro - mesh helical cut intermediate speed and constant mesh gearbox.
			3. Safety glass.		5. Down Draft Carburettor
4. Stylish, modern, dignified.	3. Riding ease.	3. Constant efficiency.	4. One piece wheels.		6. Fully automatic ignition control.
					7. Roomy bodies
5. Luxurious convenient interior.		4. Smooth flexible satisfying performance.	5. Large brakes.		8. Safety glass.
	4. Pleasant effortless driving.				9. Rustless steel.
					10. Value for above the price.
6. Pride of ownership.			6. Owner protection.		11. Sign order here.

LEFT *The 1932 Michigan State Fair was to be the venue of Ford's biggest outdoor exhibition during 1932. Here members of the public are trying out the ride of a V8 Fordor over a simulated railroad crossing. The railroad was just one section on a half mile oval track which included a gradient, one-wheel ramp and a rough rough road section*

especially Chevrolet, to get almost five months lead on him, nor did he anticipate the unreliability of the car he had spent millions of dollars on developing, and he especially didn't understand the fact that although he was prepared to risk everything to stimulate the economy, that wouldn't be enough. During 1932 Ford was to lose almost $75 million. Nevertheless he launched his dealers on an impressive sales campaign.

It began with the nationwide dealer shows and exhibitions in New York at 1740 Broadway, in San Francisco and a permanent display of 19 versions of the new range at Detroit's Woodward Avenue Showrooms at Ford's old Highland Park plant.

Sales were, unfortunately, as slow in forthcoming as cars. In April only 4967 V8s were built, but at last these were to be supplemented with the four-cylinder Model Bs. By May production was beginning to pick up and Ford was obviously finding it easier to make fours, perhaps because he had to hand plenty of parts. 19,499 V8s were produced, but this figure was far exceeded by the numbers of Bs – 30,571. Sales for that month, however, only reached 23,556. Where were those 200,000 customers Ford had claimed placed orders during the weekend of its announcement?

It was becoming obvious in those Depression-torn days that those members of the public who did have the money to buy a new car were not going to be such an easy sell as they had been in the past. Consequently, Ford sent out to its dealers literature describing how a salesman might go about securing a sale.

In the US and Canada this literature took several forms. There were, among others, the Sales Manual and the Sales Presentation Guide. In England and most other countries there was merely the Salesman's Reference Book, which was a small but expanded reprint of the Sales Manual. All dealt with the correct procedure for what Head Office thought was the logical presentation of the car which would result in a sale.

The American Sales Presentation Guide consisted of a brown leatherette folder, titled 'The New Ford', containing 41 sales presentation cards. Each one was 11 × 14 in and described, with drawings and photographs, aspects of the new Ford.

The Sales Manual was, in America, a loose-leaf folder containing a description and specification of the new models. In Canada, where sales were even worse, this manual took the form of a bound book and was much more comprehensive.

Eventually this book was reprinted and reissued as the 1932 Selling Programme. Even their Sales Presentation cards were superior, again being bound in leatherette and containing over 50 cards all illustrated with photographs not drawings.

All of this literature is now extremely rare, but Ford of England do have a copy of the Salesman's Reference Book, which is perhaps more interesting than its North American counterparts because it deals with the four-cylinder models in as much detail as it does with the V8. The Model B received scant attention in its homeland, but in Europe, and especially the UK, the four-cylinder, which was cheaper to operate, was consequently more popular.

The book begins with a short précis of Ford history and what the development of the new models meant. It then goes on to describe the early thirties as 'an age of aggressive selling where few prospects hunt up a salesman. Continual contact with potential buyers and proper presentation and sales methods are most essential to influence buyers to purchase one make of car in preference to another.' It continues, 'You must have prospects. Prospects are your stock-in-trade. Day and night you should be on the alert for them. Make some new contacts each day, take advantage of every opportunity to meet people, to make new friends and to let them know you are a Ford salesman.'

From there the salesman was guided through the approach saying, 'Before you can sell cars you must approach people. It is the first step in every sale.' It went on to say how the salesman should create a feeling of respect, arouse a friendly attitude and interest, obtain information about the prospect and then make him a friend.

From there the Logical Presentation took the salesman along a charted course which would result in a sale.

The strong point made in all of this literature was 'Driving means buying'. Fords were renowned for their vibration, and according to designer Joe Galamb even Henry Ford loathed the four-cylinder's vibration and that was why he didn't care what it cost to develop the V8. But the V8, and even the four, were different from their predecessors – both had rubber mountings for the engine plus plenty of other rubber insulation. The V8 was an inherently more balanced engine and it possessed terrific acceleration. Ford knew that once you got a prospect to drive the V8 you had him sold. Consequently he handed down instructions to 'Get the V8 out on the road'.

With company guidance, dealers organized 'Open Air Salons' at which the public were invited to drive. Much of this campaign was aimed at overcoming public resistance to an unreliable motor car.

Ford's grandest official outdoor exhibition was held in September during the Michigan State Fair. A small village of marquees housed the Ford exhibits, which included the various models, a cutaway chassis and other interesting displays plus some more lighthearted entertainment in the form of films and musicians. Free literature was handed out to every visitor by staff of the Rouge plant.

The centrepiece of the display was a half-mile circuit around which the public were encouraged to drive. The exhibition was a resounding success and by the time it was all over Ford had taken 63,000 people for a ride.

The event may have impressed the public, but it made little impression upon the sales figures. They fell, for the third month running, to 25,000.

Domestic sales of the V8 were infinitely better than those abroad. The V8 had come too late for the London debut of the Model Y, and although some Bs were to hand none were shown at the Albert Hall exhibition in February. Instead they were announced in May but didn't go on show until the Ford Motor Exhibition at the White City between 13 and 22 October. In France, where there were heavy import restrictions, the V8 cost three times its American equivalent. Only 2500 Fords of any kind were sold in Australia, hardly more than 1000 went to Sweden, and Canada had a disastrous year, producing fewer than 30,000 vehicles of all types, and many were for export.

In desperation Ford launched another sales incentive with the slogan 'Driving means buying'. The National Fall Sales Drive lasted from 21 October until 31 December and during this period dealers were encouraged to canvass from door to door in order to get the public to buy. If they took all their allotment prior to 16 December they got a $20 bonus and they received an extra $20 for each unit sold over the allotment.

Later in the year dealers received another $5 for every unit sold, then an extra $5 for every four sold and then an added bonus of another $5 per unit if more than 20 were sold in a month.

As another winter of discontent rolled across the Great Lakes Ford could hardly boast of his achievements. The sales figures were but 20 per cent of his projected targets, however, the V8 was now almost fully sorted and certainly would be over the next year. Nevertheless, against the deepest depression the industrial revolution has ever known he made a good showing and any marketing man would have been proud of the hype generated that year. Sadly, it didn't work and sales dropped off drastically in the last months of the year. In November came the lay-offs, and the trusty, familiar Ford four had already been relegated to commercial use, but for the first time Ford readied themselves for their first annual body change. Edsel had sold his father on restyling the car for 1933, and although Chevrolet and Plymouth would both have new models out before him, Henry's next baby would be on sale by mid-February.

● Open the door for the prospect and call attention to the attractive handles and sturdy doors. Invite him to open and close the door himself. As the prospect enters the car emphasize the wide, strong running boards, with the rubber covering vulcanized to the steel for long wear. Also refer to the large door openings, permitting ease of entrance and exit. Show how the handles may be moved up to lock the doors from the inside.

In desperation Ford sent his salesmen out canvassing from door to door. He knew that people would be impressed once they got behind the wheel. He was probably right too for sales steadied slightly in November and December

● After the engine has been warmed up, make a demonstration of acceleration in high gear. Do this on a smooth, paved road and within a stretch of between 150 and 175 yards or 1/10 of a mile as indicated on the speedometer. Start between 5 and 10 miles an hour and accelerate with a full throttle. ▸ ▸ Explain to the prospect before you start just what you intend to do. Ask him to watch how fast the car gains speed. Later, at a speed of around 35 miles an hour, demonstrate the advantages of the synchronized transmission by shifting from high to second and vice versa. Also mention the quiet second speed.

● Move to the rear of the car, and point out how its attractive lines flow gracefully from the top of the radiator up over the car and down the rear to the tip of the fenders. These lines mean more than beauty alone. They actually improve car performance because of the lessened wind resistance. Direct attention to the attractive angle at which the spare tire is mounted, and how the fuel tank is formed and located to fit inconspicuously into the lines of the car.

● Upon entering the car and before starting the engine for the road demonstration, attention should be called to such features as the following:

Roominess of bodies . . Deep, comfortable seats . . Quality of upholstery . . Interior hardware . . Windshield wiper mechanism enclosed in header . . Beautifully designed instrument panel and conveniently placed controls . . Coincidental ignition and steering lock, 3-spoke steering wheel, etc.

In both the V-8 and the 4-cylinder cars stress accessibility of starter. Be sure to start slowly and smoothly—don't race the engine.

> **A DEMONSTRATION PROPERLY MADE IS AN EFFECTIVE SALES STORY**
> ●

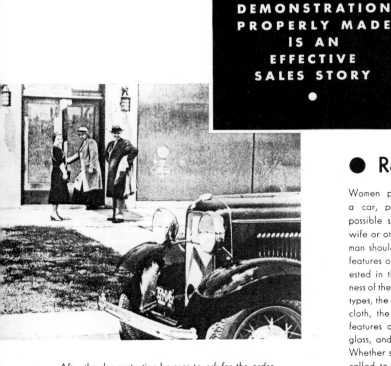

● After the demonstration be sure to *ask for the order*. The advantages of the U.C.C. deferred payment plan should be carefully explained. ▸ ▸ A trip through your dealership should also be made and the prospect should be introduced to the dealer and the department heads. ▸ ▸ Whether the order is obtained or not, explain fully to the prospect all the features of the particular body type in which he seems most interested. Also present him with a piece of literature illustrating this type.

● Remember This —

Women play an important part in the selection of a car, particularly cars for the family. Whenever possible see that the prospect is accompanied by his wife or other feminine member of the family. The salesman should courteously call to the lady's attention such features of the car as appeal to her. She will be interested in the various color combinations, the attractiveness of the interior appointments, especially in the de luxe types, the quality, durability and variety of the upholstery cloth, the depth of the seat cushions and the comfort features of the car, the protection afforded by safety glass, and the economy in upkeep and operation. ▸ ▸ Whether she is a driver or not, her attention should be called to the ease of driving, the convenience of the controls, and the adjustable driver's seat. ▸ ▸ If she makes any inquiry regarding any mechanical feature of the car, the salesman should give a clear, simple explanation. This explanation should not only include the construction of the part, but also the quality of material, the function it performs, and the reason why it is used. Be sure she fully understands your explanation.

Again—Proper Demonstration means an order

6 They are in no way a sudden development

Proclaimed the Salesman's Reference Book, and I suppose if you repeat a phrase often enough and loud enough people should believe you. But nothing could have been further from the truth when discussing the 1932 Ford V8.

Edsel understood better than his father the need to 'Meet the public's demand for something new and better at a price the average man can pay.' It is therefore likely that he encouraged his father to go ahead with the introduction of the V8, but after their hour-long meeting on 7 December in Edsel's office at the Dearborn laboratories, things began to hum, causing James Sweinhart to say of the period, 'Henry Ford personally became the dynamo of the works. He was here, there, everywhere, ordering, directing, changing.' Even Edsel said of his father, 'I have never seen him give such attention to detail as he is now.' Nevertheless the speed with which the Model B was halted and the V8 scheduled worried Edsel and although they had experience of building V8 engines for their Lincoln range, they had not been mass produced in anything like the numbers which were now proposed. Laurence Sheldrick recounted of Edsel, 'He was fearful that we would have trouble, and we did have trouble.'

Quite a few prototype engines had been built by the year's end and it could be seen that the major mechanical difficulties had been overcome, but the engine was far from refined and many production problems had yet to be surmounted. Nevertheless, the blueprints were resurrected, requests went out to suppliers for help with the design and supply of the ignition and induction systems and numerous other components. New manufacturing machines to cope with the complexity of V8 production were quickly designed and ordered and in just three short, hectic months, as Laurence Sheldrick recalled, 'This thing was whipped into shape.'

Commendable though this feat was it did mean that there was little or no time for testing. There had never been anything other than prototype four-cylinder models and V8 cars were not assembled until three weeks before introduction. Hardly time to mount a proper test programme, so they went on sale almost untried.

Nearly all of the first 2000 motors would need their camshafts, push rods, valves, valve guides and front cover changed. While the next 2000 or so would need a new front cover, even then none of these first 4250 cars could be sold; instead they were to be used as demonstrators.

Edsel's reservations were therefore justified; as soon as the cars reached the public and were put to use so the letters of complaint began to flood into the Dearborn offices. In their wake came an equal and opposite flow of service and change letters from the Ford Motor Company. They were fairly detailed and sometimes included photographs and diagrams. Some dealt with minor changes like a new oil filler assembly, whereas others instructed dealers to totally dismantle the engine for a bearing modification. Nevertheless, the sheer volume of paperwork and the detail contained therein testifies to the hurry in which the V8 was put into production.

Ford was, however, trying to do something about the problems both with the product and with its maintenance. Development work was continuing and many of the initial problems would be eliminated by the year's end. Ford also instigated the establishment of service schools, which would teach branch mechanics the correct way to service the new model.

To quote Service Letter 67 dated 26 May 1932, 'Advise by return mail the total number of dealers' mechanics that have been trained in the branch service school, the number of mechanics attending each class, the time required to complete each class; also how many dealers have been called upon to see if the mechanics trained in the school are actually putting these instructions to good use, and if the information they received is being passed on to the rest of the mechanics in the dealer's service department. In your reply please cover each point mentioned as well as giving us any other

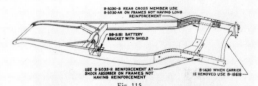

B-5030-B REAR CROSS MEMBER USE
B-5030-AR ON FRAMES NOT HAVING LONG
REINFORCEMENT

B-5151 BATTERY
BRACKET WITH SHIELD

USE B-5033-R REINFORCEMENT AT
SHOCK ABSORBER ON FRAMES NOT
HAVING REINFORCEMENT

USE B-1430 WHEN CARRIER
IS REMOVED USE B-18618

Fig. 115

FRAME

During July reinforcements were added and welded in place on both frame side members as shown in Fig. 115.

The addition of these reinforcements removes the necessity for the B-5033-R frame reinforcement at the rear shock absorber on all frames equipped with the new reinforcements as shown in Fig. 115. It is, however, extremely important that the B-5033-R reinforcements be used on all frames not provided with the long reinforcement as shown in the illustration.

The addition of these reinforcements to the frame side member also necessitates the use of a shorter rear cross member as follows:

B-5030-B rear cross member (short) used on all frames reinforced as shown in Fig. 115.

B-5030-AR rear cross member (long) used for replacement on all frames manufactured prior to the addition of the reinforcements to the frame side members as illustrated in Fig. 115.

The B-1430 spare wheel carrier shown in the illustration (Fig. 115) also acts as a frame cross member, greatly contributing to its rigidity. In instances where this spare wheel carrier is removed, as on fender well installations, it should be replaced with B-18618 bar. Either the B-1430 spare wheel carrier or the B-18618 bar must be in place on all cars and commercial chassis.

BATTERY SHIELD

Fig. 115 also illustrates the BB-5151 battery bracket now used in production having a flange at the front affording maximum protection to the battery from flying stones, etc.

A new battery shield, B-5167-R, as shown in Fig. 116 is now available for all chassis manufactured prior to the adoption of the flange at the front of the battery support base as shown

in Fig. 115. These B-5167-R battery shields are easily installed by removing the floor board and battery and inserting the shield in the battery bracket with the high flange toward the front of the car. (See Fig. 116.)

When the battery is reinstalled it will hold the shield in place.

B-5167-R BATTERY
SHIELD

Fig. 116

STEERING GEAR

Due to a slight difference in the angle of the "B" Commercial Chassis Steering Gear, as compared with the passenger car chassis, these steering gears were originally provided with a different steering gear cover assembly B-3583-B. To remove the necessity of dealers carrying this part in stock, the B-3583-B housing cover has been obsoleted, and when present stocks are exhausted, will no longer be supplied.

The steering gear housing cover bolt holes in the frame side member are now elongated on all current production, as shown by the dotted lines (see Fig. 117). The elongation of these holes permit sufficient variation in the angle of the steering column, thus making the B-3583-A steering gear housing cover adaptable to both the car and commercial chassis.

ABOVE *An inherant frame weakness. Sorensen had persuaded Ford that the original tubular, rectangular section, crossmember designed by Farkas was unnecessary. Several attempts, both before and during production, failed to eliminate the problems. Farkas' design would therefore be adopted for 1933*

Ford Motor Company
Dearborn Office
Subject:

In answering
Refer to No. SERVICE LETTER #79 Replying to No:

B-45288-9 R & LH Cowl & Pillar Panel Reinforcement at Belt Rail (Cont'd)

Where this breakage occurs in service and dealer is not equipped to make satisfactory repairs, the car should be returned to the branch and the reinforcements and reinforcements assembled. In cases where dealers can install these reinforcements and make satisfactory repairs, we will absorb the dealer's actual labor cost for the installation, based upon (4) hours labor. In these cases the reinforcements will be supplied the dealer, no charge.

COWL SIDE &
PILLAR
PANEL
REIN-
FORCEMENTS

B-79272-3 To reinforce cowl side and pillar panel assemblies of closed cabs, and panel bodies, reinforcements B-79272-3 have been released for production and service.

The same instructions apply to these parts as outlined above.

FRONT
PILLAR
PANEL

In instances where the front pillar panel cracks on the upper part or about the line where the roof panel and pillar panel meet, you will make a small V shape indentation between 1/4" and 1/2" in width and 1/8" deep, all around the pillar panel as shown in sketch below. You will then fill this indentation with weld, metal finish and repaint.

Where break occurs at this point
make indentation 1/8 deep, 1/2"
wide and fill with weld:

B-45288-9 Reinforcement fit
to cowl. Then at points
marked X, spotweld for Prodn
Drill holes and weld for
service.

ABOVE *Chassis flexing caused body cracking; reinforcement panels would counteract this. The first of these were for the right and left hand cowl and pillar. For cowls not assembled to bodies they were to be spot-welded in position with eight welds! For assembled cars eight holes were to be drilled and then the patch welded in. Afterwards refinishing took place. This was necessary for all sedans, Standard and Sport Coupés, Convertible Sedans and Victoria*

BELOW *Reinforcement of the rear deck quarter panels in production required at least 15 spot welds. In service they had to be both bolted and welded in position. In service operation, dealers were allowed two hours labour per side (including refinishing) and Ford absorbed the costs*

Ford Motor Company
Dearborn Office
Subject:

In answering
Refer to No. SERVICE LETTER NO. 79 Replying to No.

B-46630-1 COUPE
B-41160-1 RDSTR
DECK DRAIN
TROUGH SIDE
BRACE TO
QUARTER PANEL
REINFORCEMENT

To prevent breakage of the rear deck quarter panels at lower corners of the deck door opening, reinforcements B-46630-1 for coupes and B-41160-1 for Roadsters have been released for production & service.

These reinforcements should be used in production on all Coupe or Roadster side panels not assembled to bodies. On above units these reinforcements should be spot welded in place with at least 15 spot welds located according to the drilling of holes as outlined in sketch below.

When necessary to install these reinforcements on bodies in service, remove the deck lower panel to quarter panel bolts. Then bolt reinforcements in place. Drill (15) 3/16" holes thru rear quarter panel and reinforcement, 5 of them evenly divided in the bead. Weld at these holes, also to side sill extension and deck drain trough side brace; metal finish and repaint.

When installation of these reinforcements has been completed, remove the old style No. 7 body bolts and install new type bolts 350524-S7, washers 34707-S7, spring B-32060, Nut 34030-S7, as outlined in chassis change letter #28.

Where dealers are equipped to install these reinforcements, we will absorb their actual labor cost of the operation, based upon two hours labor when one side only repaired and 4 hours if both sides require reinforcements.

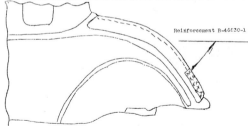

Reinforcement B-46630-1

Where breaks in metal have occurred in service on Coupe or Roadster bodies at upper corners of deck door opening, you will make a small V shape indentation, 1/4 to 1/2" in width and 1/8" deep, the full length of the crack; fill with weld, metal finish and repaint.

Where dealers are equipped to make this repair we will absorb their actual labor cost of the operation, based upon one hour labor when one side only is repaired, and two hours if both sides.

BELOW *Quarter panel to back panel reinforcements B-46640 were also released for all sedans, Standard and De Luxe Coupés and Victorias. Again Ford would absorb the dealers' labour (3 hours) if they were able to execute a satisfactory repair*

Ford Motor Company
Dearborn Office
Subject:

In answering
Refer to No. SERVICE LETTER NO. 79 Replying to No.

B-46640
QUARTER
PANEL TO BACK
PANEL
REIN-
FORCE-
MENT

A quarter panel to back panel reinforcement, B-46640 has been released for production and service, for all standard and De Luxe Coupes, Standard and De Luxe Tudors, Standard and De Luxe Fordors and Victoria.

These reinforcements should be assembled on all bodies not built into bodies. They should be assembled over the weld joint of quarter panel and back panel and as near the end of weld as possible and not interfere with the assembly of roof assembly. These parts should be spot welded in place, as per sketch.

To repair bodies in service where cracks have developed at the weld line of the quarter panel to back panel, remove rear seat back assembly, back curtain, quarter window moulding, back window moulding, rear quarter trim, and drop head lining at point opposite to crack in panel. Then install one or more of the reinforcements, (depending upon length of crack in metal.) Place reinforcement over the crack and drill (6) 3/16" holes from inside of body thru each reinforcement and outer panel, then weld at these holes; metal finish and repaint.

In cases where dealers can install these reinforcements and make satisfactory repairs, we will absorb the dealer's actual labor cost for the installation, based upon 3 hours labor. In these cases the reinforcements will be supplied the dealer, no charge.

REINFORCEMENT B-46640
Use quantity required to
reinforce break:

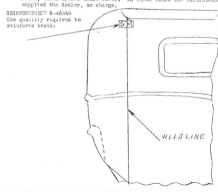

WELD LINE

information you have covered with this work.'

Unfortunately, even by September it was obvious that the training scheme had not been entirely satisfactory, as Service Letter 75 of 9 September confirms: 'The training of dealers' mechanics or getting dealers' mechanics to service the V8 and improved 4-cylinder cars properly has not been accomplished by the Branches. After four months' work by the Branch Organization, you can find dealers' men who are not familiar with methods of analyzing and locating possible troubles that may arise from the operation of the units, or they do not make any attempt to locate the trouble. We are daily encountering such instances, and feel that we have spent sufficient time on the subject, and now should take definite action in determining whether the dealers' organization desires to handle this work, and have a very plain talk with them, providing you know that the Branch Service Organization has been properly instructing them.

'It is not necessary for the dealers' mechanics to alter the construction or make changes in the design of unit assemblies. We have observed

ABOVE *Precise instructions and special tools and gauges wre shipped to dealers in April 1932 so that they might modify the oil grooves in the main bearing*

RIGHT *New connecting rod bearings, 18-6211, were also supplied*

FAR RIGHT *Subsequent to tests being carried out on Van Born Road these and other rather sketchy reports were passed on to Sorensen, Bricker, Dragsdorf and Petersen on 18 April 1932*

BELOW *This photograph of frost covered pipes surrounding a V8 test rig, taken on May 19, 1932, in the cold room, proves that Ford were at least making some attempts to sort out the engine's problems. With it's tendency to overheat it may, however, have been more beneficial to construct a hot room.*

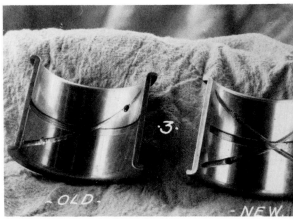

instances, however, where items such as the float level of the carburettor has been changed by dealers' mechanics. The stop on the front brake carrier plates has been altered. Where the unit cannot be adjusted or repaired in accordance with instructions covered by Service Bulletin, Service Letters or Service Schools, the unit should be replaced and forwarded to us for our inspection, as, if a change in design is necessary, we should have the facts and have it come through our Engineering Department. Please acknowledge, outlining the program that is laid out by your Branch Organization to improve this service condition, and to assure us that dealers' mechanics can properly service these units. If there is anything further required from here, please state what additional help we can give you.'

The first major problem to come to light was the chassis weakness. Sorensen's cost-cutting demands for chassis construction resulted in a weakness which had an adverse effect on the steering and caused flexing and subsequent cracking in the bodywork. The first attempts to cure this were made even before the V8 went into production and consisted of heavier gearbox cross-members that now enveloped the rear of the transmission case, instead of merely supporting it, plus heavier, full-height K members. In addition to this modification the frame side rails were stamped with that distinctive '32 pressing, which presumably imparted a little torsional strength to the chassis.

This was, however, not enough and after only 500 or 600 units had been made it was found necessary to install braces between the side rails and the centre cross-member. Service Letter 65 of 22 April instructed how this operation was to be carried out on cars already in dealers' hands.

Within a month more frame-strengthening plates, this time to be mounted to the side rails above the rear axle, with a narrower rear cross-member, had been shipped to dealers for fitting free of charge.

The problem would not be eliminated until the introduction of the Model 40, when Farkas pushed through his original concept of a sturdy X-member.

Most of the body styles suffered some cracking in one place or another and eventually reinforcement plates had to be shipped to dealers with Service Letter 79, dated 18 October, which contained instructions and diagrams for their fitment.

A further Service Letter, No. 85, dated 30 December, contained a sketch and instructions for the repair of cracks around the door opening of the Panel Delivery.

Another major problem quickly realized centred around the V8 bearings and lubrication system. Tool and diemaker Clem Davis recalled, 'They had trouble with the bearings. The bearings just wouldn't hold up. They wouldn't take the pounding.'

A Service Letter dated 29 April contained specific instructions, photographs, tools and gauges to enlarge the oil grooves of the main bearings in the block. New, three-groove, connecting rod bearings were also supplied.

Eventually, for 1933, Ford introduced new copper-lead insert bearings made for them by Cleveland Graphite Bronze. This was a strip bearing previously used only in trucks. It seemed, however, to cure the problem.

Further attempts to improve the lubrication quickly followed and on 7 June a new camshaft

(18-6250) was released with spiral-cut oil grooves on the front and centre bearings so as to provide additional oil flow at these points. The cam change was effective on 2 June, commencing motor number 18-33621.

Excessive oil consumption was another great source of embarrassment for Ford's V8 as Clem Davis remembered: 'When the V8 came out, they had trouble with motors using oil. They came out with it in too much of a hurry. When they were using a quart of oil for 50 miles, you know what that meant.'

Several minor changes had to be made to cure small leaks, but by July a new, highly efficient oil pressure regulator (18-6660) had been developed. It required no adjustment and was factory fitted from engine number 18-76601. Service Letter 71, of 15 July, requested dealers to, 'Install as quickly as possible,' on engines prior to that number.

A further precaution against owners operating their cars with insufficient oil in the crankcase came on 16 September, when a change was made to the oil level indicator. The dipstick was made 1 in shorter and had its 'Low' mark raised 1 in, thus making the spacing between the 'F' and 'L' level 2 in instead of 3 in. This effectively increased the oil capacity and reduced the likelihood of running dry.

No more major modifications were made to the lubrication system, but several small changes were made to that highly efficient oil pressure regulator early in 1933, when the engine was being built for the Model 40.

Overheating was another troublesome trait. Some testing had taken place – in the early days on the road to Georgia, in the cold room at the Dearborn laboratories and, once in production, on Van Born Road, but the conditions were not as severe as those experienced by the motoring

---

VICTORIA-Mot. 3377   (Cont'd from page 2)
Bolt loose in valve cover right side
Coil screws loose holding coil to distributor
Gas tank rubs bumper bracket bold right side
Motor cut out at high speed changed coil and did not improve it. Changed
     distributor assembly and still did not improve. While motor was
     cutting out, I throwed ignition switch off and pushed the
     clutch out so fuel pump would not pump any more gas from tank
     and stopped the car and carburetor man took screws out of cover
     on float chamber and found the gas to be one quarter inch below the
     correct lever in cowl showing the fuel pump did not deliver sufficient
     gas for speeds of 78 to 80 M.P.H. Came back in the garage
     and installed new fuel pump and found we could hold car at a speed
     of 78 to 80 M.P.H. for four and five miles at a stretch
     without any cutting out.
This car was driven for 182 miles, it developed a slight knock in number
     2 cylinder when accelerating quick, also transmission became very noisy
     at 78 to 80 M.P.H. or 40 to 42 M.P.H. in second. I took Mr. Smith
     from Motor Bldg out and let him hear both motor and transmission.
     He asked me to have motor pulled as I told him that most of the
     182 miles were driven at speeds from 60 to 80 M.P.H. He thought it would be
     a good job to check into for scores and bearing trouble.
Motor was pulled Saturday 4-16-32 by night shift and sent to Mr. Smith
     in Motor Bldg.

VICTORIA-Mot. 3377 - Driver: Murray
Noisy time gears
Fan belt hits front motor support at high speed.
One noisy valve
Gas tank rubs on bumper bolt right side

public, particularly those living in the south-western United States, where temperatures often exceed 100 degrees F. Initially, Ford engineers dismissed the claims, presumably because the colder climate of the Great Lakes region had given them no cause for concern. There is certainly no indication of overheating problems in the road test reports conducted by drivers Gentry and Murray, which were passed to Sorensen and others on 18 April 1932. Instead the engineers tried to blame the condition upon loose fan belts or out-of-tune engines, but the complaints persisted.

Conceding that there might be something wrong, a new four-blade fan and larger fan pulley were introduced on 6 May. Eventually, on 15 July, a new series of $2\frac{3}{4}$ in radiators, manufactured by both McCord and Long, were announced. To be fitted free of charge if that was the only way of satisfying the customer, these radiators, identified by the numbers 1, 2 or 3 stamped on the top tank, went some way towards alleviating the problem. However, when the problem persisted it became necessary, on 28 October, to increase the number of bonnet louvres from 20 to 25 to improve airflow around the engine.

Unfortunately, as we have seen, the cooling problem would not be licked until 1937, when the water pumps which Henry Ford wanted on top of the engine were removed to the bottom, where they could do their job properly.

Incidentally, on the early 20-louvred bonnets the rear louvre was open, but on the later 25-louvre bonnets, the rear louvre was closed and the louvres were repositioned to align with the bonnet hinge. Bonnets with 20 louvres on a raised panel, similar to that found on the Model A, were used on foreign-made vehicles.

Although Gene Farkas had increased the brake drum diameter from 11 to 12 in, and the total lining area from 168 in (Model A) to 186 in, braking ability was nevertheless poor, especially when one took into consideration the V8's increased power-to-weight ratio compared to the Model A.

Very little was ever done about the problem other than an increase in brake plate thickness on 13 May, heat treatment of the cross shaft lever to prevent it bending when the brakes were applied and a new front brake rod support, which became made of strap steel instead of wire on 21 September.

There had always been some worry in the back of ignorant minds that pistons laying on their side would wear unduly, or that a V8 would use a lot of fuel or cause vibration, and for all the wrong reasons these notions were proved correct. The engine vibrated because the design of rubber mounts was still in its infancy. They were, however, improved for the following year.

A Fordor sedan undergoing a water test on 13 May 1932

Fuel consumption was high, about 16 mpg (Imperial) according to *The Motor Magazine*'s road test, but this was probably due to the poorly designed, restrictive induction system, which was also improved by the end of 1933.

Piston wear was a more serious and less easily remedied complaint as Clem Davis recalled: 'We were in piston difficulty there for quite a while. As soon as they would wear out a set of pistons, they would go back and the dealer would replace the pistons. They would be good again for a little while, and then soon people would be in again. The company would reimburse the dealer for the labour and give them the pistons. We gave away millions of pistons.'

The fuel system consistently gave trouble; the carburettor received several modifications and would eventually be replaced by the dual-throat carburettor for 1934. It was, however, the A.C. fuel pump that continually plagued owners, especially in winter.

In fact Service Letter 67 of 26 May referred to Instruction & Assembly Change Letter No. 6 and said, 'All fuel pump assemblies on the V8 Display cars now being returned to branches for changeover as instructed in our letters of April 22 and 29 should be replaced with the new-style fuel pump, and the old-style pump returned to the Rouge Plant. If the owner is having any difficulty with the fuel pump, even though not serious, the unit should be replaced if it has the cadmium-plated operating sleeve.'

Head of truck engineering, Dale Roeder, recalled: 'There was a tremendous amount of trouble on the early V8s with condensation around the fuel pump. In winter, this condensation would freeze up the pump mechanism; then the engine couldn't be started.'

Eventually, for 1934, this problem and another of pump corrosion, also caused by the condensing crankcase vapour, was overcome by the use of baffles and improved crankcase ventilation.

Though he had worked long and hard, Emil Zoerlein had still not managed to satisfactorily smooth out the engine by the time it went into production and recounted: 'It went into production, but we still kept working on the ignition to smooth out the rough spots.'

According to Laurence Sheldrick, 'You simply cannot devise a firing order for a 90 degree V8 with a 90 degree crankshaft with a single manifold that gives proper distribution to all cylinders. The manifold has to be broken up into two sections, half for each cylinder block feeding one stratum of the manifold. The No. 1 cylinder was always the orphan – the No. 1 cylinder of the right-hand bank.

'All sorts of firing orders were devised to try to overcome this without going to the extent of the over-and-under manifold. But that was the only cure then and it's the only cure today. All modern V8s are using the over-and-under manifold.'

Introduced in 1934 the over-and-under manifold was principally designed by Dave Anderson of the Bohn Aluminum Company, who supplied Ford with pistons, cylinder heads (for 1933), oil pans and distributor cases, as well as inlet manifolds. Bohn were in fact just one of many outside suppliers who were called in to not only manufacture parts but to design and engineer them as well.

An impossible firing order wasn't the ignition's only fault, the one-piece coil/distributor demanded by Henry Ford and made by Emil Zoerlein was an unreliable piece of equipment which was difficult at best, and impossible for the layman to maintain. Initially, it was not the 50,000 trouble-free mileage distributor that Mr Ford had envisaged.

Zoerlein came up with another coil design late in 1932 nicknamed the 'Hedgehog', but this too proved unreliable as it broke down at 4100 rpm under test conditions. Eventually Zoerlein licked the problem by going to an eight-, instead of four-, lobe cam with twin breakers acting as a make and brake system. This system eventually proved to be extremely reliable and a credit to the man who developed it with very little in the way of experience or equipment. It is interesting to note, however, that many of the service letters dealing with the return of faulty distributors indicate that there was little if anything wrong with most of them and their replacement was due almost entirely to inept or inadequate servicing by local mechanics.

The electrical system as a whole was somewhat troublesome. Several changes had to be made not only to the distributor but also to the generator and starter.

With every major facet of the engine's workings causing some sort of problem – in the induction and fuel supply, the bearings and lubrication and the electrical system – it is little wonder that the exhaust system, as simple as it was, should also be troublesome, but as Clem Davis recounted, 'They also had trouble with the cylinder blocks. They would crack very easily near the valve ports.' Blocks also suffered from sand holes and sometimes had to be exchanged.

But Clem went on to say, 'They fought that out, and they licked it too.' Just as they did all the other teething troubles.

Certainly by 1934 most of the wrinkles had been ironed out, the new engine produced a reliable 90 hp, returned about 20 mpg and had a maximum speed of almost 90 mph. It was just unfortunate

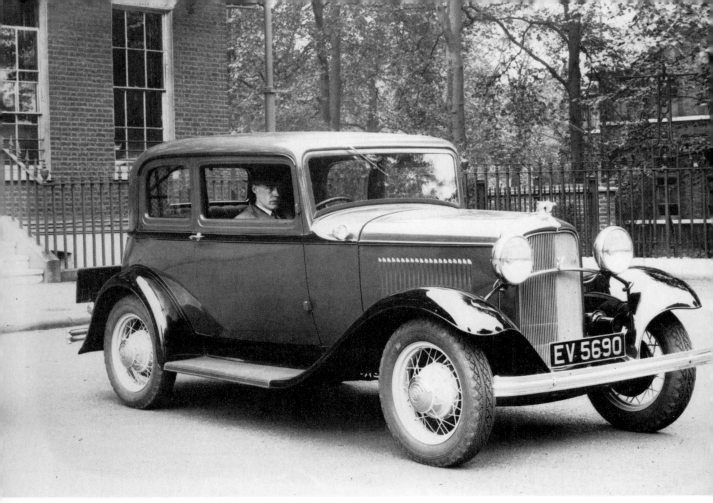

ABOVE The Motor, *in their road test of this V8 Victoria on 14 June 1932 were more than impressed with its phenomenal acceleration declaring its features as 'Exceptional Acceleration and Hill-climbing, Quiet Running and a High Maximum Speed'. Though The Motor indicated that the Victoria would not be marketed in England several models were imported and a few, possibly half a dozen, still survive*

BELOW *The results of* The Motor *test*

TABULATED DATA FOR THE DRIVER

CHASSIS DETAILS

Ford V-Eight: Victoria coupe; eight cylinders in two banks; side valves: 76.5 mm. × 95.5 mm. (3,630 c.c.); tax £30. Coil ignition, automatic timing.

Gearbox: Three forward speeds, Synchro-mesh change, central control. Ratios: 4.33, 6.96 and 12.22 to 1. (*Note.*—A 4.1 to 1 rear-axle ratio will probably become standard.)

Engine Speed: 1,040 r.p.m. at 20 m.p.h. on top gear.

PERFORMANCE

Speeds on Gears: Top, 76 m.p.h.; second, 57 m.p.h. Minimum speed, top gear, 4 m.p.h.

Petrol Consumption: Over 90 miles, including heavy traffic and Brooklands tests, 16 m.p.g.

Acceleration: Rest to 60 m.p.h. through the gears, 16⅜ secs.

DIMENSIONS, ETC.

Wheelbase. 8 ft. 10 ins.; track, 4 ft. 8 ins.; overall length, 13 ft. 9¼ ins. width, 5 ft. 6½ ins

Turning Circles: Left, 39 ft.; right, 38½ ft.

Weight: Unladen, 23 cwt.

Price: Model tested will not be marketed. A coupe will be available at £255.

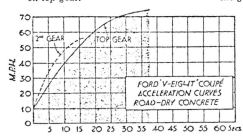

FORD 'V-EIGHT' COUPÉ
ACCELERATION CURVES
ROAD-DRY CONCRETE

BRAKES

SPEED m.p.h.		STOP feet
20	—	16
30	—	36
40	—	67
50	—	103

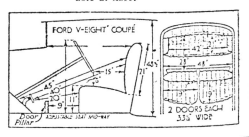

FORD V-EIGHT COUPÉ

2 DOORS EACH 33½ WIDE

that Mr Ford, in his eagerness to stimulate the economy, unwittingly perhaps but nevertheless, lumbered the public with the unenviable task of road-testing his revolutionary creation.

Regardless of all these faults the motoring press were enthusiastic about the V8's appearance. I suspect their glowing reports were a result of all too short a test period, where the cars' excellent power-to-weight ratio resulted in terrific acceleratation, unknown in a car of its price range at that time.

The Motor Magazine of 14 June 1932 stated, 'When an eight-cylinder engine of 30 hp rating is harnessed to a car weighing only 23 cwt complete, something phenomenal in the way of acceleration is to be expected.' They went on to say, 'The new Ford V-Eight, which complies with this specification, fulfilled our expectations to the utmost.'

The Autocar of 8 July that year said, 'The driver is conscious of the unusual ratio of power to weight. . . . Furthermore, acceleration is devoid of hesitation, the car veritably shooting forward the instant the throttle is depressed.'

Had these journalists had to live with the car for several weeks they may have uncovered some of its less exciting tendencies. The test driver of the *The Motor* only covered 90 miles, and J. Harrison, writing for the *Ford Times* in May, only manoeuvred the new 14.9 hp model in the close confines of a garage.

It's my opinion that these journalists were not the cynical, pampered, opinionated members of the motoring press we know nowadays, and rather than look for faults they felt it their duty to praise the car. After all, Mr Ford had done his bit to get the economy moving, now it was their turn to bolster the illusion.

Journalists, of course, were not the only sector of the public to acclaim the V8. Mechanically minded men soon learn to fix anything and the Ford engineers were definitely not sitting back congratulating themselves, indeed they were not allowed to sit. Walter Reuther recalled that one day he was sitting at his bench at Highland Park and the next he was standing up at the Rouge, with Sorensen saying, 'You can't work with these fine tolerances sitting down, you need to be firmly planted.' In one position or another the problems were overcome mostly within six months of production start-up and to prove its reliability the Standard Oil Company of New York shipped a V8 Fordor with a glass bonnet to Moose Factory on Canada's James Bay on the Hudson Bay for oil and petroleum tests. Similarly, Pennzoil had racing driver Eddie Pullen and his crew drive a total of 33,301 miles in 33 days around the Mojave Desert. In temperatures averaging between 110 degrees F and 114 degrees F the Victoria recorded an average

speed of 41.8 mph, returned 19.64 mpg (US) and used only 1½ pints of oil every 1000 miles.

These endurance tests did more than anything to convince the public that the V8 was as reliable as the good old Ford four. One group easily convinced of the engine's attributes were the racers. It wouldn't be until the following year that the full potential of the V8 would be realized, when Ford V8s took the first seven places in the Elgin Road Race, but perhaps an indication of what was to come was Fred Frame's 1932 victory lap of Indianapolis in a Ford V8 roadster.

The V8 had in fact already claimed its first victory, in French Indo-China, where a Madame A. Dassier won a 10-kilometre race during a Ford Day in Hanoi.

Mechanical defects were not Mr Ford's only cause for concern in 1932. The deepening Depression, signalled by Black Thursday's Wall Street Crash, reached its nadir in 1932, and nowhere more so than in the city of Detroit, which declared bankruptcy in 1931. As the calendar peeled back on a new year almost 50 per cent of its population (accounting for 70 per cent of the State of Michigan's total unemployed) were on welfare and 14 per cent of those had been laid off from the Ford Motor Company when production of the Model A ceased.

The auto trade was notorious for its poor treatment of labour, and although Mr Ford considered himself a humanitarian, and to some degree he was, the Rouge had the very worst reputation.

Workers throughout the industry were hired and fired as the production demanded. Men stood all day, were not allowed to talk or even smile and spotters made certain they didn't. Toilet breaks, when a relief was available, were two or three minutes and lunch lasted but a quarter of an hour.

Lay-offs were common, especially during a model changeover or the three-week inventory period, and then the older, more experienced and thus higher-paid men were unlikely to be rehired, the company preferring cheaper, hungrier labour. Ford was accused of causing a depression within a depression.

With the announcement of a new model, on 11 February, Ford began hiring, but plans only called for the re-employment of 30,000; there were still over 50,000 Ford workers idle. Mr Ford also announced that he would continue to pay a minimum of $6 per day. The 'prosperity dollar' introduced on 1 December 1929 had been cut in 1931, Henry Ford saying, 'That was the hardest thing I ever had to do.'

Unfortunately, trouble was just around the corner, or, to be precise, along Miller Road, where 5000 men, induced by the Communist Party, were approaching the Ford gates. The Young Communist League, sponsored by the Unemployment Council, applied to the City of Detroit for a parade permit for 7 March. It was granted and Mayor Frank Murphy instructed the Detroit Police not to interfere. At a rally on 6 March well-known communist leader William Z. Foster, who also left town that day, proposed that they march to the Ford works. With their demands listed in the magazine *The New Force* the marchers set off with a police motorcycle escort to the Dearborn line.

There they were met by the Dearborn police under a different master, Carl Brooks, a former Ford plant guard, who was said to have received two salaries, one from the city and another from Ford. Brookes' reaction to the march was a barrage of tear gas. Possibly luck but certainly the wind was with the protesters as the air cleared and they marched on towards the Rouge plant.

At the gates the leaders of the Ford Hunger March, as it became known, intended, some say, to make a peaceful protest handing out leaflets. Other opinions would have them take over the factory and blockade the gates. Neither occurred. Instead they had their spirits dampened by the hoses of the Dearborn Fire Department, a trick Ford first employed in 1914 to disperse unemployed men queuing for jobs.

Mr Ford, Edsel, Sorensen and others were at lunch as usual at the round table at Dearborn Laboratories. Harry Bennett, meanwhile, having heard about the march, had driven up to Gate 4, the scene of the trouble. According to Harry Bennett in his book *We Never Called Him Henry* a woman shouted, 'We want Bennett, and he's in that building.' To which Bennett replied, 'No, you're wrong, I'm Bennett.' As Bennett climbed

A facsimile of how the demands were listed in The New Force

The demands as listed in the proletariat magazine **The New Force** were:

1. Jobs for all laid-off Ford workers
2. Immediate payment of fifty per cent of full wages
3. Seven hour day without reduction in pay
4. Slowing down of the deadly speed-up
5. Two fifteen-minute rest periods
6. No discrimination against Negroes as to jobs, relief, medical service
7. Free medical aid in the Ford Hospital for the employed and unemployed Ford workers and their families
8. Five tons of coke or coal for the winter
9. Abolition of service men (factory guards)
10. No foreclusures on homes of former Ford workers – Ford to assume responsibility for all mortgages, land contracts, and back taxes until six months after regular full-time re-employment.
11. Immediate payment of lump sum of fifty dollars winter relief
12. Full wages for part-time workers
13. Abolition of graft system in hiring workers
14. The right to organize

out of his sedan a shower of missiles forced him to the ground. To protect himself he dragged 19-year-old Joe York, an organizer of the Young Communist League, on top of him. As York tried to stand up the police opened fire. York and three others, including an organizer of the Young Pioneers, were killed, 19 were seriously injured and more than 50 police and demonstrators received minor injuries.

Bennett was taken to the Henry Ford Hospital, where he was treated, with many of the other casualties, for his injuries.

Surprisingly few photographs of the events of that day remain, supposedly because Bennett's men took care of the press in an attempt to prevent any adverse publicity regarding the Ford Motor Company.

Most reports would have it that none of the demonstrators were, or ever had been, Ford workers, indeed many of them had never worked, and few came from Detroit.

According to Bennett's book, Wayne County Prosecutor Harry S. Troy conducted a grand jury investigation into the event, and while the jury criticized the action of the Dearborn Police it laid no blame for the deaths on the Ford Motor Company.

The Hunger March was just one of many labour-related problems which continued to dog the Ford Motor Company and most of the other major motor manufacturers for the rest of the year and throughout the thirties until the right to belong to a union was established under President Roosevelt. And, as we have seen, it has never stopped!

Unfortunately the Depression was deepening, banks were closing their doors at an alarming rate and money was scarce. The relentless progress of the industrial revolution towards automation, though probably not recognized at the time, was also contributing to the number of unemployed.

Sorensen said of the developments, for which he was largely responsible, 'High costs of labour and materials are danger signals. To see costs climbing and not do anything about it does not make sense. With the V8 and the Rouge plant Ford Motor Company again became the example to the industry of the United States on how to reduce the handling of materials.' And thus the number of workers.

In 1929 Ford's average number of payroll employees was 101,069, with an average wage of $36.97 for a 40-hour week. That year the company paid out $181.5 million to Rouge wage earners.

In 1930 this figure was cut to $145 million, and by 1931, when the minimum wage was cut to $6, this figure fell to $76.7 million. By 1932 the average number of workers was almost half the 1929 total

Harry Bennett is lifted from the ground in one of the few surviving photographs taken on 6 March 1932, during the Ford Hunger March. The United Press International headlined: '4 slain, 30 hurt in idle riot at Ford plant'

at 56,277 and the average weekly wage was down to $31.53.

Similarly, General Motors had employed an average 233,286 men in 1929, but by 1932 that number was halved to 116,152.

During 1932 Ford paid $6 for a skilled man, $5 for semi-skilled and $4 for labourers.

In November of that year 2500 men were on $6, 12,000 were on $5, 9600 were on $4 and 400 got less than $4. That only adds up to 24,500, the others had been laid off because of falling sales.

Incidentally, Henry Ford's earnings for 1929 had been $14 million and Edsel's were 8$ million.

Henry Ford could hardly expect his cars for the masses to be bought by the masses if they couldn't work to earn the money to pay for them. Instead of hiring one man a week, the company might employ one man for two days and another for three. With heads of families desperately seeking places, jealousy and suspicion ran rife. Accusations of favouritism were numerous, as worker Ernest Grimshaw related: 'I remember very well, certain individuals who were friends of the foreman worked every week; other fellows wouldn't get any work at all.'

So, Mr Ford's V8 would not be the magic ingredient which would drive the country out of the Depression.

Part of the problem was the fact that in 1932 he had too many assembly plants. It is generally agreed that there were 32 domestic plants, but I

71

**Ford assembly plants in the order in which they
appeared on the 1932 assembly record sheets**

Atlanta, Georgia	Edgewater, New Jersey	Oklahoma City, Oklahoma
Buffalo, New York	Houston, Texas	Omaha, Nebraska
Charlotte, North Carolina	Indianapolis, Indiana	Pittsburg, Pennsylvania
Chester, Pennsylvania	Jacksonville, Florida	Portland, Oregon
Chicago, Illinois	Kansas City, Missouri	Richmond, California
Cincinnati, Ohio	Long Beach, California	St. Louis, Missouri
Cleveland, Ohio	Louisville, Kentucky	Salt Lake City, Utau
Columbus, Ohio	Memphis, Tennessee	Seattle, Washington
Dallas, Texas	Milwaukee, Wisconsin	Somerville, Massachusetts
Denver, Colorado	New Orleans, Louisiana	Twin City (St. Paul), Minnesota
Des Moines, Iowa	Norfolk, Virginia	Dearborn, Michigan

put the number at 33 (most historians omit the Salt Lake City plant, which manufactured a small amount of truck bodies throughout 1932). Nevertheless, there were a lot of them and they had all been entirely necessary in the years preceding 1932, those pre-Depression days when demand for new Ford cars exceeded 1¼ million. Full capacity was around 2 million units. By 1932, however, Ford was to produce little more than 25 per cent of his 1929 total, just over 300,000 vehicles.

Plants were undoubtedly slow to begin production, especially when Dearborn and the Rouge had hardly got the problems sorted out themselves. Consequently only Dearborn appears in the domestic production figures for March. Walkerville, Canada, was the only other plant to begin production in March.

By April only 16 of the 33 American plants had produced anything, and for some, like Charlotte, North Carolina, production meant but one chassis.

By May everybody was working, including three other foreign plants; Asnières in France, Copenhagen in Denmark and Dagenham in England.

June, usually a slack month, saw things begin to pick up. Sales at 53,322 were almost double that of May and were almost as much as Chevrolet and Plymouth added together. Production for June topped 80,000 units, but by July it could be seen that the demand was just not there. Sales fell back, production was halved and wages were cut to $4 minimum.

Banks continued to close and in America by the end of the year the total had reached 1456.

By August it was obvious that the four-cylinder Model B had been a good stop-gap while the V8 was put into production (almost 50,000 Model B engines had been produced before Henry announced his V8 at the end of March 1931), but now it was obvious that if the public could be persuaded

to buy a car at all then it wanted a V8. Though the engine would be offered as an option for Ford cars until 1934, its end, except as a commercial power plant, was in sight.

For the next three months production hovered around the 20,000 mark, but it gradually tailed off along with sales. A massive sales drive in October helped, but November would see lay-offs and over three-quarters of a million Michigan workers unemployed. The figure had only been half a million in January.

The presidential elections took place on 4 November, and as election day approached notices appeared at the Ford plants saying, 'To prevent times from getting worse and to help get them better, President Hoover must be re-elected.' Henry Ford was obviously solidly behind Hoover, but Roosevelt, offering a 'New Deal', the rescue of the 'Forgotten Man' and 'Social Justice Through Social Action', won by six million votes. In Wayne County, where many Ford workers lived, he received 100,000 more votes than Hoover.

By December, four plants, Atlanta, Jacksonville, Milwaukee and Oklahoma City, had shut down and seven others were producing only one or two truck bodies, production fell well below 20,000 and sales were down to 13,121.

Ford was in fact getting ready to introduce the new Model 40, a car which Edsel had pushed for and which set a precedent for yearly changes for Ford. Nevertheless, minimal production of the 18 and B units continued, but by January 1933, 23 domestic plants had closed down, many of them never to reopen. February saw the start of Model 40 production in eight plants, Chester, Chicago, Cincinnati, Edgewater, Kansas City, Norfolk, Richmond and the Rouge, while the last 249 32s were made at Kansas City, and that was it as far as America was concerned. Total domestic production had been a little over 300,000, a far cry from Henry's predicted one and a half million cars.

The United States was not the only country in the world producing cars and 1932 Fords continued to roll off foreign production lines, in more or less their original form, until 1935. The last complete cars were built in Dagenham in September 1935 and consisted of ten Model B Tudor sedans for the police.

Early in 1933 newspapers were reporting that Ford had lost in the region of $75 million the previous year, and indeed the annual report filed each year with the state of Massachusetts indicated a loss of $74,861,644 for the year 1932. That averages out at a $250 loss for every car sold, but Mr Ford didn't see it that way, saying to Charles Sorensen, 'We did not lose it. We spent it. Most of it went into wage envelopes, the rest for taxes; but we did not lose it – we used it. If we had dropped it on the stock market, that would have been losing it.'

The total income from both Ford and Lincoln for 1932 was almost 50 per cent down on 1931 at $254,680,000, of which nearly 20 per cent had been earned on parts sales – nothing compared to the amounts earned from the sales of Model T spares, but nevertheless a healthy and welcome income.

Whether it was a loss or merely an investment is arguable, the balance sheet for 1932 showed a profit and loss surplus of $580,440,603 held in real estate, machinery, inventory, cash and accounts receivable. The surplus was $75 million short of the 1931 figure and was lower than it had been for many years, but it was still an intangible sum that Mr Ford could easily afford.

Other Ford companies with nothing like Henry's piggy bank to dip into fared even worse. Sales for Ford-Canada slumped by 60 per cent, its cash resources dwindled and in 1932 the company lost over $5 million.

The new baby, Dagenham, was having teething troubles and was all set to lose a great deal of money until it persuaded Dearborn to cut its $½ million bill for the design and development of the Model Y. Even with a £1 million loan from Ford-Holland, Dagenham still managed to post a loss of £681,828. Ford of France lost over $¼ million. Only Belgium, Holland and Denmark made money that year.

More news items declared that Chevrolet outsold Ford in 1932, which they did, but the figures don't look so good when we compare the months in which Ford was properly in production. Ford hardly produced anything for the first three months of the year as it readied itself for the introduction of the V8. At that time they were merely selling leftover Model As. Once Ford were competing with Chevrolet on an even basis Ford pulled up, outselling Chevy for the last seven months of the year.

1932 retail sales by the 'Big Three'			
	Ford	Chevrolet	Plymouth
January	13,566	34,516	4,801
February	9,572	28,525	4,372
March	7,878	29,929	5,605
April	6,307	45,712	14,161
May	23,556	43,500	17,325
June	53,322	37,068	16,701
July	39,634	24,869	11,018
August	31,023	23,875	9,490
September	25,283	19,361	7,689
October	19,608	14,950	4,582
November	13,997	7,990	5,197
December	13,121	10,036	10,651
TOTAL	256,867	320,331	111,592

Source: **Motor** magazine, November, 1932, and later issues.

For 1932 General Motors showed a rather small loss in comparison to Ford's, of $4,559,000, while the other member of the Big Three, Chrysler, lost just over $10 million.

So Ford spent a lot of money and saw little return in the way of sales, but by the end of 1932 he had the most modern mass-production facility in the world capable of meeting any demands in the years to come.

In the 1932 Ford he had one of the most beautiful and classic cars ever to be made in steel, and although the dies were only to be used, in America at least, for one year, many of those cars still survive. They became the instant favourites of racers the world over and although many were to be wrecked at the hands of those enthusiasts it is because of that love for the Deuce that so many have survived.

That it was a good-looking car was probably immaterial to Henry, all that concerned him was its V8 engine. But that too survived, once the bugs were sorted out, almost unchanged and un-challenged for 21 years. During those two decades Ford sold 25 million V8s, and if that doesn't prove that the money was well invested then I don't know what does.

Sadly, as 1933 dawned Ford was still behind, the new Model 40 would not be on sale until mid-February and already Chevy was topping the sales charts with its new CA Master, as it would continue to do throughout the year.

7 Worldwide production

Though a grand idea, Henry Ford's 1928 plan was, by 1932, beginning to look a little shaky. Business in the mid-twenties had been good, there was a postwar boom, and America had discovered that the world its immigrant population had left behind was nothing other than a huge market place. By 1929 the United States produced 85 per cent of the world's automobiles and their export ranked third in the US behind raw cotton and machinery.

Henry's plans, bolstered by an enthusiastic Percival Perry, rehired on 1 May 1928 to head European operations (after his resignation in 1919 over a disagreement about the running of the British company), were to launch a new company called the Ford Motor Company Limited, to replace the Ford Motor Company (England) Limited. Incidentally, upon hearing the news of Perry's hiring, Sorensen is quoted as saying: 'The best news you could have brought me.' With a capitalization of $7 million, but 60 per cent of the stock controlled by the parent company, Ford-America, Ford and Perry intended the Dagenham-based company to be the largest manufacturing plant outside of the United States, Henry saying, 'I want an English company that will be the Detroit of Europe.' Production was aimed at 200,000 units per year, with Ford-Britain having sole rights to manufacture, assemble, distribute and market Ford products in the United Kingdom, Irish Free State, Channel Islands, Isle of Man, Europe with the exception of European Russia, Asia Minor, Palestine, Syria, Arabia but not Aden, Iraq, Persia, Afghanistan, Egypt and others parts of Africa.

The rest of the British Empire was supplied by Canada under an agreement reached on 10 August 1904. For a fee, Henry Ford and the American company agreed to supply the Ford Motor Company of Canada Limited, founded by Gordon B. McGregor, all patents, plans, drawings and specifications needed to build Ford automobiles. Ford-America also oversaw construction and in return the new company had 'the sole and exclusive right to manufacture and sell its automobiles in Canada and the British colonies, possessions and dependencies'. By the late twenties the Canadian company had established operations in South Africa, Australia, New Zealand, India and Malaya.

Windsor was, however, only just across the river from Detroit and not 4000 miles away as was Dagenham. Although both Ford-Canada and Ford-Britain were established upon the same principles of local management and direction, with respective nationals holding a substantial portion of the shares but Ford-America retaining control, the geographical closeness gave the two North American companies a special kind of relationship Dagenham never enjoyed. Indeed Sorensen wrote to Perry on one occasion of Campbell, 'He is so close to us that his men who contact our engineering as well as manufacturing end sometimes sense changes that are coming along before even the drawings are completed.' It is said that Campbell frequented the Ford Engineering building when the V8 was being designed, and watched, enquired, prodded and even advised on its construction. When Perry complained about engineering charges levied upon Dagenham by Dearborn, Sorensen wrote: 'We have never had any arguments with Ford of Canada on the cost of engineering charges,' and suggested that Perry talk to Campbell to learn how Windsor and Dearborn got on so well together.

Fortunately for Canada, though, they did not have the same problems as Dagenham. The Canadian company had been established longer, did not need massive investment to first build a factory before it could build cars and it did not need to build special cars for its markets. What sold well in America also sold in Canada and served equally well in the South American, Australasian and Far Eastern markets.

Meanwhile, Ford-Britain had acquired the assets of Ford companies in Germany, France, Italy, Spain, Ireland, Belgium, Holland, Den-

Ford's foreign automotive operations

Anybody interested in the 1932 Ford will notice instantly that the accompanying list of Ford's foreign automotive operations differs greatly from those usually reproduced. The 13 plants commonly listed as Ford's only foreign operations are certainly to be found on the Production Department's assembly record sheets. But had the researcher bothered to glance further down the page he would have found record of Canadian production. Being the second biggest producer of Fords after Dearborn, at the Rouge, this is quite an omission and no doubt very annoying for the Canadians.

Had they looked further-down the page still, as of November 1932, they would also have seen the addition of Cork in Ireland, where bodies were mounted on chassis received from Dagenham. Even this extended list does not include countries to which both the United States and Canada exported knockdown shipments for local assembly. Countries such as Australia, South Africa and India, plus Panama (Cristobal), Peru (Lima), Uruguay (Montevideo), Brazil (Permambuco-Recire, Porto Alegre, Rio De Janeiro), Cuba (Havana), China (Shanghai), and the Phillipines, all of which are mentioned in records of foreign plant deliveries to dealers for 1932. Obviously some of these operations, however small, may have been supplied by the nearest assembly plant, but this is unlikely in the case of Peru which is hundreds of miles from the nearest

Country	Year of formation or incorporation of first company	Year Ford assembly started	Year Ford manufacture started	Year of termination of activities
Argentina	1913 (Br); 1959 (Co)	1916	1961	—
Australia	1909 (Br)	—	—	1918
	1925 (Co)	1925	1925	—
Belgium	1922 (Co)	1922	—	—
Brazil	1919 (Br)	1920	1959	—
Canada	1904 (Co)	1905	1908	—
Canal Zone	1927 (Br)	—	—	1949
Chile	1924 (Br)	1924	—	—
China	1928 (Br)	—	—	1948
Cuba	1922 (Br)	—	—	1949
Denmark	1919 (Co)	1919	—	—
Egypt	1926 (Br); 1932 (Co)	1950	—	—
England	1909 (Br); 1911 (Co)	1911	1912—Manchester 1931—Dagenham	—
Finland	1926 (Co)	1946	—	—
France	1908 (Br); 1916 (Co)	1913—Bordeaux 1926—Asnieres 1939—Poissy	1934—Strasbourg 1939—Poissy	1954
	1954 (Co)	—	—	—
Germany	1925 (Co)	1926—Berlin 1931—Cologne	1931—Cologne	—
Greece	1932 (Co)	—	—	1946
Holland	1924 (Co)	1932	—	—
India	1926 (Co)	1926	—	1954
Ireland	1917 (Co)	1919 (tractors) 1923 (cars)	1919 (tractors) 1921 (car parts)	—
Italy	1922 (Co)	1922	—	—
Japan	1925 (Co)	1925	—	1940
Malaya	1926 (Co)	1926	—	—
Mexico	1925 (Co)	1925	—	—
Peru	1926 (Br)	—	—	1931*
Portugal	1932 (Co)	1963	—	—
Puerto Rico	1926 (Br)	—	—	1927
Rumania	1931 (Co)	1936	—	1946
South Africa	1923 (Co)	1924	—	—
Spain	1919 (Co)	1920	—	1954
Sweden	1924 (Co)	1948	—	—
Turkey	1928 (Br)	1929	—	1944
Uruguay	1920 (Br); 1955 (Co)	1920	—	—
Venezuela	1926 (Br); 1959 (Co)	1962	—	1927

*Cars sold in 1932

plant in Chile but nevertheless accounted for 41 V8s and 21 Bs in 1932! The same can be said of the Phillipines, which is miles from any generally recognised plant, where 393 V8s and 261 Bs were sold. Presumably all of these cars are accounted for by either the American, Canadian and maybe British knockdown exports but unfortunately there is no record as to exactly what models went where. The list of Ford's operations above, which was compiled from information in the Ford Archives, should go some way to explaining where all those knockdown shipments for export may have ended up

mark, Finland and Sweden from both the parent company and the Ford family (Henry Ford having had another plan in 1919, where the family had complete control.) Of the remaining shares 40 per cent were sold off locally in order that the nationals might get involved and not consider Ford a foreign company. Although Dagenham would eventually lose control of France and Germany it did take over supervision of branches in Egypt, Greece, Portugal, Rumania and Turkey.

Unfortunately, Henry had failed to consider certain points or foresee several events. The Wall Street crash of October 1929 stemmed the flood of dollars, and though Ford had preached against it, America introduced the Smoot-Hawley import tariff in 1930.

There was a worldwide retaliation, but nowhere stronger than in Europe. Italy's nationalistic tendencies, under the dictatorship of Mussolini, had already led to a Royal decree, in 1929, forbidding the construction of any car without Government permission, and that permission was not forthcoming. Mussolini told Perry's assistant for European co-ordination, F. G. Thornhill-Cooper, that the Government would only back 100 per cent Italian manufacture. Talks with Fiat were suggested, as was an international combine to build Isotta-Fraschinis in Detroit and Fords in

Italy, but land purchased early in 1929 at Livorno went undeveloped when Italy introduced her own tariffs.

Spain too reacted with import taxes. In protest Ford's Barcelona manager closed down his plant, but to no avail. It eventually reopened with a reduced workforce. Two revolutions had not helped either.

Things were not much better in France, however, fast action by director Maurice Doll-fuss, with the agreement of Edsel Ford, enabled them to import a nine-month supply of cars before import restrictions were imposed. Protests to the French Government failed to get a response and in fact government policy dictated that Model A prices were the highest in Europe, almost three times their American price.

The Polish Government had rejected plans for a plant, and though things had got off to a good start in Cologne a far-reaching merchant bank crash in Austria caused the plant to close. When it did reopen in 1932 Ford-Germany had fallen from second to ninth place among German manufacturers. The surge of nationalism was also calling for an increase in locally manufactured content, which would, by early 1933, have to be 100 per cent.

In Holland a site had been located in Rotterdam, but when Henry Ford arrived to lay the cornerstone he found no water for the shipment of ore and consequently declared, 'No water, no plant.'

However, a plant, on water, was eventually opened at Amsterdam. There had been hope of building a plant in Yugoslavia, but negotiations failed. Meanwhile, the Constantinople plant continued to run at a loss until it was eventually closed. Only in the Low Countries and Scandinavia was expansion progressing smoothly.

The troublesome Irish plant at Cork, though a pet of Henry's because his family originated near there, was also cause for concern. Production costs were higher than at Dearborn and a promising future producing Fordson tractors for the USSR faded in 1931 when Russia was unable to obtain credit and the relationship between the two powers petered out. The machinery was moved to Dagenham, leaving Cork a small car and truck assembly plant and producer of the 14.9 hp AF engine. This engine, recognizable by its sunken spark plug seats, had been introduced in 1928 as Ford's first real concession to foreign needs, apart from left-hand drive and small styling differences, to counteract a horsepower tax which was crippling UK sales of the Model A.

The Motor Taxation Act of 1920 introduced on 1 January 1921 by the then Liberal government imposed a tax of £1 per year per horsepower for all cars with engines exceeding six horsepower. Unfortunately, for Ford especially, it was calculated on the Royal Automobile Club's formula, which only took into consideration an engine's cylinder bore. Calculated with an assumed piston speed of 100 ft/min, a mean effective pressure of 90 lb/sq in and a mechanical efficiency of 75 per cent,

$$\text{Horsepower} = \frac{D^2 n}{2.5},$$

where 'D' equalled the bore in inches and 'n' equalled the number of cylinders. Piston stroke was not taken into account and the system, which was used until after the Second World War, was very unfair to many engines manufactured in the thirties.

The horsepower tax had not been a problem in the mid-twenties, when Ford was riding the crest of the Model T wave, because it was one of the cheapest cars on the market, the Model T costing some £30 less than an Austin 7.

All waves eventually break, as did Ford's, and the tide began to turn when other manufacturers adopted Ford's mass-production methods but tailored them to suit local demands and restrictions. The T's replacement, the Model A, was viewed by European automobilists as typically American and therefore no great threat. It was greeted in England not only with the horsepower tax but also by a 'Don't buy American' campaign, quickly followed by a petrol tax in 1928.

At that time though Henry Ford was not about to change his product. He liked over-square engines, i.e. those with a piston diameter to stroke ratio of something like 1.1:1, as was the Model A. He liked thin crankshafts too, and an over-square engine with a short stroke meant less cylinder wear and piston wear, less stress on the crankshaft and consequently more reliability. The introduction of the horsepower tax, which didn't take into account stroke, heralded the development in Europe of the long stroke, high-revving engine. Not a Ford engine at all. Nevertheless its exponents, Austin and Morris, were both doing well. Ford wasn't even one of the top three manufacturers in 1931 and in fact sold only five Model A cars in the last quarter of that year.

Something had to be done because not only were sales pitiful but the new European Rouge, Dagenham, was behind schedule and way over budget. Perhaps the buckling of Edsel Ford's silver spade, on 16 May 1929, as he dug the first sod at the Dagenham site was some indication of the problems to follow. If it was then just as surely it was not an indication of the soil. It seems that nobody had seen fit to survey the Thames estuary site properly, the fact that it was 'on water' being sufficient to go ahead. Had they done so they would have seen that the 310 acres acquired was nothing but marshland, as the Rouge had been, and to build the factory more than 22,000 14-in-square concrete piles had to be sunk, sometimes to a depth of 80 feet.

Perry was already borrowing money to finance the project and in desperation he turned to Detroit and pleaded once again for a small, economical car for Europe.

Henry Ford eventually relented and work started on the Model Y, code-named Mercury, in October 1931 under the direction of Laurence Sheldrick.

The body of Ford's first small car was designed by Eugene T. Gregorie and was a scaled-down version of the 1932 improved Model A destined for the European market. Body mouldings, bumpers and many other items were Model B miniatures, but where Gregorie did deviate slightly was on the grille design. Edsel liked the

RIGHT *Edsel Ford's smile belies the problems which followed the bending of his silver spade as he attempted to dig the first sod at the Dagenham site on 16 May 1929*

BELOW *The Dagenham site was chosen because it was 'on water' but nobody discovered that it was full of water until work began. Subsequently, to support the factory, more than 22,000 reinforced concrete piles had to be sunk, sometimes to a depth of 80 feet*

styling so much he gave Gregorie the go-ahead to proceed with designs for the full-size 1933 Model 40.

A very uncommon practice indeed for Ford where body styles changed gradually, not drastically. This time factor confirms the fact that the 1933 Model 40 was based on the Model Y and not the other way around as is generally supposed.

At the same time the first Model A, actually a 30 cwt AA truck, rolled off the line at Dagenham; the factory was at last operational, but would not be in full production until the end of summer 1932.

Meanwhile, after a slow but healthy start, Ford-Canada was facing similar problems due to the far-reaching effects of the Depression. A healthy profit of almost \$5½ million in 1929 turned, in just three short years, to a similarly large loss. Production fell and with it sales, by almost 60 per cent, in all markets from Australia to India and its position in the production of Fords fell from second, behind the United States, to fifth behind England, France and Germany.

When Model A sales had been rising in Canada they had been doing likewise in South America and a 1929 United States Department of Commerce report stated, 'Argentina is the most important automobile market in South America', where Ford held 54 per cent of new registrations. With a minimum of 50 per cent of new registrations in almost every other South American country, Ford was expanding everywhere, though conditions and communications were difficult.

As the Depression began to bite the markets shrank. Governments became unstable, those in power imposed foreign exchange controls and there were revolutions in Argentina, Bolivia, Brazil and Peru in 1930 and in Peru, Venezuela, Bolivia, Chile, Ecuador and Paraguay in 1931. Expansion and building plans collapsed, Ford-Argentina, in one month in 1932, managed to sell only 11 cars, three As, two V8s and six Model Ys, and for the first time General Motors outsold Ford in South America.

After an exploratory visit to China, W. C. Cowling, General Sales Manager, advised against any further development because of China's own slow progress in establishing a new order. Besides, they were under attack from Japan, whose own assembly plant consequently became jeopardized.

Only in Mexico, where an assembly operation was approved in 1929, did plans go ahead for expansion. A new assembly plant had its grand opening on 14 September 1932 and production would soon reach the capacity of 100 units per day.

Certainly the outlook at the beginning of 1932 was bleak; Henry had had to cut wages from \$7 to \$5 per day, there was labour unrest as the unions tried to establish themselves in Fords' factories, there was capital expenditure on a colossal scale, but worse still there was very little in the way of income. Henry's enthusiasm for the V8 was nevertheless immense and, as Edsel had predicted, 'Faith is catching.'

Confidence gradually returned, sales slowly picked up and abandoned plans were dusted off

Production of Model B and 18 passenger cars at this factory in Mexico City lasted from June until December 1932

and re-examined in the hope of regained prosperity.

Canada, of course, came out with the Models 18 and B on the same day as Ford-America, Campbell correctly believing that that was the kind of car Canadians wanted. In England, however, Ford officials were struggling with their two recalcitrant infants, Dagenham, the Detroit of Europe, and the Model Y. They did have on hand English prototype versions of the Tudor and Fordor Improved Model As, both with suicide doors. These had been completed and photographed at Dearborn as early as October 1931. One commercial chassis and the prototype Mercury were strapped to the deck of the Mauritania and shipped to England for inspection. Unfortunately, the saltwater corrosion was so bad that, upon arrival, the cars almost fell apart. This first meagre offering was quickly followed by two complete Bs, one Fordor and one Tudor, but a cable from Charles Sorensen forbade A. R. Smith, General Manager of Dagenham, from showing them, along with the Model Y, at its public presentation at the Ford Exhibition in the Royal Albert Hall in London between 19–27 February 1932. Ford-Britain would have to wait patiently until Henry announced the V8 at the end of March.

When Henry Ford finally presented the Model 18 and, in passing, the Model B, at the end of March, Dagenham still needed time to prepare for production. An extra 191 acres had been purchased at the Dagenham site, and estimating that he would need only 112 acres, Perry established an industrial estate to house suppliers such as the Kelsey-Hayes Wheel Company Ltd. and Briggs Manufacturing Company Ltd., both of whom had been encouraged to go to England to supply the new factory. Perry cabled Sorensen on 23 March to say that Briggs were ready to deliver bodies, but that the 14.9 hp AF engine would not be in production until the end of April.

Ford-Britain eventually announced, on 12 May, the Model B, known in England at first as the Improved Ford Models A and AF and then as the AB and ABF or just B and BF. Because they were close to the action and knew in advance what was going on, the English edition of the *Ford Times* carried, in its May issue, a four-page impression of the new offerings: 'The Improved Ford Models A and AF.' See page 80.

Ignoring the rather dated language it is nevertheless interesting to note that the writer regarded them as new models and not just improved ones, which is correct, as they had little in common with the Model A though there was a strong family resemblance. Mr Harrison did not seem to have much inside information, but perhaps that is how they reviewed cars in those days. However, he was impressed with such odd details as the steering wheel, dashboard cubby holes, adjustable seats, wide doors and a left-side filler cap, which of course it was on all models! Strangely, he liked the styling, which has always been viewed as very boxey when compared to the more rounded American sedans. One wonders why Ford decided to build this special English model; they had never made those kind of concessions to a market before and the tooling investment costs, whether paid for by Ford or Briggs, can never have seen a return. Were European and American tastes really so different in 1932, or was it perhaps a trick to make the anti-American Europeans think this really was a car of their own?

This report was quickly followed by road tests in *The Motor* and *The Autocar* magazines, where it was fairly well received. Sadly, both models suffered the same inadequacies as their predecessor, the Model A. The 24 hp AB was too expensive to run because of the cost of petrol and the horsepower tax (£24 per annum) and the 14.9 hp ABF, though souped up to give 40 bhp at 3000 rpm, compared to its previous output of 30 bhp at 2600 rpm, was still underpowered for what was now a much heavier car.

As yet there was no sign of the V8; indeed Perry, already overextended and wanting to concentrate on one car, the Model Y, did not want to produce the V8 car at all. He had no V8 engine manufacturing facilities and because of the low volumes and higher costs Dagenham could in no way match Dearborn prices, and he wrote in July 1932, 'I am satisfied that Dagenham can never produce at dollars and cents which can match Detroit.' There was, however, a demand for the V8, and various examples had been imported for and had been tested by the press. As a result Perry contacted Campbell with regard to a reciprocal agreement, 'To ensure that the supply of Ford cars . . . throughout the British Empire should be derived from an Empire factory, i.e. either Dagenham, England, or Walkerville, Canada.' This would mean that the Model Y could be sold in Canada's traditional market place, while the V8 could be sold in England's.

By importing from Canada rather than America, Ford-Britain only had to pay $22\frac{2}{9}$ per cent *ad valorem* duty instead of $33\frac{1}{3}$ per cent. It could also get right-hand-drive models made by Ford-Canada for their overseas markets. This arrangement worked well and Canadian-made V8 engines were also imported for fitment to the British-built sedans. However, the fact that Dagenham built only 911 V8-engined cars in almost three years of production attests to the general unpopularity of the model. Production costs were higher in

THE IMPROVED FORD MODELS A and AF

BY J. HARRISON

I MUST PREFACE these remarks by saying that, except for manœuvring the new 14.9 h.p. model in the close confines of a garage, I have not yet driven the new Fords. I have, however, had oppourtnities of subjecting them to a more critical examination than it is possible to give at a public exhibition.

The new 8 h.p. Ford is designed to provide fast, safe and comfortable motoring for four adults at the minimum cost. In the past the criticism that has been levelled against the " eight " is that, while it provides accommodation of a sort for four persons, it is not large enough to give real comfort even to one. Having sat in the Ford with three other broad-shouldered men, I can say that this does not apply, for there is adequate head, elbow and leg room. I did find that the pedals were rather close together, but this will be remedied in the production models, in which there will be even more elbow-room, because the body is being made two inches wider.

The engine is the largest that has yet been built to come in the £8 tax class, for it has a swept volume of nearly 950 c.c. This should give a satisfactory performance, especially as the gear ratios have been happily chosen. They are : Top, 5.42 to 1, second, 9.53 to 1, and first, 16.63 to 1.

THE AVERAGE 8 h.p. car is somewhat rough running and when driven fast the engine makes its presence felt in a rather unpleasant manner. The Ford Motor

The Frontal Presentation of the Improved Models A and AF

Company are to be congratulated on their determination to cure this defect, and give us smooth, silent running. They have certainly not stopped at half-measures, for the engine is extraordinarily sturdy.

In the interest of rigidity, the cylinder-block is cast in one with the top half of the crank-case, and in the same good cause the crankshaft is supported on three bearings, instead of the two usual in a motor of this size. The crankshaft is a truly massive affair, for the diameters of its bearings are no less than those previously employed on the 24 h.p. model.

Those who have driven a Model A for tens of thousands of miles, without appreciable crankshaft wear, know that a shaft of these dimensions is ridiculously " oversize " for an 8 h.p. unit. On the fact of it, it is a most un-scientific selection of dimensions, because it is obvious that the shaft must long outlast the rest of the car. It was not a search for longevity, however, that caused its adoption, but a desire for extreme silence and smooth running.

The Instrument-Board and Controls

I F YOU STRIKE a small piece of metal, such as a half-crown, with a hammer, you will send it flying ; but if a big anvil is hit with the same force it takes the blow without a tremor. If four little pistons and connecting rods deliver 7,000 hammer blows per minute on a spidery, two-bearing crankshaft, noise and vibration are set up, but the big Ford crank-shaft is so much " oversize " that it is unaffected.

To further the same end, an entirely new type of engine mounting has been devised. There is a rubber carrier at the rear end of the gear-box, and there are two rubber supports at the front end of the engine. As there is no metallic contact between the power unit and the frame, any engine vibration and sound-waves that may be set up are damped out before they can cause body drumming. I feel safe in predicting that, as the result of these drastic measures, this Ford will set a new standard among relatively small cars in the matters of silence and smooth running.

and it is dropped between the axles, to give a low floor-level. Across the frame, just aft of the power unit, is a singularly strong cross-member, and it is to this that the rear of the power unit, and the front axle radius-rods, are anchored.

The steering link-work and shock-absorber bearings have rubber bushings that require no lubrication, and do not rattle or squeak. Much ingenuity has been exercised in the design of the shock-absorbers, which are of the servo-brake type. They are adjustable, and the servo action takes place on the rebound only, when the shock-absorbers exert three times the resistance that they do on the upward motion of the spring.

One cannot but be impressed by the sturdy, well braced front mudguards.

THE EDITOR SAYS that the 14.9 h.p. and 24 h.p. cars are " improved models " and as editors are powers before whom

The Tudor Saloon, with either 14.9 or 24 h.p. engine, remains £180, at Works

Realising that on an 8 h.p. car more use must, of necessity, be made of intermediate gear than on a larger one, synchronising clutches have been embodied in the top and middle gear-changing mechanism. These will greatly simplify changing. The helically toothed second speed and constant-mesh gears are a big step forward, because they make the car as silent on second gear as it is on top. In conjunction with rubber engine-mountings, they should make gear over-run " whirr " a thing of the past. Further to simplify driving, the ignition timing is automatically varied to suit the engine's demands.

LOOKING UNDERNEATH the car one sees some sound engineering. Ford designers, instead of trying to accommodate the body to the chassis, have done the logical thing, shaping the frame to suit the body. It is wider at the rear than at the front,

even kings tremble, they are just "improved models." I, however, prefer to regard them as new *and much better* cars. It is true that they are directly developed from the Models A and AF, and that mechanically they have a strong family likeness to their forebears. It is also true that many parts of the new cars are the same as those used on their predecessors ; but nevertheless, their characters are different.

On first lifting the bonnet one would think that the old type of power-unit was installed, for a casual glance shows no constructional differences. This is because the overall size of the cylinder-head and block are the same as formerly, and many of the parts that gave satisfaction on the previous model have been retained. They have not been changed. A change in shape would have involved the scrapping of several hundred thousand pounds' worth of jigs and special-purpose machine tools.

More careful examination reveals the fact

that a new water pump has been evolved ; and the absence of the oil-return pipe speaks of a new lubrication system, in which the main and camshaft bearings are pressure-fed. The oil filler is now higher than before, so that it is easy to reach, and so that oil-mist cannot be blown out over the generator. The carburettor is different, as also are the inlet and exhaust manifolds. The last-named is a particularly fine piece of work, giving a much easier flow to the gases than did that formerly used.

Depressing the accelerator pedal, one is immediately made aware that the new engines are much more responsive and have more " kick " in them than had their predecessors, facts that lead one to suspect higher compression-ratios, and a different cam design.

The specification reveals that the 24 h.p. engine now develops 48 b.h.p. at 2,400 r.p.m. (as against 40 at 2,600). The new 14.9 h.p. engine actually gives more power than

The De Luxe Fordor Saloon also is still £225, at Works, with either 14.9 or 24 h.p. engine

the previous " Twenty-four," for its output is no less than 41 b.h.p. at 3,000 r.p.m. (as against 30 at 2,600). These performance figures speak for themselves, and justify my contention that these are *not* merely " improved models," but new and altogether better engines.

HAVING LEARNED HOW a really stiff crankshaft can give a sweet and silent performance to a small engine, the Ford engineers have applied their lesson to the larger cars, in which they have stepped up the diameter of the main bearings from 1⅝ ins. to 2 ins., and the diameter of the crankpins from 1⅜ ins. to 1⅞ ins. A two-inch diameter main shaft on an engine the cylinder diameter of which is only five-hundredths of an inch over three inches, should make for smooth running and exceptional longevity.

As on the small car, the engine is supported at three points on rubber and if, with the bonnet open, one suddenly steps on the accelerator and

races up the engine, it is interesting to watch the manner in which it heels over on its rubber mountings, to take the torque reaction. Repeated jabs at the accelerator cause the engine to rock from side to side on its mountings, but not a tremor is felt in the driving seat.

As on the 8 h.p. car, a silent intermediate gear is provided, and synchro-mesh clutches facilitate gear-changing. I expect greatly increased speed from these new models, because of the enhanced power output, and at the same time, the top gear acceleration should be better, for although the top gear ratio is the same, the road wheels are one inch smaller in diameter and the gear ratio has, in effect, been lowered.

The new front axle beam is a beautiful piece of work. Any teacher of applied mechanics would welcome it to show to his pupils as a good example of how metal can be economically used to give the greatest strength for the minimum weight. I should imagine that it is lighter than the old axle, but it is deeper in section, and obviously stronger.

The brakes have very stiff *cast*, instead of pressed, drums. Each has a deep fin cast around it. This acts as a cooler for the brakes (in a manner similar to that in which the fins on a motor-cycle cylinder dissipate the heat). It greatly stiffens the drum and therefore makes the brake action smoother. It also acts as a thrower-ring to any water that finds its way on to the brake drums.

DURING THE PAST two years I drove the Model A in seven long-distance reliability trials and won five gold and two silver medals on it. I drove through water, over ploughed fields and boulders, and round Brooklands track. The way she stood the racket was wonderful : not a frame rivet started, or bolt loosened.

The new frame is even stronger than the old one. In addition to the strong cross-members

over the springs, there is a very stout channel-sectioned member in the centre of **the** chassis. It supports the rear end of the power unit, and forms the anchorage for the front axle radius-rods.

The ends of this member are well splayed out, and they make a very powerful chassis-brace. In addition to these there is a tubular member joining the front ends of the side members. This stiffens the front of the chassis, and should make the steering very positive. At the rear end the spare wheel carrier and tank-cover combine to make a stiff triangular brace. As on the 8 h.p. car, the frame follows the body-line. It is deeply dropped between the axles, so that the floor-level is lowered by a considerable amount, without sacrificing more than half an inch of ground-clearance.

The new models are easily the most shapely that the Ford Motor Company have produced to date, the new Tudor being of particularly handsome design. The wheelbase is now three inches longer than it was, and the bodies are even more roomy ; but they are so well-proportioned that they look longer and slimmer than they actually are. The eddy-free front and the enclosed windscreen-wiper mechanism improve the frontal aspect, while the curve of the bottom of the body—which all but eliminates the valances—and the small road wheels with their impressively large-sectioned tyres, make the car look very substantial and road-worthy.

IN MY OPINION it is the details—the hundred-and-one things that make for comfort and convenience—that lift the superlative car above the ranks of the moderately good. Here are some of them that impressed themselves on my memory : The new thin-rimmed large-diameter steering wheel is the most comfortable that the Ford designers have produced to date. The dash cubby-holes, which are felt-lined to prevent one's possessions from rattling and becoming scratched, are a much-wanted improvement. The old-type instrument board was practical but, in my opinion, " homely ". The new oval sunk panel is good to see, and the needle type, 80 m.p.h. speedometer has white figures on a black face. They are large enough to be seen at a glance, a valuable feature to the motorist who drives fast.

The petrol tank is now at the rear. Its quick-opening filler is on the near side, where it can be easily reached by the garage man. There is a petrol gauge on the dash. Tyre inflation has been facilitated by the new Schrader tyre valves, so inclined that the pump connection can rapidly be pushed on. A stout bumper now protects the whole of the rear of the car, including the spare wheel.

AN INGENIOUS ADJUSTER has been fitted to the driving seat of both models. A spring tends to pull the seat forward against a ratchet controlled by a trigger. To move the seat nearer to the pedals, lift the trigger and the seat will come forward of its own account. When it is in the correct position, release the trigger to lock it. To move the seat back, lift the trigger and press the seat back until your feet are the correct distance from the pedals. Then release the trigger to lock it in position. The adjustment is instantaneous.

On the Fordor saloon the lower part of the rear doors can be felt-lined, so that it is easier to enter the car than it was. The Tudor's doors are now so wide that it is possible to enter the rear

A Glimpse of the interior of the De Luxe Fordor Saloon

seats without asking the front seat passengers to vacate their places. There is also a roof light in the Tudor.

The new door handles come easily to hand. To open a door, push the handle down and to lock it, so that it cannot be opened from the outside, lift the handle beyond its normal locked position. The head-lamps have been increased in size and they are now in a better position, higher off the road. I would judge them to be more powerful than any previously fitted to Ford cars as standard equipment.

The clutch and brake pedal shanks are provided with thick rubber washers which, when the pedals are in their normal ' up ' position, completely close the holes in the floorboards through which the pedals project. They absolutely exclude draughts.

These " improved " models will, I am sure, have a wide appeal, for they should have all the reliability of their dependable ancestors, and, in addition, they are better looking, easier to drive, and should give greatly enhanced road performance.

Dagenham not only because of the low volume but because they were using untrained labour, and because British workers did not work as hard as their American counterparts. W. J. Squire contrasted Dearborn and Dagenham saying, 'I was as mild a young man as you would want to see when I went to work at Dearborn, but two weeks after I arrived I saw that it was either get tough or get out, and I got tough. Henry Ford paid a high wage, but he wanted a hard day's work. You did a son-of-a-bitch day's work at the Rouge. It was a lot more of a day's work than the English ever thought of doing.' England had also seen a wage cut, of 10 per cent, in April 1932, actually on All Fools' Day, but it didn't help to bring prices down. Dagenham was indeed in trouble and purchasing manager Patrick Hennessy said of the time, 'No one outside really knew how bad the situation was. We would pay off one supplier, and then another, keeping the secret successfully.'

Continental plant managers complained about Dagenham's high prices and asked if they could buy from Dearborn. Eventually, Edsel ruled that they could buy in the cheapest market.

This made life even more difficult for Perry, who saw his empire and potential market, as forecast in 1928, shrinking. Production in 1932 hardly reached 60 per cent of the intended 200,000 and both Ford-Germany and Ford-France pushed for 100 per cent home manufacturing. Indeed, they were forced into it, Germany because of the searing rise of nationalism which made it impossible to sell an imported car and in France because the government continued to discourage imports with high tariffs and there was a national campaign to 'Buy French First'. A V8 which cost $550 in America cost the equivalent of $1484 in France. It was, however, a popular car and Managing Director Maurice Dollfus pushed hard for his own manufacturing plant.

Both Canada and the US were, from March 1932, exporting, through the office of R. M. Lockwood in New York, B and 18 models in both knock-down (KD) and built-up form before the rest of the world officially saw the new models. They were to go on display in many countries in May and, ironically, Asnières was one of the first plants, along with Dagenham and Copenhagen, to begin production. In that month the French factory produced 27 Tudors and seven Fordors, significantly more than Copenhagen's five Tudors and two Fordors and Dagenham's meagre four Fordors. Incidentally, all were standard and had four-cylinder engines.

As the new models went on display they were well received. London saw no special show, that would come later, but the cars were on permanent display at Ford's Regent Street showroom.

ABOVE *One of each English Model Bs, a Tudor (this one) and a Fordor, were shipped to England early in 1932 but Charles Sorensen forbade A. R. Smith from showing them alongside the Model Y at its London debut in February 1932*

ALL LEFT *Road test of the improved Models A and AF from the* Ford Times *May 1932, page 318*

BELOW *French advertisement of 1 June 1932. Sedans sold in France were mainly English bodied with front-opening doors but here are American bodies. The artist illustrated them with English raised louvre bonnets which, of course, would be right if they had English style bodies. Though reasonably popular the French V8s cost almost three times their American equivalent*

In Denmark dealers saw the new models on 12 May, while the press reviewed them the following day. In Stockholm, over the same two days, 25,000 people visited the Ford A/B presentation. Other displays in Sweden were similarly well attended. For some reason Norwegians would have to wait until 21 May before they could see the 1932 offerings.

All of the V8-engined cars seen around the world were imported from either Canada or the US, but the majority of the parts for the European sedans, including their angular bodies, came initially from Dagenham. Other parts were made locally and it was this situation, allied to differing construction and safety regulations, which gave rise to the anomalies found in models offered in various countries.

For example, there were three slightly different braking systems in use: the American, the German and the English.

As the English-made two- and four-door sedans had entirely different bodies from those made in either Canada or the US there are many minor differences. The most noticeable was the longer cowl, which necessitated a longer steering column and a different, more sunken, dashboard, which had twin glove pockets and no wood graining.

Upholstery differed greatly as bodies made by Briggs at Dagenham were shipped in either knock-down or built-up form, the latter being un-

FORD-NYT

2. AARGANG | JUNI 1932 | NUMMER 6

PRÆSENTATIONEN AF
Ny Ford 4 — Ny Ford V-8

Danske Fordforhandlere tager de nye Fordmodeller i Øjesyn i Teknologisk Instituts Udstillingssal i København.

EN NY VOGN FOR EN NY TID

Præsentationen af de nye Ford-Modeller fandt Sted den 12. og 13. Maj i Teknologisk Instituts smukke Udstillingssal for henholdsvis Forhandlere og Pressen. Ved Forhandler-Præsentationen afsløredes Vognen af Grosserer A. E. D. Bruhn, Esbjerg, — de danske Ford-Forhandleres Nestor — medens Direktør S. Kyhl, Forenede Danske Motorejere, foretog Afsløringen for Pressen.

Spændingen havde været stor, Forhandlerne havde endnu Fremkomsten af Ford Model A for fire Aar siden i frisk Erindring og imødesaa nu med store Forventninger, hvilke nye Fremskridt Henry Ford og Ford Motor Company denne Gang havde præsteret.

Resultatet var overvældende. Alle Forhandlere, Pressens Repræsentanter og de tilstedeværende Motorsagkyndige, som her for første Gang fik Lejlighed til at tage de nye Modeller i Øjesyn, udtalte deres uforbeholdne Anerkendelse af de nye Vognes smukke Udseende og det gennemførte Kvalitets- og Præcisionsarbejde.

Her var i Sandhed en ny Vogn for en ny Tid — en helt ny Maalestok for Automobilers Værdi.

UDSØGT SMAG FORENET MED MODERNE ELEGANCE
karakteriserer de nye Ford Karosseriers hele indvendige Udstyr.

NY 4 | FLUGT | EN NY VOGN FOR EN NY TID | STYRKE | V8

De nye Ford Karosserier staar paa Højde med det bedste og dyreste paa hele Automobilmarkedet. — Al ønskelig Hensigtsmæssighed, Komfort, Skønhed, og Ydeevne er indbygget i dem. Ved første Øjekast vil man se at her er et helt nyt Automobil. Fra den moderne V-formede Køler til Benzinbeholderen bagi Vognen, giver de bløde Strømlinier

en Ynde og Flugt, som tillige udtrykker Kraft. De nye Linier, som harmonerer med de fuldtkronede Skærme og de lange, brede Trinbrædder, fremhæver Vognens Skønhed og bidrager til at forøge dens Præstationsevne, idet det skraatstillede Vindspejl, den lave Taglinie, de afrundede Bagpaneler, formindsker Luftmodstanden under Farten.

Det skraatstillede Vindspejl og den afrundede Taglinie, uden Solskærm, fremhæver Skønheden af den Nye Ford.

Det nye 52-Eger, elektrisk homogent svejsede Staalhjul. De store Navklapper skjuler Navbohene, og er af rustfrit Staal.

FORD Karosseriernes nye Strømlinier naar deres højeste Charme i Victoria Coupéen. Set bagfra kurver Karrosseriet frem-og opefter fra Benzintanken til den afrundede Taglinie og giver en særlig elegant Fremraden, alt imedens Luftmodstanden derved mindskes.

SKØNHED

PRISER	
	Ford 4 + Ford V-8
	Kroner
Roadster	3535 + 3950
Phaeton	3795 + 4210
Tudor	3595 + 3990
Sports Coupe	3660 + 4080
Coupe	3695 + 4115
Fordor	4095 + 4515
De Luxe Roadster	3785 + 4200
De Luxe Phaeton	4075 + 4495
De Luxe Tudor	3790 + 4190
De Luxe Fordor	4335 + 4755
samt De Luxe Coupe, Cabriolet, Victoria, Convertible Sedan.	
Alle Priser f.o.b. København,	
ekskl. Omsætningsafgift.	

Dette Interiør fra De Luxe Fordor Sedan er typisk for De Luxe Karosseriernes Komfort og Luksus. Læg Mærke til Dørene, Askebægerne og Haandstropperne. — Der er ligeledes Loftslys og Plaidholder. Selve Polstringen er udsøgt blød og dyb og fremtræder i prima Udførelse og Materialer.

KOMFORT

trimmed. Therefore, interior fittings, materials and style had no consistency. Even the British steering wheel was unlike its American counterpart, being a two-piece assembly having the rim screwed to the three spokes.

External fittings were also different. British lighting regulations called for mandatory wing-top-mounted side lights, cowl lamps being a de luxe or optional item in the US. Twin rear lamps were also mandatory in the UK, the second one being optional in the US. The British headlamp lenses were also different as were the various styles of door handles fitted, Dagenham probably using whatever was available to get the job done.

The English-made bodies were not the only ones which differed from their North American counterparts. On the other side of the world in Australia, where the 1932 models were not introduced until 25 August, the Ford plant at Geelong would eventually produce its own versions of both the Phaeton and the open pick-up.

The Phaeton is discernible as Australian by its lack of beaded seams in the rear panel. Instead, these were welded and ground smooth like other body seams.

Of the open pick-up there were in fact two versions: the type 302 Standard Utility Car, which had smooth pick-up bed sides, and the type 304 Welltype Utility Car, which had shelved pick-up bed sides. The latter was probably more popular because of its extra carrying capacity.

Later in the year Lewis T. Bandt would begin to design a vehicle peculiar to Australia. The marriage of a coupé and a pick-up, utility as the Australians call them, resulted in a 'Ute', which would, however, not be available until 1934, when Ford was marketing the Model 40.

Just as it was taking the American plants some months to get into production, so it was in the rest of the world. By June, however, Antwerp, Barcelona, Cologne, Mexico City, São Paulo and Yokohama had joined the other three. Initial production wasn't particularly high anywhere, São Paulo managing 41 trucks and Yokohama 24 Fordors.

By July everybody was in the picture except Buenos Aires and Santiago, but Istanbul managed only one four-cylinder chassis. Production there was never much above 100 units. Meanwhile on 29 July, 400 cars arrived in the free port of Stockholm from Canada. The car was popular there if nowhere else.

The first big push of the new models from Dagenham came in October, when Ford and their dealers staged an exhibition at London's White City coinciding with the Motor Show at Olympia. During the 10-day show thousands of people thronged the hall, which was open for 12 hours

LEFT ABOVE *Two piece steering wheel of the English sedan*

LEFT BELOW *British Construction and Use Regulations demanded sidelights. These were placed atop of each front wing. Twin rear lamps were also mandatory*

ABOVE *Type 302 Standard Utility Car peculiar to Australia was basically a Roadster pickup with locally made straight-side pickup bed. It is not known how many of these half ton trucks were produced but it was probably less than 100, hence the use of this less than perfect photograph. Little else is known about the vehicle except the pickup bed dimensions which were: length 60 in.; width 46 in.; height 20 in.*

BELOW *Cars were assembled in Geelong, Australia, from knock-down Canadian shipments. The Australian Phaeton is detectable by the absence of body seams in the rear panel*

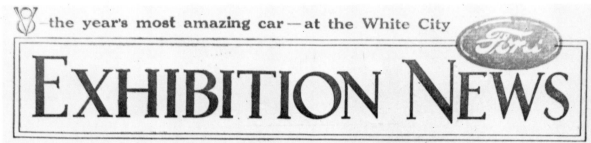

the year's most amazing car — at the White City

EXHIBITION NEWS

Forecast in Pictures and News of the Ford Motor Exhibition at the White City, London, W., Oct. 13-22, 1932

THE LURE OF THE "V-8"

Combined with acceleration and speed hitherto confined to a few high-powered sports cars are a remarkable luxury of appointment and appearance. Yet it is a most inexpensive model.

This picture, and that below (taken in Regent Street, London) reveal the intense interest already created by the V-8. The crowd that flocked to the Ford exhibits in the country is shown in the lower left-hand photograph. From the day it appeared it was the centre of remarkable attraction, and even non-motorists were excited.

The V-8 is a car that gives a new zest to motoring — breath-taking performance, luxurious comfort and appearance — at an amazingly low price. It will be one of a host of almost equally interesting exhibits at the great Ford Motor Show to be held at the White City, London. No motorist can afford to miss this event, which will include something new in value and performance for every class of car-owner, while one of the most comprehensive displays of commercial vehicles ever gathered under one roof will be yet another feature.

ABOVE *The front cover of the* Exhibition News, *Ford's official publication describing the new models which would be on display at London's White City*

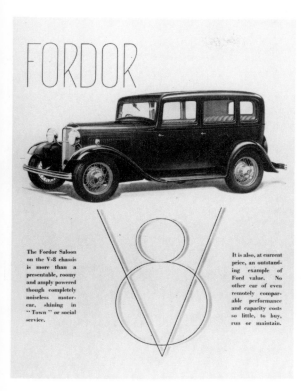

FORDOR

The Fordor Saloon on the V-8 chassis is more than a presentable, roomy and amply powered though completely noiseless motor-car, shining in "Town" or social service.

It is also, at current price, an outstand-ing example of Ford value. No other car of even remotely compar-able performance and capacity costs so little, to buy, run or maintain.

Ford V-8 Cabriolet, Completely Equipped, £295, at Works, Dagenham
Illustrated Catalogue on request

The V8 Cabriolet

The V-8 Cabriolet is a dual-purpose model, in the sense that it can be used as either a completely open or a completely enclosed car.
The mechanism by which the head is folded, at will, is of the simplest, most easily operated, yet is rattle-proof, open or closed, and in the rear is an uncommonly roomy and comfortable dickey seat, so that in all this model will accommodate four people.

Ford V-8 Cabriolet, Completely Equipped, £295, at Works, Dagenham
Illustrated Catalogue Forwarded on Request

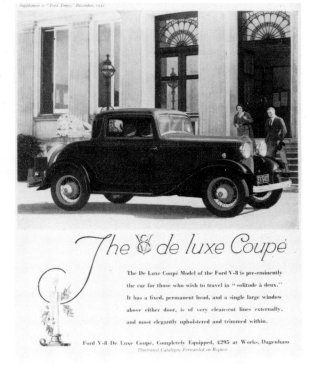

The V8 de luxe Coupé

The De Luxe Coupé Model of the Ford V-8 is pre-eminently the car for those who wish to travel in "solitude à deux." It has a fixed, permanent head, and a single large window above either door, is of very clean-cut lines externally, and most elegantly upholstered and trimmed within.

Ford V-8 De Luxe Coupé, Completely Equipped, £295, at Works, Dagenham
Illustrated Catalogue Forwarded on Request

ALL ABOVE *When Ford-Britain eventually offered the V8 it was only available in five body types; the English bodied Tudor (£230) and Fordor (£260) with three engine options and the imported Victoria, (£285) De Luxe Coupé (£295) and Cabriolet (£295). The imported cars were advertised only with V8s but some examples have been found with four cylinder engines. The Cabriolet was the only convertible offered. The Fordor De Luxe was, however, fitted with a sunshine roof and cost £275. Leather upholstery was optional on the English bodied sedans for £7 10s extra*

87

Sports bodied specials such as this one built by W. J. Reynolds of East Ham, London, did well in motoring events. This is Reynolds taking part in an observed section of the 1937 Welsh Rally

every day to view not only the standard Fords but also a uniquely interesting selection of what the British termed 'specials'. It seems strange that although the products offered by Ford were not particularly popular, and by all accounts this was due to their expensive running costs, there existed a huge market for specials based on not only the four-cylinder but also the V8 chassis. It didn't matter which body style one chose, the horse-power tax was rated on engine size, and yet here were people clamouring to buy V8-engined hot rods. Special builders such as W. J. Reynolds, Dagenham Motors Ltd. and W. Harold Perry Ltd. were cashing in on the lack of open-topped models. Ford, at the time, were offering the British public only the sedans with three engine options and the imported Cabriolet, Victoria and De Luxe Coupé, all mainly with V8 power. For a nation brought up on such classic open tourers as the Bentley and Jaguar, the lack of both Roadster and Phaeton left a very big hole in their range. The hole was quickly filled by the special builders, who unfortunately never managed, in my opinion, to get it quite right. Nevertheless, they were riding a wave of success in such motoring events as the Welsh Rally, the Shelsley Walsh hill climb, various off-road trials and an MCC high-speed trial at Brooklands. At that event John Harrison driving a 14.9 Tudor

averaged 64.67 miles for one hour, even after spinning several times due to a waterlogged track. Everybody in the motor sport fraternity was talking about Ford's pulling power and from October on Dagenham did good business in both B and 18 chassis. In November they sold 423 and in December 377. The sales continued well into 1933, averaging about 200 per month. Many of course were used as the basis for commercial vehicles, but it was, nevertheless, good business.

Though they did attract a lot of attention, specials were not the only things on display at the White City. Ford had on show its now extensive array of vehicles ranging from the expensive Thrupp & Maberly-bodied Lincoln to its £120 Model Y. There was a huge display of commercial vehicles alongside Fordson tractors, industrial power units and the facilities plant.

Entertainment was provided by various artists, including the RAF band, Messrs. Flotsam and Jetsam and Mr Norman Long, entertainers of the time. This lighter side to the show may not have gone down as well as expected, because the reporter, Iolaus, reviewing the show for the

November edition of the *Ford Times*, remarked, 'A majority of the entertainers hired by the BBC should be hanged, drawn, quartered, burned at the stake, and then be made to listen to gramophone records of their own performances.'

Nevertheless, the show was a resounding success and was followed by the British Exhibition in Copenhagen, where the Ford Motor Company A/S had the only automobile stand in the Tivoli gardens. Besides a much-travelled model of Dagenham all the Ford models were on display and the V8 attracted by far the greatest interest. There was also a great deal of comparison for Model A owners with the new AB and ABF models. The 14.9 hp ABF was, however, never sold through the Danish company, the Nordic drivers much preferring the V8.

There were similar shows by dealers and companies alike in places as diverse as the Limerick Horse Show and Alexandria, Egypt.

The Irish plant at Cork commenced production in November, trimming and mounting bodies on

chassis received from Dagenham. They managed 163 units that month, both Tudors and Fordors, five of which were V8s. Production would unfortunately never reach that figure again, and for the next three years Cork produced on average 100 vehicles per month.

By December, when the rest of the world was just getting going, 11 plants in the US had ceased production. For some unexplained reason the records also show that there was no production for that month in Cologne.

Nevertheless, Cork was doing better than some, for example in Santiago, Chile, production never actually got going, operations there having ceased because of the political and economic situation.

Although there had been a lot of interest worldwide when the new cars had been introduced, most people had come to look rather than buy. In Sweden Ford managed to sell only 1080 vehicles of all types and the car received a favourable reception there. In Europe, Holland, Belgium and Denmark continued to make a small profit, whereas France, Egypt, Rumania and Greece made a small loss. England and Germany were the main causes of the year-end total loss for the European operation of $4 million. This was no doubt due to grossly underestimated costs incurred during plant construction.

Ford of Canada lost over $5 million that year and

Although both Tudors and Fordors sold in Scandinavia had English suicide door bodies it is obvious that they too found them boxy compared to the American versions. This artist's impression, taken from a Danish brochure, depicts an English sedan with front-opening doors but with softened contours and the angular windscreen removed. The raised louvre panel is also missing; cars were sold there with and without that feature

TUDOR SEDAN

En elegant fem-Personers Sedan, der for sin
Pris byder enestaaende Værdi, og som saaalan
har vundet universel Beundring. Sæderne er
rummelige og komfortable.

DE LUXE TUDOR SEDAN

Denne Vogns elegante Udstyr indbefatter
Gulvtæpper, Plaidholder, Askebæger, Loftslys,
og andet Luksusudstyr. Polstringen er elegant
og smagfuld.

ABOVE *Production at Cork, Ireland, which consisted of mounting two and four-door sedans only on chassis received from Dagenham, began in November 1932 and lasted until December 1934. Assembly in the background, trimming on the foreground*

BELOW *The rise of the Nazi party was causing Ford –Germany and Britain– much hurt. The Nazis were demanding 100 per cent local content which drastically reduced Dagenham's market and eventually caused the seperation of the two companies. Here is the Cologne plant with a replacement V8 being fitted into a De Luxe Coupé*

sales fell in practically all of its markets. Only in Australia did sales rise from a 1931 total of 1607 to 2590 in 1932. By 1933, though, assembly operations in Adelaide and Sydney would be suspended.

As the world woke up to 1933, Dearborn had given up the Models B and 18 and was instead getting ready to launch, in February, the new Model 40. Only ten of the domestic plants were still in production and soon some of these would close along with the others, never to reopen.

Canada was also to cease producing the '32 models in June 1933 in favour of the 40, but the rest of the world, especially Europe, was still hard at it. The economic situation was unfortunately hardly improving and this was reflected in both production and sales.

Only Dagenham was producing over 1000 units per month, while all of the other foreign plants averaged about 200, but Dagenham still had more than its fair share of problems. Despite a reduction in design and development costs from Dearborn for the Model Y, from $535,360 to $210,000, and a loan of £1 million from Ford-Holland, Dagenham closed the year with a loss of £681,828. Almost immediately a new financial crisis was upon them concerning the operation of their coke-ovens, blast furnace and by-products plant. Extra capital would be needed and A. R. Smith could see no market for the production surplus to Dagenham's requirements. Suggesting economies and that associated European companies advance additional funds Sorensen insisted 'that it was essential in the interests of economy and manufacturing efficiency to make and control the quality of iron used in the factory and that he and his USA colleagues were convinced as to the wisdom of operating power house, blast furnace and coke-ovens as early as possible.' Of course he would be proved right in the long term, but at the time Dagenham was in real difficulty. However, the directors voted to complete all the projects.

In Germany the Nazi party was now the largest group within the Reichstag and in March they seized power. The manager of the Cologne plant, Edmund C. Heine, consequently wrote to Thornhill-Cooper on 24 March stating that, 'After 20 May the Cologne organization must manufacture or procure motors, transmissions, front and rear axles locally, if we are to be considered a national German product, and if our business is not to be jeopardized by arbitrary taxation.' Connections with Dagenham would be almost severed as the Reichsverband der Automobilindustrie gave three successive directives: first that practically all automobile parts must be made in Germany: then that the cars must be made entirely of German materials; and finally that all cars must

have standard parts, interchangeable from one German automobile to another.

The Ford plant never managed to comply, especially with the last directive, and Heine, who was pro-Nazi but with few allies even in his own government, proved inadequate for the task and eventually had to be replaced.

Though it had got off to a good start at the beginning of 1932, France was now facing a year of massive losses.

By May the plants in Buenos Aires, Istanbul, São Paulo and Mexico had ceased production of 1932 models. This left only Japan and Canada on the international scene and they didn't produce 40 vehicles between them. The rest of the production was centred in Europe with bodies still coming mainly from Dagenham. Sedans constituted by far the largest proportion of production, but there were a few Victorias, Coupés, Roadsters and Phaetons, though they were only being manufactured in single numbers, in plants other than Dagenham.

The special market was obviously still large in Britain, where Ford were still producing, on average, 200 chassis per month, of which 95 per cent or more were four-cylinder types. No other country enjoyed this trade as much as Dagenham, but there was a steady flow of chassis from both Cologne and Copenhagen. The German coachbuilders such as Deutsch and Drauz seemed, in my opinion, to make a much better job of their conversions than did their English counterparts. They were, however, building rather more luxurious, upmarket cars than the British, who were, in the main, building lightweight sports models for competition.

Towards the end of the year sales in Europe of the '32 models began to erode as the new, sleeker Model 40 became available. The English sedans, with their boxey bodies, looked like leftovers from the twenties in comparison. Sales were so bad for Denmark that they reduced prices on the V8 Tudor from 3990 Dk to 3700 Dk and on the Sport Coupé from 4080 Dk to 3500 Dk. All B models were 200 Dk cheaper.

The situation was no better in England and Ford decided to introduce three new models at their Albert Hall Exhibition between 12 and 21 October 1933. The first two were not really new models but rather facelifts of the two- and four-door sedans. Though to be renamed the Ford Fourteen they retained, in essence, the original English bodies. Closer inspection, however, reveals that new body dies were in fact made. The windscreen was altered from its original flat-top shape with a piano hinge to the more conventional curved top with hidden hinges. The rear section of the body was also altered to be more barrel shaped, in fact almost

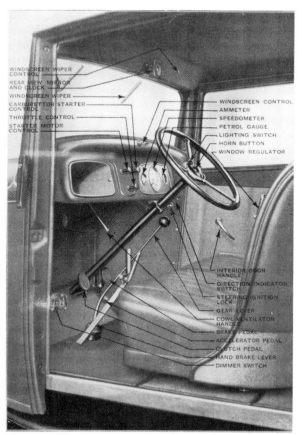

WINDSCREEN WIPER CONTROL
REAR VIEW MIRROR AND CLOCK
WINDSCREEN WIPER
CARBURETTOR STARTER CONTROL
THROTTLE CONTROL
STARTER MOTOR CONTROL

WINDSCREEN CONTROL
AMMETER
SPEEDOMETER
PETROL GAUGE
LIGHTING SWITCH
HORN BUTTON
WINDOW REGULATOR

INTERIOR DOOR HANDLE
DIRECTION INDICATOR SWITCH
STEERING/IGNITION LOCK
GEAR LEVER
COWL VENTILATOR HANDLE
BRAKE PEDAL
ACCELERATOR PEDAL
CLUTCH PEDAL
HAND BRAKE LEVER
DIMMER SWITCH

three inches deeper, thus affording more space inside. The doors were also made slightly longer and the body appears to be sitting lower on the chassis rails. The moulding on the bottom of the cowl, which was also deeper, now had a distinctive S shape in order to align with the bonnet moulding. These changes were obviously made to give the car both more room and a more modern appearance.

The most noticeable changes were made to the front and rear wings, which now sported skirts similar to, but deeper than, those on the Model 40. Atop the front wings were perched new, streamlined, side lights and the headlights were now supported on a straight, Model A-style, bar replacing the original curved bar. The headlights

ABOVE *In 1933 Ford-Britain revamped the 1932 models with new body dies making the back more rounded, thus increasing interior space. Model 40 style skirted wings were fitted front and rear and the doors were made longer. The lower cowl beading now takes on a distinctive S shape to align with the bonnet moulding. These new models were called the Ford Fourteen*

LEFT *The Fourteen had a 1933 Model 40 style dashboard similar to the American commercial dashboard. Whilst the dash panel retained the engine turned patterning the ammeter and petrol gauges were round rather than oval. The 1933 lighting switch was fitted to the English two-piece steering wheel*

RIGHT *The windscreen shape resembled the 1932 American cars, gone was the square top and piano hinge. The distinctive corrugated bumpers were replaced with straight, Model 40 section, bumpers. The new 'acorn' headlights are mounted on a slightly dropped, straight headlight bar, not the curved original. The mandatory wing-top mounted sidelights are not streamlined. This particular car was restored by its owner, Dennis Smart of Horsham, Sussex*

were in most cases not shaped like the originals but instead had peculiarly shaped buckets which became known as acorns. They were, however, still made of stainless steel.

Lastly, Henry Ford's distinctive corrugated safety bumper had been replaced with a Model 40 section bumper, which was straight rather than dipped in the centre.

Inside, the car had changed almost as much. Gone was the deep-set dash panel with its twin glove pockets and in its place was a new Model 40-style dash. This was similar to the American commercial dashboard in that it lacked the cigar lighter and ashtray but retained the windscreen crank handle. Interestingly, although the American-style engine-turned dash panel was retained the gauges were round rather than oval.

Apart from retaining the two-piece steering wheel of 1932, the Fourteen utilized the same combination switch and electrical switch mechanism as the Model 40.

Upholstery materials, door panel design and door cappings were all different from earlier models.

V8 engines were no longer offered as optional by Dagenham, but production records do show that in May 1934 three V8 Fordors were produced.

The only Dagenham product offering the V8 was the third new model. Production records from Dagenham show this as the 7-Passenger Sedan, but it was known generally as the V8 Imperial Limousine. Strangely, there are no records of its production in the Ford Archives at Dearborn.

Exactly why Ford built this model nobody knows, the Ford-Britain files having long since been lost. Some historians would have it that the British Army ordered some with solid rather than welded-spoke wheels and run-flat tyres. Research at London's Imperial War Museum resulted in no evidence to support this theory. There is, however, evidence to confirm that the Limousine was used in Europe as a taxi. According to Dagenham records only 60 were built between 6 October 1933 and 20 June 1934. It would also appear that Dagenham supplied the same, or a similar, 122 in wheelbase chassis, to at least Denmark and Germany. They are certainly listed in Danish Ford literature as 6–7 passenger sedans and chassis, but it would appear that coach-builders in both countries produced specialist limousine bodies for the Ford frame.

Unfortuantely, all three of these big American-style cars were even less popular than they had been two years earlier. Sixty per cent of the

LEFT *This ugly hotch-potch was called the V8 Imperial Limousine. Supposedly, with balloon tyres mounted on solid wheels, it was built for the British Army. No record appears in the Imperial War Museum, but the run-flat tyres which were British military issue for desert use, plus the roof vent, might indicate army use*

RIGHT ABOVE *From December 1934 only Cork and Dagenham were producing Model Bs. The small production line at Cork, where they also assembled Model Ys, shows a few Fourteens with chrome windscreen surrounds but curved, 1932 style, headlight bars. Presumably this was leftover stock*

BELOW LEFT *The Imperial Limousine was, however, sold as a taxi. Its 7-seater body, an amalgam of British 1932 and 1933 Tudor and Fordor parts, was mounted on a special 123 in. wheelbase chassis fitted with an aluminium headed Canadian V8. Only 60 were built at Dagenham between 6 October 1933 and 20 June 1934*

LEFT *When sales of the Fourteen slumped towards the end of 1934, it was decided to tart them up with the addition of a chromed grille shell, windscreen surround and door latches plus other luxury items. It is doubtful if the ploy worked as this Fordor was not registered until June 1935*

RIGHT *The last ten Model Bs produced were police cars at Dagenham in September 1935. Unfortuntely no photographs of these exist, however, here are two 1932 police cars. Note the use of the rear blind as a stop sign, and the fabric roof, a legacy of the Model A*

vehicles sold in Britain were rated at less than 10 hp in 1933, whereas that figure had only been 25 per cent in 1928. Ford were now placed third in the league of volume automobile manufacturers behind Austin and Morris. Though there would be no dividend for shareholders that year the books showed a credit balance of £388,170. Some of this surplus had come from the Danish, Dutch, Belgian and Spanish Ford companies, who had reduced their capitalization by 40 per cent. There never would be much cash to spare though, as Sir Percival Perry was like Henry Ford in that he saw the best use of profits when they were reinvested in plant and machinery, Ford saying, 'No use being all worn out when the tide turns. Take it easy and get ready.'

In France sales had been poor because of import tariffs and a dislike of the very English models, especially the Y. Dollfus was concerned enough to state, 'There is no other future for Ford S.A.F. than the one that can be found in local manufacturing.' Perry was not so easily convinced and wrote to Sorensen, 'I have my doubts as to whether the small production (in France) will be profitable even having regard to the enormous duties which are imposed on imports into France at the present time.'

At the end of November Dollfus went to Dearborn, and accompanying him was E.E.C. Mathis, another established French automobile manufacturer. Dollfus's proposal was a merger between the two companies which would result in both manufacturing and assembly facilities at Asnières and at Mathis's Strasbourg factory.

Sorensen and Edsel listened to the Frenchman and in the new year would send Ford officials to investigate the situation. Nevertheless Ford-France ended the year with a $1¼ million loss.

Even Canada's output was still below its 1929 figure. Ford-Britain, however, closed the year with a profit of almost £1½ million. This was partly due to favourable exchange rates created with President Roosevelt's devaluation of the US dollar, excellent sales of the Model Y and income from the few profitable European companies. This large influx of money enabled Perry to clear up his debts and have some left over for development of Dagenham. Notwithstanding the loss of the French and German markets the future for Dagenham looked bright.

In January 1934 only eight plants, Amsterdam, Antwerp, Asnières, Barcelona, Cologne, Copenhagen, Cork and Dagenham were still producing the B and 18 models. Total production for that month was only 1113 units, the majority of which were still two- and four-door sedans, but Dagenham still churned out 234 B commercial chassis.

Perhaps in North America, where on 13 March the Canadian company managed to raise its wages, the worst of the Depression was behind them. Europe, unfortunately, was facing something much worse – war. Ford-Britain sold back to Dearborn most of its stock in the French and German companies, but in Germany the Nazis were looking towards the production of military vehicles.

In France the law demanded Ford do its own manufacturing and in April production of the Dagenham sedans ceased. That, however, was not the end of the line for the V8 in France. On 27 September the amalgam of Ford and Mathis, Matford, would begin manufacture, in the Strasbourg plant, of its own V8.

By September it was all but over, only Copenhagen, Cork and Dagenham being left on the map. Production was now only sedans, Bs in England and Ireland, and V8s in Denmark.

A last-ditch attempt by the sales office to get rid of the remaining stocks was a tarting-up job. The Fourteens as they were still called were given the glitter treatment with a chrome grille shell, chrome windscreen surround, chrome door latches, etc. The ploy obviously didn't work, because one I found in Sussex, England, had not been registered until June 1935. So if you ever see somebody driving a 1932 Ford with a chromium-plated grille shell and funny looking wings don't accuse him of customizing it, it probably came that way from the factory.

Copenhagen produced its last three cars, V8 Tudors, in November 1934 and paid its shareholders a reasonable 7 per cent dividend. Other companies to pay dividends were Sweden 8 per cent, Holland 12 per cent and Belgium and Spain 25 per cent each.

Dagenham managed to make a profit of about £½ million, but sales were falling, even of the Model Y. By 1935 chief buyer Patrick Hennessey was hammering suppliers for even lower prices until Perry could announce the first £100 saloon.

For the Model B it was the end of the road, production running on at both Cork and Dagenham at sometimes one per month for Cork and ten for Dagenham. The last ten sedans, Tudors for the police, were shipped on 9 September.

From then until early 1936 Dagenham, Cork and occasionally Wellington, New Zealand, and Geelong, Australia, produced a few 106 in wheelbase commercial chassis, but as far as the cars were concerned that was it.

8 The greatest thrill in motoring — pre-war

Practically all of the well-known names in automobile history have had their day on the race tracks of the world. That's how marques such as Bentley, Jaguar, Ferrari and Porsche became household names and in the beginning it was no different for Ford.

Henry Ford's first and last race, at the age of 38, took place on 10 October, 1901, at the Grosse Point one-mile oval. Organized by the Detroit Driving Club, this ten-miler had only three entrants, one of whom dropped out even before the race began, thus leaving Ford to race favourite Alexander Winton.

Ford was totally inexperienced at racing. Nevertheless, with friend and mechanic Ed 'Spider' Huff crouched on the running board he managed to win and not only took home a cut glass punch bowl with matching cups but also $1000. To many the money might have been incentive enough to make a career of it, but Ford's comment was 'Once is enough.'

Rather than do his own driving Ford acquired the services of Barney Oldfield and put him behind the wheel of the infamous 999. This team went on to win numerous races all over America, but Henry stayed firmly on the ground, except when taking rare demonstration rides.

Ford did, however, take one more ride on the wild side, in the winter of 1903. He was after the land speed record, and on January 12 took the Arrow, 999's stablemate, to a frozen Lake St Clair. With Huff once again on the running board, this time working the accelerator because the icy bumps were jarring Ford's foot off, they set a new record of 91.37 mph.

When Barney Oldfield moved on Ford engaged Frank Kulick to do his winning and win he did, at the oval tracks, in hill climbs and in road races. Unfortunately, in 1907, Kulick suffered an accident which left him limping for the rest of his life and Ford with a bad taste in his mouth. The rules were unfair towards his lightweight cars and he didn't want to see his friends killed, but by 1910

Kulick was back at the track winning races and setting new records.

Ford was still unhappy about the situation and after one successful record attempt he gave Frank $1000 to quit. It wouldn't happen right away, but by 1913 Henry Ford was out of racing.

His cars, however, were not. Until the Model T appeared motor racing had been the pastime of gentlemen with enough money to race cars like Millers and Duesenbergs, but Lizzie, with her good power-to-weight ratio and a host of after-market speed equipment available, made a racing driver out of every backyard mechanic who had a mind to be one. They raced their Ts, they raced their As and when it appeared they raced their V8s.

It didn't matter which, it mattered only that they chose Ford and in its turn the V8, which was eventually to make an even bigger name for itself on the race tracks than the Model T.

Ultimately, it was all attributable to Henry – the V8 engine was his idea and he was the one that decided to drop it into the Model B. The fact that people have been doing likewise ever since is indisputable.

I will agree that some of the modifications performed by the so-called hop-up chop-up set have been, over the years, less than pretty, but the perpetrators probably had a lot of fun doing what they did.

I think we have a lot to thank those guys for. Sure they may have butchered a few cars on the way, but by doing what they did they made a rather ordinary Ford a classic with a history a lot more colourful than many of its contemporaries. What follows is a tribute to those fun-loving guys of yesteryear who raced, rallied and rodded the 1932 Ford. Thankfully, many of them are still doing it.

Indy: Brickyard Blues

Americans were perhaps a little slow to realize just what they had in Ford's flattie. Sure V8 versions of the Cabriolet and Roadster would be the official

ABOVE *V8 versions of the Roadster and Cabriolet were the official cars for the 20th running of the Indianapolis 500 mile race in 1932. Winner Fred Frame would make his lap of honour in the Roadster*

BELOW *The first Ford V8 to race in the Indy 500 was entered by local dealer C. O. Warnock. It sported an almost stock chassis with a crude racing body and even cruder split rear radius rods. Daytona 18 in. wheels supported Firestone Balloons. With a speed of 104 mph the car failed to qualify*

CHAS. CRAWFORD, Dr. — M. TOTTON, Mech.
Indianapolis Motor Speedway, 1934.

ABOVE *The car returned the following year disguised as the Detroit Gasket Special. The appearance of the car was so poor it was quickly painted black before the race. Driver Charlie Crawford qualified 3rd slowest at 108.784 mph but a head gasket blew on the 110th lap. They were credited with 16th place. The car was wrecked the following year during practice*

BELOW *Also in the 1934 race was this lovely Bohn Aluminiun & Brass Company racer built by Don Sullivan. Again the 1932 chassis was used but out front was the latest Model 40 grille. Unfortunately driver Chet Miller took himself and mechanic Eddie Tynan over the wall on the 11th lap*

CHET MILLER, Dr. — EDDIE TYNAN
Indianapolis Mo

cars at the 20th Indianapolis 500 Mile Race in 1932, and winner Fred Frame would make his lap of honour in the Roadster, but the V8 would never do well at the Brickyard.

Indianapolis, just like the rest of America, was affected by the Depression and in an effort to reduce the cost of racing and eliminate the all-conquering 'thoroughbred' Millers and Duesenbergs, the organizers introduced in 1930 what became known as the 'Junk Formula'. Structured for modified two-seater production cars with a minimum weight restriction, a maximum capacity of 366 ci and no supercharging, it failed miserably and the 91.5 ci racers continued to lead the way home.

Nevertheless, 1933 became the real debut for the Ford V8 when local dealer C. O. Warnock entered a rather tacky special. It was little more than a stripped-down V8 with a stock chassis, knock-on wire wheels with Firestone Balloons, a racing body and outside exhausts. Prepared by Robert M. Roof, designer of Laurel equipment for Fords, it had an almost standard engine except for two stock Detroit Lubricator carburettors atop a home-made manifold.

With Doc Williams driving and Milton Totten as mechanic, the car failed to qualify with a best run of 104.538 mph.

It was to return the following year disguised as the Detroit Gasket Special. Rebuilt with Bohnalite aluminium heads, a large single Stromberg carb and Charlie Crawford behind the wheel it managed to run at 108.784 mph, and qualified, the third slowest. Unfortunately, for the sponsor, the engine blew a head gasket on lap 110 and the car was subsequently placed sixteenth.

Also running in the 1934 race was another V8 special based on '32 rails entered by the Bohn Aluminum & Brass Company. Built by Don Sullivan the car had a '34 engine with Bohn aluminium racing heads, 30 thou. oversize pistons with a compression ratio of 8.5:1, racing camshaft and a Bosch magneto. It also had a Sullivan-designed inlet manifold with two Stromberg 97s mounted sideways so that they aligned with the centrifugal forces. It was a cheap but well-built car producing 140 hp at 4400 rpm.

In the hands of driver Chet Miller and mechanic Eddie Tynan the car qualified at 109.252 mph, but unfortunately sailed over the wall on the eleventh lap after hitting a patch of oil spilt by Wilbur Shaw. Interestingly the car had its front radius rods split and mounted to either chassis rail, a suspension modification favoured later by hot rod builders.

In 1935, Warnock's car was back at the Brickyard. Renamed the Harry Henderson Special and with a new 1934 grille shell and four Winfield carburettors, it was unfortunately written off before the start when driver Doc Williams took it over the inside wall on the south turn.

The infamous Harry Miller also had a fleet of factory-backed Ford V8-engined racers in the 1935 event, but their miserable failure was to keep Ford officially out of racing for the next 17 years.

In the lower echelons of oval track racing, i.e. the dirt tracks, the 1932 Ford did not really make much of a showing. It was too heavy in comparison to the stripped-down track Ts which were winning, and the V8 was grossly under-developed when compared to a hot four-pot. Nevertheless, the '32 would have its day in the dirt, but not until after the war.

Road races

Practically every American town had its half-mile or mile oval, usually a converted horse track, but apart from Indianapolis there were no major motor races in the United States until 1933. That year, 26 August would see the reinstatement, by the American Automobile Association, of the Elgin Road Race for Stock Cars. The term Stock Car, at the time, loosely ascribed to stripped-down, fenderless and almost screenless roadsters with strictly stock engines not exceeding 231 cu in.

Indy winner Fred Frame collected the Weidenhoff Trophy as the first to finish the 203-mile race, with an average speed of 80.22 mph. Only eight of the 15 starters finished, but the first seven of those were Fords, several of them '32 models. Fred's car was a 1933 Roadster with a very special V8 engine supposedly supplied out of the back door of Dearborn. Yes, Ford were 'officially' out of racing, but the publicity was definitely welcome and Ford made the most of it.

The road races proved to be an ideal venue for the Ford V8, it being light, fast and above all cheap. Elgin, unfortunately was deemed too dangerous and the event was never staged again. Other races would follow and in the new year attention was centred as usual on California.

Mines Field in Inglewood, California, was to be the scene of a 250-mile race, probably the first to be staged on an airport. Mines Field is now Los Angeles International Airport, but then more than 60,000 people turned out on 24 February to watch 'Stubby' Stubblefield take the Gilmore Trophy in his '33 Roadster with an average speed of 62.37 mph. Other drivers in the 26-car field included Chet Gardner, Pete DePaolo, Lou Meyer, 'Shorty' Cantlon, Rex Mays, Al Gordon, Bill Froelich and 'Wild Bill' Cummings. Swede Smith was one of several '32 drivers, but most of the other 22 Fords were Model 40 Roadsters. Fords would take the first ten places.

The Gilmore Gold Cup Race was held on 24 February 1934 at Mines Field, Los Angeles (Los Angeles Municipal Airport). Here at the start Rex Mays (21) pulls away from Al Gordon (15) who at one time thought he was the winner. However, he was nosed out by Stubby Stubblefield (8) who covered the 250 mile course in 4 hours 46 seconds with an average speed of 62.367 mph. Pete de Paolo (2) took 3rd place, Lou Meyer (1) 4th and Rex Mays 5th

Less than a month later the action had moved over to the Ascot Legion Speedway at Valley and Soto Streets in Los Angeles, where, on 21 March, there was a 150-mile event called the American Targa Florio, staged partly on Ascot's half-mile oval and partly in the surrounding hills. Lou Meyer won the event, but the promoters lost out when many of the spectators sneaked through the hills to watch. With no control of the paying public the promoters and reluctantly the racers went back to more orthodox oval racing. Apart from a few minor races, Stock Car racing as it was in 1934 was finished.

The '32 Ford would make few appearances in the serious side of American motor racing in the years to follow as they were no match for the purpose-built European road racers. But their engines, both the four-cylinder and the V8, would find themselves swapped into all sorts of sports car bodies and doing very well thank you.

The California Kids

At about the same time as those good ol' mid-Western farm boys and backyard mechanics were beginning to realize just what Ford had in his V8 engine there was another group of Ford fans going off in an entirely different direction. Instead of racing round and round in circles the California kids were speeding in straight lines across the dried-up lake beds of the Mojave Desert.

The lakes had been used for record runs since the beginning of the twentieth century and their use by the AAA in the twenties and thirties brought worldwide attention. For the big boys, though, not the hot rodders who ran hopped-up Ts and As.

There was already plenty of speed equipment about for Ford's four-pot, but the lakes proved to

be a breeding ground for a new generation of innovative engine tuners – tuners who ran their engines near to melting point and coined the phrase hot rod. As soon as the more streamlined 1932 models appeared they were adopted as the racer's favourite, especially the 'air-flow' grille shell which was tacked on to the front of Ts and As alike.

The V8 was at first rejected as being possibly unreliable but certainly less powerful than a good racing four. Speeds of up to 120 mph were possible with parts such as Riley four-port heads or Winfield's red or yellow heads. Nevertheless, as Ford improved the design of the V8 to increase its output and speed equipment manufacturers began to make parts for it, so the racers came to love it. They still do, but it would be 1937 before Richie Richard's stripped-down '32 V8 Roadster topped 100 mph. With milled heads, a Betry intake manifold and no fenders the car ran at 104.04 mph. Karl Orr, the first guy to exceed 120 mph in a Deuce, would increase the speed to almost 140 mph by the time war broke out, but in the thirties the four bangers were never far behind.

At the time it was 'cool' to own a stripped-down hot rod and drive it around Los Angeles all week, covered in lakes dust. At the weekend it was a 100-mile drive out to Muroc (eventually to become Edwards Airforce Base and home of the space shuttle), the largest and most popular of the lakes, where early the next morning, before the sun got too hot, the races would take place. In those days, after solo heat runs, everybody raced at once and only the guy out front could see. Everybody else was clouded in fine white alkali dust. The ensuing mêlée was the cause of many accidents, eventually attracting the attention of the police. Organization was necessary, if only to safeguard the continuation of the fun, and so, in 1937, the Southern

LEFT *They may have had too little money or maybe they were too busy but the lads racing at the lakes took few photographs. Seen here screaming across the dust in the late thirties or early forties is the Porter Muffler car from Los Angeles*

ABOVE RIGHT *This typical late thirties lakes racer awaits his turn on the dried and cracked course of Muroc. Stripped of its wings, lights, bumpers, windscreen and silencer it does, however, wear the badge of a lakes racer, a covering of white dust*

BELOW RIGHT *Veda Orr at the wheel of her husband Karl's Deuce Roadster. In 1937 she broke her own record and ran 114.24. In 1939 Karl went 121.62 and became the first man to exceed 120 mph in a Deuce. He used a thick wall Canadian truck block with Indian motorcycle pistons. He says 'they popped up about $\frac{1}{4}$ in. so I took cast iron heads, cut 'em out into the water jackets and brazed cups into 'em. The welds would give way pretty quick, but boy that motor went good.' It eventually ran 125.82 mph*

California Timing Association was born. With its own newspaper, a few rules and plenty of guidelines the rodders got organized.

Activity at Muroc ceased in 1940 when the government-owned land was taken over by the army. America was not yet in the war and consequently the racers merely moved to one of the other dry lakes, either El Mirage, Harper or Rosamond. The war for America was but a year away and all racing at the lakes stopped in 1942, but the rodders would be back.

When the V8 did become popular, ironically it was the forged-steel crankshaft, only used in 1932, which most engine tuners sought out, believing it was stronger than the later cast cranks.

Speed trials

Dry lakes are rather rare in Europe, but there has never been a shortage of places to run fast cars or for that matter men to drive them. Unfortunately, the activities of those early speed merchants went, for the most part, unrecorded.

England of course had Brooklands, a purpose-built 2¾-mile track with banked corners, situated to the south-west of London near Weybridge, Surrey. Built in 1907 by Hugh Fortescue Locke King, a renowned civil engineer, whose projects included the Sydney Harbour Bridge and whose wife, Dame Ethel Locke King, would be the eventual proud owner of a Ford V8 Coupé, the circuit became the centre of European motor racing until the advent of the Second World War.

Twice a year, usually in May and September, clubs such as the MCC (Motor Cycle Club) or JCC (Junior Cycle Club) held high-speed reliability trials there. During these events members of the club could try their car against the clock. Competing cars ran in oddly mixed groups for one hour, at the end of which their completed distance was computed against the time to give an average speed. These events were not particularly big on the motor racing calendar, but they were well supported by the drivers.

Ford themselves took over Brooklands in the summer of 1932 to produce a film which would be shown at the forthcoming White City Exhibition. Depicted racing around the track were a Lincoln, a V8 De Luxe Coupé, Tudor and Fordor B models and the 8 hp Model Y. Luckily the film survived and is now preserved on video tape at Ford-Britain's head office.

Sadly, Brooklands was not to survive; it encircled two very important aircraft factories – Hawker Aircraft Co. and Vickers-Armstrong, where Hurricane fighters and Wellington bombers were made. The vast expanse of concrete surrounding them was thought to be a perfect landmark for German bombers and it was therefore decided to camouflage it. The last race was held over the August Bank Holiday in 1939, after which trees were planted in the cracks between the unreinforced concrete slabs caused by the constant pounding of heavy, high-speed racing

ABOVE *Reliability Trials were the thing to enter in England in the late thirties and the Ford V8 was popular; its good power to weight ratio being ideal. Seen here barrelling over the finish line of the Caerphilly hill climb section of the 1938 Welsh Rally is H. Koppenhagen in one of the Jabberwok team cars. The Jabberwok team invariably drove V8 Cabriolets with bobbed fenders*

LEFT ABOVE *In 1937 a new inner circuit was built at Brooklands and named the Campbell Circuit in honour of Sir Donald Campbell. Seen here racing on that circuit is John Cleland in his 1933 V8 Cabriolet, one of the most popular models with the racing fraternity. The streamlined side lights identify it as a '33 but those aero screens are definately not standard. Incidentally, in the background is an overhead gantry built for the Ford day on which reads, 1st FOR SPEED & COMFORT THE FORD V-8*

LEFT *Shades of Muroc at Montlhéry near Paris; this streamlined Model B, nicknamed* Agathe, *established speed records between 6 and 14 March 1933. It was sponsored by Yacco oil and prepared by Cesar Marchand. During those eight days the car covered 21,101 km at an average of 125.602 km/h. In C class (cars under 5000 cc), it took ten world records.*

How would the French have reacted to a dusty lakes racer which could produce the same figures but in miles per hour?

As if that wasn't enough, Agathe II, *a Model B delivery van, loaded with 800 kg of oil, presumably Yacco, ran for six hours at an average speed of 83.462 km/h*

cars. As if that wasn't enough, an extra access road was cut right through the banking and what the trees didn't crack up the rabbits undermined.

Thankfully, part of the track still remains and one stretch of it is preserved by The Brooklands Society as a museum and a venue for their annual rally. Incidentally, the industrial estate occupying the centre of the track now houses a company called Autokraft, who manufacture the AC Mk IV, a development of Carroll Shelby's legendary Cobra – it too is powered by a Ford V8.

Speed trials were and still are held on Brighton's Madeira Drive and in 1932 J. W. Whalley driving a V8 Phaeton covered the distance. Mr Whalley was a regular competitor with his Ford V8 in various forms of motor sport. He finished the 1932 Monte Carlo Rally, won his class in the Mont Des Moles Hill Climb and competed in the reliability trials which were very popular in pre-war Britain.

Rallies and races

Obscure English events were not the only places where the Ford V8 was to appear and J. W. Whalley was not the only Ford V8 driver in the Monte. Another Englishman, T. V. G. Selby, began his journey to the Mediterranean in a Ford

V8 from Stavanger, but unfortunately retired. A Ford V8 team did reasonably well in the International Alpine Trial through Italy, Germany, Austria, Switzerland and France, while in the 1933 Swedish Grand Prix Ford V8s came third and fourth with C. G. Johansson and a Mr Bennstrom driving.

Trials: Mud, glorious mud

There might not have been any dirt tracks in England in the thirties, but there sure was a lot of mud. The English motoring enthusiast therefore spent a lot of his weekends pitting man and machine against the mountains or, at least, fairly steep hills.

Racing on the Queen's highway was and still is forbidden, but under the direction of the Royal Automobile Club affiliated groups organized cross-country Reliability Trials. These events, organized by local motoring clubs, which to this day form the backbone of British motor sport, covered distances varying from 10 to 60 miles and were mainly concentrated in the hilly areas of the

Cotswolds, Derbyshire, Surrey and Hampshire.

All competing vehicles had to adhere to what regulations there were regarding the use of motor vehicles on the road and all drivers had to be a member of a club. Apart from that it was open house. The course consisted of observed and unobserved sections and to stop in an observed section meant the accumulation of penalty points and little chance of an award. There were no winners, it was not a race.

The more famous national events included the Welsh Rally, the Land's End Trial and the Exeter Trial, and it was in these events and at various speed trials that the name Sydney Allard and Ford V8 became synonymous.

Sydney was an enthusiastic participant in any form of motor sport and he, along with others, soon saw the potential of the sprightly Ford. By the mid-thirties the 1932 Ford could be bought second-hand relatively cheaply, normal motorists being unable or unwilling to afford their high running costs. Its excellent power-to-weight ratio was ideal for trials and the extra running costs meant little to the enthusiast.

LEFT *Mud, glorious mud and Jim Mac rescues one of the May sisters from Sydney Allard's first Ford based special. This car was built from a wrecked Model 48 but many of Allard's early specials would use the 1932 frame as their basis*

BELOW *A rare for England De Luxe Coupé is seen here taking part in the 1939 MCC Lands End Trial. Notice how the headlight bar is adorned with club badges and that the car has at sometime been fitted with the 1933 Fourteen bumper*

Fords of all types, but especially the 1932 V8, became popular with the trials entrant. Any type of body style from tourer to Tudor was acceptable, but in an endeavour to improve the already good power-to-weight ratio the special was born. Sydney himself was busy engine swapping Model Bs when he managed to purchase an ex-Tourist Trophy racer built in Northern Ireland. Though based on a 1933 model, this car, with its stripped appearance and lightweight body, was to lead the way for many, but Sydney would go on to build his specials using the distinctive 1932 chassis.

His early involvement with the Ford V8 eventually led to the formation of the Allard Motor Company, which produced many fine Ford-powered automobiles. He was also to be instrumental in bringing the American sport of drag racing to Britain in the early sixties.

The popularity of cross-country trials began to decline towards the end of the thirties and died a natural death during the war. There was no time and no money for the frivolous pastime of motor racing and even if there had been there were precious few cars to compete with and even less petrol to power them.

The trials scene still exists in Britain and is seeing something of a revival in the form of Classic Car Trials. There are sadly very few '32 Fords left to compete in.

Here at an unidentified hill climb, is Mr Smith. In order to improve his power to weight ratio he has removed one bumper iron plus the front wings, running boards, one headlight and the doors. Perhaps their removal was the result of a threat to blow them off by Ken Hutchison who is ready behind him in a V12 Lincoln-Zephyr powered Allard special. Also awaiting their turn in the background are another Allard special and two Model 40s, one of them a three-window coupé

Hill climbs: OTT

Ford V8s driven by Bus Hammond, Angelo Cimino and Glen Schultz may have taken the first three places and broken production car class records at the 1934 Pikes Peak hill climb, but hill climbing has never been a popular pastime for Americans.

In England hill climbs were all part of the Reliability Trial, but they were in some cases events in their own right. It is interesting to note that they are one of the few forms of truly amateur motor racing that has survived into the eighties.

Today the sport is mostly practised on paved private roads, but back in the thirties it didn't seem to matter if it was a mud or made-up surface. A

good power-to-weight ratio was and still is the prerequisite of a hill climber, so, once again, it was no wonder that the 1932 Ford was popular. Cars didn't necessarily have to be road legal or driven to the event, but in most cases they were. In fact the participants usually used the same car for daily transport as they did for a weekend warrior in everything from speed trials to hill climbs. They were in pretty much the same situation as the California kids, but without the sunshine.

The more famous national events included Shelsley Walsh and Prescott, but there were a host of smaller venues operated by local clubs and the Fords of 1932 made a good showing at all of them.

9 The same thrill — postwar

By the time the Second World War had ended there was little of anything left in Europe – there certainly were not cars, money or petrol enough to go racing. Brooklands had been destroyed by trees, rabbits and bombs, there being three successful raids on the aeroplane factories, and the trials scene had faded from popularity.

California, on the other hand, had hardly been touched by the war; all that had happened there was that it had become a staging post for servicemen on their way to and from the Pacific theatre. On their way through they saw the kids who were too young to fight but old enough to drive cruising around in their hot rods – stripped-down Fords with more emphasis on looks than

speed. After all, the dry lakes were closed and the only thing to do was cruise the boulevards and hit the hot dog stands.

Of the guys that returned from the war some were to settle in the sunnier climes of California, where they could hot rod all year round, while others would carry the dream of what they had seen to their homes all over America, spreading the word like wandering preachers.

The shape of things to come. Ed Negley's hot rod at El Mirage in 1947 has such street-neat tricks as a louvred bonnet, filled and peaked grille shell and shortened front frame horns with a welded and peaked spreader bar. None of these modifications, nor the chrome shocks, increased speed much but they looked sharp as did the shiny black lacquer

RIGHT ABOVE *1948 saw Robert E. Petersen and friend Bob Lindsay launch* Hod Rod *magazine, the first issue completely sold out. Pete is seen here photographing a roadster streaking through the dust at El Mirage*

RIGHT BELOW *Few '32s are seen at the lakes these days, racers preferring the slimmer Model A. However, in the early seventies a team of students at Chaffey College campaigned this flathead powered car in X/GR class, (for pre-1960 engined Gas Roadsters of less than 325 ci)*

Meanwhile, the serious racers returned to the lakes and oval tracks, the war merely an unpleasant hiccup in their quest for speed.

Back at the lakes

The late forties proved to be the golden years of lakes racing, when men such as Stuart Hilborn, Vic Edelbrock, Chuck Potvin, Phil Weiand, Ak Miller and Ed Winfield made their names as tuners and producers of speed equipment. Those first names and nicknames are now mostly forgotten or even unknown by today's generation of racers, but the surnames can still be found cast into fuel injectors, manifolds, camshafts and a host of proven speed parts. Those back-yard businesses born out of necessity went on to form the Specialty Equipment Manufacturers Association, a body increasingly active in today's sometimes repressive society towards the continuation and advancement of fun with motor cars.

At that time motor sport was not as fragmented as it appears today, with near fanatical factions ignoring events outside their own circle. Instead racers might be out at the lakes one weekend, sliding into the bends at the dirt track the next and street racing every night in between. To prove my point officials of the SCTA in 1946 included Wally Parks, now President of the National Hot Rod Association, Lou Meyer, three-time winner of the Indianapolis 500, and Rex Mays, AAA Champion, and you can't get more diverse than that.

1948 was to be a great milestone in hot rodding history. Robert E. Petersen and his friend Bob Lindsay launched *Hot Rod* magazine, completely selling out their first print order of 10,000 copies at

Southern California's first hot rod show, held in January at the Los Angeles Armory. Since that first issue *Hot Rod* has grown, with the sport, to become the world's largest-selling automotive magazine with a monthly print order around one million copies.

Later in 1948 the Santa Barbara Acceleration Association staged the first organized drag races on a back road at the Santa Barbara airport in Goleta, California.

Meanwhile, back at the lakes the cars were beginning to take on a new shape. You couldn't just go out there now and race your grocery getter. Well, you couldn't if you wanted to win.

Perhaps the most significant discovery was the importance of streamlining. It was no longer sufficient to strip off all the bits that stuck out, it was now necessary to add bodywork to improve the aerodynamics.

The trend began with the addition of '32 grille shells to almost everything, progressed through belly pans and a craze of channelling (dropping the bodies over the chassis rails to reduce frontal area) and ended with the rejection of the 1932 bodyshell in favour of the slimmer Model A.

The 1932 engine never stood a chance. By the time the racers accepted the V8, 1932 was pre-war history, but the hot set-up, a Mercury V8 loaded with speed parts, was a direct descendant of Ford's first flathead.

The quest for speed was in itself about to ring the death knell of the dry lakes. Most of the traditional-style roadsters were running in the high 120s, while some of the new breed lakesters, fashioned from aeroplane fuel tanks, were capable of running at almost 150 mph. There was also a

rumour that two hot rodders, Alex Xydias and Dean Batchelor, were building a streamliner which would go 200 mph. The lakes were just not safe enough. Twenty years of racing had left the surface, which had previously lain unmolested for hundreds of years, broken, rutted and dangerous. A new, safer, faster venue had to be found.

That venue turned out to be the Great Salt Lake Desert of Utah, specifically the Bonneville salt flats. Robert E. Petersen, his general manager, Lee Ryan, and soon-to-be *Hot Rod* magazine editor Wally Parks, travelled the 700 miles to organize, with Utah state officials, the establishment of the Bonneville Nationals. The first annual speed week was held in 1949 and that rumour of a 200 mph car turned out to be true when the So-Cal Special ran at 193 mph.

Speed trials, organized by the SCTA, are still held annually at Bonneville and regularly at El Mirage, but a '32 Roadster is sadly a rare sight.

Drag racing

That first legal drag race at Santa Barbara airport was quickly followed by other impromptu events organized by the SCTA on similar temporary sites. The rapid and spectacular growth of drag

ABOVE *The world's first commercial drag strip was opened in Santa Ana, California in 1950. Same year here but Blimp Base in El Toro. Little in the way of equipment or safety structures but the crowd is large. Who won, the Model A or the '32 with dropped axle, chromed tank and '39 teardrop lights?*

RIGHT ABOVE *The Deuce has been a rare sight at the strip until the recent Yesteryear Drags and the Nostalgia Nationals. This ol' time five-window looks like they used to. It is even sports a tuned four-banger with overhead valve conversion, dual twin throat Webers and magneto ignition*

RIGHT BELOW *This may be the late-seventies or early-eighties but this fenderless, flathead, five-window was where it was at 20 years earlier. A drilled and dropped axle, front mounted gas tank, cheater slicks and plenty of racer tape don't deter this hot rod from running the quarter mile in 14.5 seconds*

racing was the result of many contributing factors – the vast numbers of young men who had decided to settle in California and take up motor racing as one way of retaining the excitement lost when the war ended; the launching of *Hot Rod* and similar magazines; the organizing of hot rod and custom car shows and a genuine concern by the police and city fathers to stop the kids racing on the street, where they were endangering not only their own but other citizens' lives.

In 1950 the world's first commercial drag strip was opened in Santa Ana, California, and pretty soon strips were opening up all over America.

Some were a full quarter mile, but many small-town strips were nothing but disused back roads with barely enough room for an eighth-mile race. Nevertheless, the sport flourished and for most people, even Californians, it was a darned sight easier to go drag racing than it was to go out to the lakes or make the once-a-year 1400-mile round trip to Bonneville.

Because the drag racers were basically the same bunch of hot rodders who had been racing at the lakes or cruising the street, the majority of the cars at the strip were Fords. Their good ol' power-to-weight ratio was once again proving to be the winning formula. Their original engines were almost invariably discarded in favour of the more powerful Merc, or, as they appeared, the overhead-valve jobs of Chrysler, Oldsmobile and eventually Chevrolet, but the '32 bodyshell was a firm favourite.

Though it remains to this day the definitive '32, the Roadster was no longer the only acceptable body style. Probably because there were not enough Roadsters to go round, Ford having only built 12,500 of them, sedans and especially coupés became familiar sights on the streets and strips. For some unexplained reason the other body styles were never acceptable, nor were other marques popular, explaining why the term Deuce, by which rodders knew the 1932 Ford, referred only to Fords and no other make of car built in 1932.

ABOVE *In the late forties the California Roadster Association organised oval track racing at several stadiums in the Los Angeles area and advertised it as the 'Roaring Roadsters'. Many of the cars were street driven and this picture depicts Bob Lindsay, who is actually driving an A-bodied roadster, ahead of an unidentified but good looking Deuce*

RIGHT BELOW *Despite chained tyres Carl Ameling slides this V8 Cabriolet across the ice during a race at Frederiksborg Slotsso in 1940. Notice the icicles hanging from the front bumper*

The popularity of the Deuce and its excellent power-to-weight ratio stood it in good stead at the drags until the sport, like all forms of motor sport, inevitably became more specialized. Pretty soon race car constructors were leaving the bodies off altogether and racing just the engine and 'rails'.

Under the various class structures formulated over the years by drag racing's governing bodies the old hot rods gradually disappeared from the strips. Thankfully, they were not junked, instead they were put back on the street, turned into show cars, restored or at worst pushed way back in the garage or yard. It has, however, taken the eighties' obsession with nostalgia to put the Deuce back on the strip on a regular basis. Now it can sometimes be seen competing in bracket drag races, but you're more likely to find them at the Street Rod Drags or the Nostalgia Nationals held annually in

California. Ironically, Los Angeles, the birth place of hot rods and drag racing, now has no permanent drag strip.

Oval tracks

While one group of guys were racing flat out across the desert under the sanction of the SCTA and another group were accelerating hard over the quarter mile under the watchful eye of the NHRA, yet other groups were chasing their tails around the oval tracks just as they had been before the war.

There were so many divergent groups of oval track racers spread across America in the immediate pre-war and postwar period it is almost impossible to chronicle their development. However, as we are concerned only with the involvement of the 1932 Ford our task is somewhat simplified.

Probably because of the weather California was obsessed with the roadster, but what happened there is not necessarily what happened elsewhere in America. Nevertheless, a group of racers formed the California Roadster Association and began organizing low-buck circle track events and calling it Hot Rod Racing.

Weekly meetings were held on tracks around Los Angeles at Bonelli Stadium, Saugus, Huntington Beach Speedway and at Carrell Speedway in Gardena. The cars, called track jobs, were mostly Model T-bodied roadsters powered by Model B or Mercury V8 engines with, among other modifications, Cragar heads, Offenhauser manifolds, Winfield cams, etc. Almost all of them, like the lakes racers, were fitted with '32 grille shells, but '32 Roadsters were few and far between.

Eventually, as drag racing grew in popularity and roadster bodies became harder to find so the 'Roaring Roadsters', as they were advertised, became less popular. The CRA eventually changed its name to the California Racing Association and remains active in the organization of sprint car racing, the direct descendant of Hot Rod Racing.

In the mid-Western and East Coast states oval track racing developed into stock car racing, what we now know as NASCAR, but in the early days it was less than organized and therefore took many forms. At the bottom of the heap came the jalopy races, little more than destruction derbys using up the so-called junkers of the late twenties and thirties, many of them Fords.

You rarely saw a roadster in a jalopy race, but in the height of its popularity in California in the fifties you saw plenty of 1932, 1933 and 1934 coupés – indeed the majority of Californian racers would only use Ford coupés of that vintage. They must have wrecked thousands of them, but the kids who sat and watched televised events from Ascot Speedway loved every minute of it.

Across the pond

The extremely diverse American oval track scene led to confusion and the widespread misuse of terms when the sport was imported to Europe. What became known in Britain and France as stock car racing bore little resemblance to the NASCAR action, its origins being more akin to jalopy racing. In Denmark, however, stock car racing in the late forties and early fifties was not a destruction derby and could be equated more easily with serious American stock car races. The first Danish track was established at Hobro in northern Jutland on 20 July, 1947.

Stock car racing, in whatever guise it appeared, was not the only form of motor racing that attracted the Scandinavian Ford V8 owner. Between the early thirties and the fifties they were seen competing on the racing circuits, including the Swedish Grand Prix, at trials, hill climbs, car rodeos and even ice races held on frozen lakes.

Stock cars

Stock cars were introduced to France by Andy Dickson in 1953, when races were held on a cinder track built initially for motorcycle speedway, in the centre of the Buffalo Stadium in Paris. This was a high-banked, wooden board Velodrome built for cycle racing.

These destruction races, using mostly American coupés and sedans, attracted the attention of British motoring journalist John Bolster, then technical editor of *Autosport* magazine, who

LEFT ABOVE *On the start line at Hobro sometime in the late Forties. At the far end in 22 is Nellemann in a special aluminium bodied '37 V8 Roadster. Behind him a Model A Tudor, two '32 De Luxe Coupés, two Cabriolets, 33 driven by Bachmann, a Roadster with special wheels (Sorensen) and a Tudor driven by Rasmussen*

ABOVE *Later on the same day but in a different race we have a '36 Roadster driven by Andersen leading Rasmussen in his Tudor and Preben Sorensen in his Roadster*

LEFT *Seen here in the Danish-Swedish hillclimb on 5 August 1951 is Arnold Jensen from Roskilde driving his well lit Convertible Sedan. Notice the skirted front wings which are similar too, but not exactly like, those fitted to the 1933 British models. Probably these were similar products made by the Danish factory. Note that the rear wings are not skirted*

journeyed from England to France to participate.

Reporting upon his experiences in the November issue Mr Bolster predicted that the sport would soon hit Britain. He couldn't have been more correct, because at that time an Australian entrepreneur and showman, 'Digger' Pugh, was already negotiating with the Greyhound Racing Association to stage American-style stock car races on the cinder ovals built inside greyhound tracks for speedway racing. The outcome of his negotiations was the offer of New Cross Stadium in South London and the date set for the first meeting was 16 April 1954.

John Bolster gave the events leading up to the first race full coverage in the pages of *Autosport* despite angry readers' letters deploring the coverage of what was regarded as little more than a 'cowboy' circus attraction.

Similar events had been taking place in the North of England, where two men, Arthur Cheetham and Ernest Appleby, with backing from Sir Henry Shiffner, formed the Northern Stock Car Racing Company. The company made a deal with Sir Henry Hornby to hold their first meeting at Bradford's Odsal Stadium on 26 May 1954.

That first meeting at New Cross was a staggering success. John Bolster had been instrumental in arranging for a French team to participate and had even persuaded the British customs to allow the French to drive their somewhat illegal stock cars the 80-odd miles from their port of entry at Southend to New Cross. Publicity stunts such as this and coverage in almost every daily newspaper precipitated a sell-out. A capacity crowd of 26,000 was locked into the

stadium hours before the event began in order to keep a further 20,000 out.

After four heats the final was won by Frenchman Chevalier D'Orgeix, but the star of the show was Tanya Crouch, the only British woman driver, who won the fourth heat in her 1934 Model 40 Fordor.

American coupés and sedans were chosen by the stock car racers for various reasons. The sport was an American import, so it was logical to use whatever suitable American cars could be found, especially as they were much stronger and more powerful than the small-bore European jobs being built at the time. It was because they had such big, powerful engines that they went unwanted by the motoring public, who in postwar Britain were still on rationing. Nobody wanted a big gas-guzzling yank, so nobody minded when the stock car racers cleared up what the wartime scrap metal drives had left. Fords were of course the most popular, being not only common but also ideally light, fast and fairly robust.

1954 and 1955 saw the sport mushroom with almost 250 meetings held at over 40 tracks, but it proved to be a flash in the pan. Tracks began to close as crowds diminished, and unprofessional squabbling by the promoters really did give the sport a poor image. By 1956 there would be half as many events at half as many venues and not until the late seventies did the sport manage to get itself organized and recognized.

Even by the end of the fifties the Ford was finished; it was too light to compete against the purpose-built racers that were bashing their way to victory. Sadly, the damage was done, hundreds of Bs, known as Fourteen-nines because of their 14.9 hp engines, 18s and 40s, etc., were destroyed in the frantic fifties of British Stock Car racing.

10 Hot rod — one history

It is unlikely that so many Deuces, or for that matter any other thirties Fords, would have survived without the hot rodders. I doubt that many restorers would agree with that statement however. Most restorers or collectors do not worry about cars until they are old and rare and then, more often than not, they care only for the prestigious, expensive models. Hot rodders, however, latched onto the V8-engined '32 as soon as Henry announced it and ever since have been searching them out and hoarding them away in part or whole for future projects. Many a hot rodder's garage is full of engines, chassis, bodies, etc. Without their interest it is unlikely that so many would have survived the scrap metal drives and jalopy races. I'll agree that few of the rodded cars are exactly as Henry built them, but hasn't it always been that way? Wasn't the model 18 nothing more nor less than an improved Model A with a V8 engine? It is sufficient that they survive, regardless of their condition.

There are no doubt many examples to prove my point, but one hot rod in particular epitomizes my statement. The car, a Hiboy roadster, was built back in the forties by Bob McGee and made its first claim to fame by gracing the cover of the October 1948 issue of *Hot Rod* magazine. Since then the car has seen a full and active life in all aspects of the hot rod sport in the hands of its present owner, Dick Scritchfield.

Scritch had been interested in hot rods and in particular the Deuce a long time before he purchased this car, his love affair having started in Washington DC in 1948, where Scritch was a drummer with the US Navy. There he purchased his first '32, a Sport Coupé which was immediately stripped of its fenders and fitted with through-body exhausts, a neat trick of the time, plus a set of sealed-beam lights to replace the dim originals. The Sport Coupé served Scritch well until they were both shipped out, he to Puerto Rico and the Coupé back home to the family farm in Missouri.

Visiting home on leave Scritch traded the car for

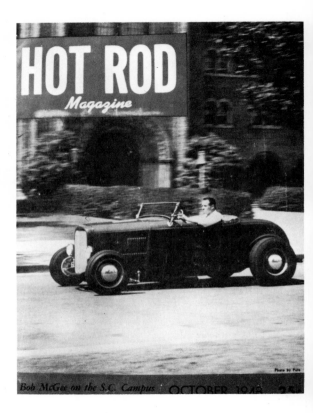

ABOVE *Bob McGee driving his Deuce Roadster across the cover of the October 1948 issue of* Hot Rod *magazine. Note photo credit for Pete Petersen, founder of the Petersen Publishing Company. Car was radical in 1947 having a dropped front axle and a zee'd frame, chopped frame horns and a welded and peaked spreader bar, filled and peaked grille shell, a three-piece bonnet and a chopped screen*

RIGHT ABOVE *When Scritch bought the car in 1956 it was bright yellow with some hot rod headers. Notice how the lower deck panel was made part of the boot lid. Also the lack of door hinges and door handles. In 1957 it appeared in its first film,* Hot Rod Gang

RIGHT *In 1960 Scritch applied one of the world's first metalflake paint jobs in bright cherry red. A year later the car was on TV being driven by Max Baer in an episode of* 77 Sunset Strip – *the cult show which introduced the world to the hot rod, specifically Kookie's fad T*

In 1962 the car was used as a prop for the singing trio the Lennon Sisters whilst appearing on the Lawrence Welk TV show

The Safety Safari turned out to be a roving public relations exercise aimed at convincing the police and other officials that hot rodding was not such a bad thing after all.

The Safari resulted in a move to warmer climes and a job at NHRA headquarters in Los Angeles. On the way home from work one day Scritch spotted a yellow Deuce Roadster parked in a service station. Eventually he found the owner and pretty soon both cars changed hands without either person having driven the other car. Thus began an association lasting to this day.

The car, built in 1947 by Bob McGee, was one of the first '32s to be modified Hiboy style. It was Bob's second roadster and was, for the day, very radical, some of its features being regarded now as eighties trends, but this car proves that nothing is new.

To begin with the stock '32 frame was zee'd in the rear to lower both the body and frame over the axle. The front was similarly lowered by the fitment of a dropped axle, and the front frame horns were shortened and fitted with a moulded and peaked spreader bar.

Mechanical specifications included a '34 V8, which was ported and bored out to 237 ci and fitted with a Bertrand cam, 21-stud Federal Mogul heads, a Burn's manifold with twin Stromberg 97 carburettors and a Spalding Zephyr-type ignition.

Behind the engine was a Zephyr transmission mated to a Ford differential.

Stopping the narrow Ford front wheels and Zephyr wide base rears were hydraulic brakes.

Bodily the car had received various modifications – the grille shell was filled and peaked, the original hood was replaced with a louvred three-piece aluminium job, the trunk lid was extended to include the lower panel and thus made full length, the door hinges were removed to the inside and the windshield posts were chopped by 2 in. Bill Summers handled the bodywork, while Whitey Clayton built the custom dash moulded around the steering column. The leather upholstery was the work of George Fabry.

All of those features made for a very unusual car back in 1947, but that didn't stop Bob trying it out at some of the Southern California Timing Association's dry lakes meets, where it returned respectable times. It was also chosen to represent the SCTA, when the group joined the National Safety Council in Los Angeles.

The essence of a hot rod is, however, change, and Bob was already building a new engine to increase his speeds at the lakes and planning to replace the bright red paint job with the yellow one, which attracted Scritch.

He wasn't the only one it attracted though. A Hollywood stunt driver saw the car one day and

a chopped and channelled five-window, which became, upon his return, the first hot rod on the island of Puerto Rico. There Scritch worked part time in a garage and was soon called upon to organize the island's drag racing before his discharge and subsequent return to the mainland.

A couple of visits to the Bonneville Speed Trials forged a lasting friendship with the National Hot Rod Association's Wally Parks, which in turn led to him becoming the NHRA's first regional advisor in 1954. Scritch covered the mid-West and helped to turn several abandoned highways and airfields into drag strips. He was never too busy to race though, and at one meet to which the Coupé was driven he made 13 runs, won his class and drove it right home afterwards.

The Missouri winters eventually persuaded Scritch to return to the warmer climate of Puerto Rico and a partnership in that garage, which soon became a speed shop. There he taught himself body- and paintwork, skills which have stood him in good stead to this day.

Then a letter arrived from Wally Parks inviting him to participate in something called the Safety Safari. Not knowing what it was, but raring to go, he sold the Coupé to pay the freight bill on a recently acquired 1948 Lincoln Continental complete with ohv Caddy power.

ABOVE *The time August 1971: the place, Bonneville Salt flats; the man, Dick Scritchfield; the car, carburrated small-block Chevy powered '32 Roadster running in C/STR (306 to 372 ci-street roadster); the speed, 167.212 mph*

BELOW *Old style, new wheels and tyres are fitted; new, also, is the licence plate. Incidentally, Scritch carries membership card number one of that club of clubs*

asked Scritch if he would be interested in renting it to the studios. This most famous of hot rods made its first screen appearance in the 1957 film *Hot Rod Gang*. Since then it has had a better career than some human stars, making cameo or even starring performances in such TV shows as: *Doobie Gillis, The FBI, Dragnet, 77 Sunset Strip, The Lawrence Welk Show, The Real McCoys* and more recently *Happy Days* and *Fantasy Island*. Film roles included *Love in a Goldfish Bowl* in 1960 with Tommy Sands, Fabian and Diana Dors, *Hometown USA* and recently *The Hollywood Knights*, directed by Max Baer, who first encountered the car in an episode of *77 Sunset Strip*.

Hiboys have always been of timeless style, but Scritch was often first with a new trend. The yellow lacquer soon gave way to one of the first metal-flake paint jobs, a bright cherry candy colour applied by Scritch himself.

The roadster became not only an introduction to the entertainment business but also to another world, which has been part of Scritch's life since the late fifties. Through it he met other roadster owners, speed equipment manufacturer Phil Weiand, Tony LaMesa and publisher LeRoi 'Tex' Smith and between them they formed the world's most famous and exclusive hot rod club, the Los Angeles Roadsters. Scritch proudly holds membership card number one and is the only remaining original member. Scritch now jokes that not only the car but also its owner has to be over 40 years old to join. That's not true, but all members must have a finished car.

One of the club's prime objectives was to furnish cars for the movie and magazine business. As you have seen they easily achieved that goal, but soon the club became more of a social group. With much assistance from Tex Smith they began meeting with a San Francisco club called the Bay Area Roadsters.

The first meet was held in 1961 in Sequoia National Park and was quite an eye-opener for the LA boys because not only were most of the northern cars finished but they were of a much higher standard than the southern cars. Eventually an annual inspection of LA members' cars was introduced to maintain and improve standards of safety, engineering and finish.

The annual meeting with the Bay Area rodders became so popular that pressure from other roadster owners and clubs dictated that they have two meets and that the second be open to a wider, but nevertheless invited, group. This run eventually became known as the Roadster Round-up.

The other major event on the LA Roadsters' calendar is the annual Father's Day Roadster Exhibition and Swap Meet. Originallly held in the Hollywood Bowl it soon outgrew that venue and is now one of the biggest outdoor gatherings on the hot rodders' calendar.

So, for the past quarter of a century Scritch and his roadster have spent every Thursday evening and many weekends down at the club. In 1964 he took time out to marry his secretary, Marian Milson, and guess what, they went on honeymoon in the Deuce roadster.

Shortly after their return Scritch's second Deuce, a sorry-looking Australian-made Phaeton, arrived courtesy of Australian publisher Eddie Ford. All that had changed hands is $100 dollars, but that car became another all-time famous hot rod and originator of the repro style.

Meanwhile Scritch had landed a job as Associate Editor of *Car Craft* magazine, often working 17 hours a day building the *Car Craft* T project to meet publishing deadlines.

As if that wasn't enough the magazine began to cover more and more drag racing. Scritch had been that route, working every weekend, so he moved over to *Rod & Custom* magazine and a job as Advertising Manager.

While at *Rod & Custom* Scritch decided to pep up the roadster, and with the aid of Dave Carpenter built a 350 ci small-block Chevy which took the roadster into the record books.

The engine was a 1969 block filled with all sorts of high-performance Chevy items. Topping it off was a Weiand (what else?) tunnel ram manifold and twin 1250 Holleys. A Mallory ignition fired the fuel and a T-10 four-speed transferred the power to a Halibrand quick-change rear end.

They took the car to the Great Salt Lake for the Bonneville Nationals in 1970 and running in C Street Roadster class set a new two-way average of 165 miles per hour.

The following year they returned, ran a best one-way speed of 168.067 and averaged 167.212, setting a record which stood until 1979.

In the intervening years the roadster has covered thousands of miles, Scritch driving back East for some of the early Street Rod Nationals events, which he helped organize in the early seventies.

Like any self-respecting hot rod the car has undergone mechanical changes to keep it up to date and safe within today's overcrowded road conditions. The original dropped I-beam gave way to a chromed Bell axle fitted with Airheart disc brakes to replace the early drums. A 1956 Ford box takes care of the steering, even at 167 mph.

The interior received some new upholstery in pearl white by Ed Martinez and a set of Stewart Warner Stage III gauges adorn that original hand-formed aluminium dash.

Externally the car is more or less as it was when Bob McGee built it, only the exhausts, wheels,

ABOVE *And, although he doesn't need to prove anything, here is Scritch at that 1979 OCIR Yesteryear drag race smokin' the tyres halfway down the track and still stoppin' the clocks in 13.9 seconds*

RIGHT *The dashboard built in the forties by Whitey Clayton is still there but now it houses Stewart Warner Stage III gauges, a CB radio and that plaque —167.212 mph. The white upholstery was stitched by Ed Martinez. The inside door hinges, though 25 years old are a current trend, as are the three-piece bonnet, peaked spreader bar and general ol' timey look*

tyres, paint and 1950 Pontiac taillights are new.

Apart from a milder cam and some smaller carbs (twin 650 cfm Holleys) the engine is as it ran on the salt at over 160 mph. When I went to visit him, Scritch admitted that the car had not run for a few weeks, the Phaeton being his favourite ride at present. Nevertheless he hooked up the battery and turned the key. The Chevy made its familiar, distinctive groan, rolled over and roared into life.

Letting it idle we cleared a path out of the garage and then Scritch eased it past his recently restored Model B Station Wagon and out into the sunlight.

As we screamed off towards the hills the engine warmed to his touch, the quick-change whined in sympathy and a wry smile spread over Scritch's face. I guess he didn't even know I was there; he was just a hot rodder having a lot of fun with an old friend.

11 Development of a street rod

Henry Ford may have sat on his beloved Model T like a brooding hen, allowing no one to touch it, but by 1932 even he was made to realize that motorists wanted something more than basic transport.

Ten different body styles were offered in that year and only one of them, the Standard Coupé, was not available in a De Luxe version. Admittedly the Sport Coupé was down-graded in mid-April, but it did have some De Luxe features like cowl lamps and ash trays, and for Henry Ford, a man who loathed smoking, ash trays were a significant concession to his customers. No longer were his cars only painted black either, by the end of the year eight colours, including black of course, had been available. Even colour-coded wheels could be had on special order.

There was also a growing list of factory-released accessories that included combination fuel and water temperature gauge, oil bath air filters, Grigsby-Grunow radio, right-hand tail-lamp, right or left side-mounted spare wheel and tyre with, of course, the necessary welled wing, three types of spare wheel cover and two types of lock, sport light, trunk rack and trunk, whitewall tyres, windwings and a winterfront. Not all of this equipment was available immediately, however, indeed some of the accessories would not appear until the car was almost obsolete.

Those parts either made by Ford or for Ford and either fitted at the factory or at the dealer were not the only items or modifications which were Ford approved. The Ford Service Bulletin for August 1932 explains how to fit the De Luxe Coupe cigar lighter into the other closed cars by removing the centre screw from the front belt rail finish panel and enlarging the hole slightly.

Henry Ford was not the only man to realize that buyers of his cars might not find everything they wanted on the specification. There had built up in the days of the Model T a huge worldwide accessory industry producing all kinds of doo-dahs to improve everything about the car from performance to appearance. When Ford finally abandoned the T and brought out the A, those manufacturers were not slow to shift production to the new model nor were they when the models B and 18 were introduced.

Besides all the chrome accessory lamps, horns, bumpers, temperature gauges, etc, the big craze in 1932 was for so-called balloon tyres. At that time Ford were fitting, as standard, 5.25 × 18 in tyres, while tyre manufacturers such as Firestone, General and Goodyear were all offering 16 in diameter tyres in widths up to seven inches. These road-going, so-called balloon tyres were developed from aircraft and racing-type tyres and were sold with and without matching wheels. Supposedly they softened the ride, improved traction and reduced the likelihood of punctures because of their low pressure.

Though a craze for several years the Ford Motor Company frowned upon the use of non-standard wheels and warned against their use in the Service Bulletin for August 1933. Ford, however, along with most of the other manufacturers, would, by 1935, reduce the diameter of their production wheels to 16 in.

Out in California, driving right alongside these accessorized cars, were another group of Ford owners who, instead of adding bits on, were busy taking parts off. The lakes racers of California were stripping them down for speed, removing all the unwanted sheet metal; front and rear fenders and running boards plus the bumpers and their irons. Luckily for them the law was such that it allowed them to drive on the street like that and the kids who wanted everybody in town to know that they raced at the lakes left them that way all week.

Mostly these cars were built for go and not show and the majority of their modifications would be under the hood. There, instead of the original 50 hp four-cylinder flathead, there might be a late model V8 or more likely the B block fitted with a Riley 4-port Overhead or possibly a Riley Overhead V8 or even a complete Cragar engine.

One trend in the early-thirties was to 'accessorize' your car. This Vicky belonged to Californian hot rodder Bill Burke and sported solid wheels, '34 bumpers, dark metallic grey paint and several add-ons

Photographed in 1932 this Roadster is far from stock. Immediately noticeable are the twin horns and Firestone tyres and wheels. These 7.00 × 16 in. Firestone Air Balloon tyres were mounted on Firestone's own wheels complete with script hub caps. Wide tread, small diameter wheels were all the rage in 1932 but Ford frowned upon them.

The other non-standard item on the car, which is almost invisible because of its position, is the Victory Model B 'Line-O-Vision' Moto Meter which replaced the original radiator cap

ABOVE *By the early-forties Bill Burke had discarded both the Victoria and the junk in favour of this stripped down lakes racing Hiboy. Photographed in 1942 it was typical of Californian cars of the time. Gone were the wings and running boards. The headlights were mounted low on posts homemade from the original headlight bar and the grille shell was filled. Note the special bonnet catches*

BELOW *In Germany things were looking much better where this rather elegant 4 or 5 seater Sport-Cabriolet was built on both V8 and four cylinder chassis by Drauz. Notice the tandem wipers, luggage trunk and the windscreen post mounted indicators which were fitted to many European models*

Whatever, it was unlikely to be factory fresh. Externally the car may have had the radiator cap and emblem removed and the shell filled and possibly a track-style nerf bar fitted between the headlamps, but that was about it.

Those early hot rodders were at one end of the spectrum, while at the other were the coach-built specials of companies such as M. B. Möller, who were producing rather dated but nevertheless classic-style automobiles on the V8 chassis.

Similar restyling exercises were being conducted upon the '32 models in Europe, where German coach-builders such as Deutsch and Drauz and Belgian Willy van den Plas appeared to be making a better job of it. The same cannot unfortunately be said of England, where though there were many attempts to produce something different, few of them, in my opinion, looked worth the effort. Admittedly the British requirement was not for a luxury motor car in a style not offered by Ford but instead for a more sporting version designed for competition use.

Even as early as the Ford White City Exhibition held in October 1932 there were several firms, including W. J. Reynolds, Dagenham Motors Ltd. and W. Harold Perry who had on display two- and four-seater sports models. These were based on both four-cylinder and V8 chassis, but invariably

RIGHT *With 14 different Ford body styles, America had little need for the custom built special. Nevertheless The Möller Motor Car Company, which specialized in hearse bodies, supplied this four-door sedan bodied V8 for the Philadelphia Rapid Transit Corporation. If it wasn't for the racing stripe, this too could be a hearse, but could the RTC really be an undertaker?*

MÖLLER BODY ON FORD V-8 CHASSIS FOR 1932 WAS DESIGNED FOR PHILADELPHIA RAPID TRANSIT CORP. (Photo courtesy John E. Harbaugh.)

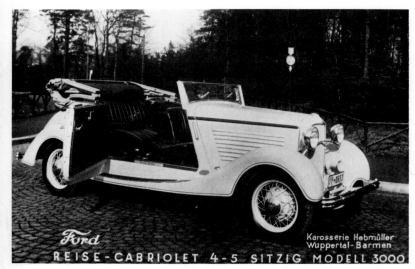

LEFT *Some more super styling from Germany. This time another 4/5 seater Cabriolet built by Hebmuller of Wuppertal-Barmen*

RIGHT *This two-door, two-seater convertible with a rather neat trunk and twin spares was built by Papler of Cologne*

CABRIOLET 4/5 PLACES   WILLY VAN DEN PLAS   SUR FORD 4 & 8 cyl PARIS Bᵈ PEREIRE
210 bis

ABOVE *The only other rather classic British custom was this Sedanca built on a V8 chassis by the famous Salmons-Tickford Company. The car was restored by its present owner Tommy Jeakins of Essex*

LEFT ABOVE *In Belgium, Willy van den Plas, who had a showroom on the Boulevard Periere in Paris, produced various special bodied Fords. Besides the 4/5 seater Cabriolet shown he also had two and four-door coaches*

LEFT *Although this photograph came from the Ford Archives in Dearborn this Sedanca De Ville was in fact built by the British coachbuilder Windover who had a showroom in London's Regent Street*

RIGHT *W. Harold Perry took stands at both the 1932 and 1933 Ford exhibitions where they displayed their range of four cylinder and V8 conversions*

Continental Coupé.

Mounted on Ford 14.9 h.p. Chassis	Price, £268 ex Wor
24.2	£278
V.8 Chassis	£318

it was only the distinctive 1932 grille shell that indicated precisely what the special was based upon. Sales of both B and 18 chassis by Dagenham between 1932 and the end of their production in 1935 attest to just how big the interest in sporting specials was.

Perhaps the most famous and lasting name to be connected with Ford-based specials was Allard. Sydney Allard's sporting association with Ford began with a Model A tourer, but he soon realized that it would never be competitive. His next acquisition was therefore an ex-Tourist Trophy racer based on a Model 40 V8 built in Northern Ireland. Stripped down and fitted with motorcycle-type mudguards and a lightweight

Value Far Above Price! Stand No. 41

THE IDEAL OPEN CAR CONVERTIBLE
for All Weathers

"CHASESIDE" SPORTS 2-4 SEATER FULLY EQUIPPED FOR COMPETITION WORK

We Specialize in Building Sports Bodies and Tuning Engines for Competitions

The above Ford V-8 Sports Model is a significant example of our workmanship. It has won a prize in every competition entered, and has accounted for no fewer than 14 Honours during the Season

Full details will be gladly given at

Stand No. 41

CHASESIDE MOTOR Co. LTD.
MAIN FORD DEALERS
ENFIELD : MIDDX.   Tel. Nos.: ENFIELD 3456-3457-3458

ABOVE *Perhaps the most attractive of all the English built specials was the Chaseside Sports 2–4 Seater. Unfortunately, the tail fin caused instability and this particular car, AMC 33, crashed and was written off. No other examples are known to have been built*

LEFT ABOVE *W.J. Reynolds of East Ham, London, produced two specials on the 106 in. chassis. There was the Continental Tourer, a 4/5 seater open model priced at £275 for the V8, £235 for the 24 hp and £225 for the 14.9. Stablemate of the Tourer was the Continental Coupé complete with sliding roof. The V8 version was priced at £318 whilst the 24 was £278 and the 14.9 £268. Bodies for both models were built from selected ash and panelled in hand-beaten aluminium and steel*

LEFT *When Ford were tarting up the Fourteen in order to get rid of them, W.J. Reynolds followed suit by fitting acorn headlights, streamlined sidelights and a chrome plated grille shell. This Continental Sports Tourer was shown at Ford's Albert Hall Exhibition in October 1933*

bathtub-like body this car performed exceedingly well in summer events. But with the arrival of winter and the trials scene it too was found to be unsuitable. Alterations were made, but it was obvious that a new purpose-built car was necessary.

The first Allard special was built in 1936 using a wrecked Model 48. The frame was narrowed, as was the rear axle, the torque tube was shortened to place the engine farther back and the whole thing was clothed in a body made up of sheet metal, a Bugatti tail section and a BB truck grille.

CLK 5, as it was registered, proved to be exceptionally versatile, winning numerous speed events, hill climbs and reliability trials. One interesting modification performed after the car's initial appearance and prior to Allard's unsuccessful attempt to climb Ben Nevis with it, was the addition of what was called an LMB split axle.

This strange device produced by Leslie Ballamy was made by cutting the original beam axle in the centre and mounting it on bushes welded to the severed axle ends and brackets welded to the front cross-member. The transverse leaf spring was retained and although the design had many faults this crude attempt at independent suspension went some way towards improving steering on the rough trials courses. In practice it worked well enough and quite a few sets were sold to competition car owners.

The result of Allard's success in competition was publicity in magazines such as *The Motor* and *The Autocar* and a subsequent flow of enquiries from people wanting to purchase similar machines. The majority of Allard's pre-war specials used the distinctive 1932 Ford chassis, though cross-members were often altered and the rest of the car was unrecognizable as a 1932 Ford.

After a short break for the war the Allard Motor Company resumed production, but a constant supply of the old Ford chassis was no longer available. Instead, Allard decided to produce his own, or at least get them produced. This fact is only significant because the chassis rails eventually stamped by John Thompsons of Wolverhampton were, in appearance, very similar to the '32 frame side members, even to their 106 in wheelbase. They did not, however, retain that distinctive side pressing.

Back in America, hot rods were big news. The craze was spreading from California to all States and concern by the police, city fathers, the media and busybody do-gooders about these speed-crazed kids only increased interest and popularity. The postwar scene was somewhat different from that which existed in the late thirties. Instead of lakes dust, dirty racers with more emphasis under the hood the new breed of hot rod in many cases

ABOVE *By the time the war was over 1932 Ford chassis had all but dried up. In an attempt to continue production Allard manufactured his own chassis. The frame rails eventually stamped by John Thompsons are very similar to '32 Ford rails with the exception of their distinctive side pressing. Even the front and rear crossmembers look similar to Ford's*

LEFT ABOVE *Over the August Bank Holiday of 1936 Sydney Allard attempted to climb the 4400 ft Scottish mountain, Ben Nevis. The mountain had only been climbed once before by an automobile and that was back in 1911 with a Model T. Unfortunately, Sydney's car turned over when the ground gave way.*
What may look like a broken axle was, in fact, an LMB split-axle – a crude attempt at independent suspension

LEFT *The first production Allard chassis was this V8 built for David Gilson in 1937. Apart from the severed front frame horns the 1932 chassis is almost intact. A crude attempt at the grille shell was made by welding a homemade front to what appears to be a 10 hp Model C shell. Hidden is an LMB axle; the original welded spoke wheels were replaced by solid wheels of 1937 vintage. Mounted with a close-coupled 2/4 seater body painted black and yellow, it was named Whirlwind and registered AUK 795*

didn't even have a hood and more importance was now placed on how sharp the car looked rather than how fast it ran. Speed equipment was still extremely important, but as much for its eye appeal as anything it might do to increase performance.

The launching of *Hot Rod* and similar magazines with nationwide circulations did much to spread the word. Clubs were forming all over America to organize reliability runs, drag races and hot rod and custom car shows.

The arrival of the custom car, invariably a 1940 or later model, lowered and customized, did much to break up the hot rod scene into different factions. From then on there would be in one corner the poor kids with their stripped-down rods, in the other the rich kids with their customized late models. That's a heavy generalization, but it has taken a long time for the two groups to get back together and realize that what they are doing is basically the same thing.

The late forties and early fifties saw a definite style of hot rod, the most coveted of which was still the Roadster. Early editions of *Hot Rod* carry several features about rodders who couldn't find the desired rag top and in desperation took the hacksaw to a coupé. As roadsters got rarer so coupés had to become more acceptable at the races, and rodders eventually refrained from chopping them up. Nevertheless the saw and the cutting torch were prerequisites for any rodder's garage.

Low was the way to go and it was every rodder's aim to get his car as low as possible. There were two ways to achieve this goal. One was to channel the body over the chassis by torching out the floor, dropping the body down over the chassis rails and then refitting the floor farther up inside the car. Sometimes this was done to the full 6 in height of a '32 chassis. The other method was to zee the frame. This involved severing the side rails ahead of the rear cross-member and rewelding them in a higher position. Boxing plates returned some of the lost rigidity. The front end was similarly lowered by the use of a dropped axle, the original Ford item being heated and reworked by a blacksmith to give a significant drop between the kingpin bosses and the suspension mounts. A really radically low stance could be achieved with a combination of both tricks and the addition, if it can be called that, of a chopped roof.

Paint and polish had not been particularly important before the war, but now it was becoming paramount. Finned heads were fine but finer still were chrome nut covers. In 1952 they were ten cents each. Performance parts were still popular and the hot items to have under your hood included multi carburettor systems, magnetos and racing camshafts, which together were an almost impossible combination for street driving. The look of an engine could be enhanced with off-the-shelf chrome parts such as fuel pumps, generator covers and air filters.

By this time the venerable flathead was rapidly losing ground to other, more modern, overhead-valve V8s. Ford may have been ahead of his time with the spectacular one-piece V8, but, as usual, when he saw no reason to change for the sake of change, other manufacturers caught up and even surpassed his designs. By 1952 there were adaptor plates available to bolt ohv V8s from Lincoln,

BELOW *Early hot rod. Gone is the dry lakes dust, here is shiny black lacquer. Gone are the bonnet side panels to reveal a full-dress flathead. The wings are in place covering small diameter wheels with shiny trim rings. The top is chopped and the headlights have been replaced with chrome King Bees. The car was owned by Gus Maanum an illustrator for early hot rod magazines and SCTA programmes*

RIGHT ABOVE *Low was the way to go in the fifties and if it meant hacking the floor out of a '32 so that the body could be channelled over the chassis, you did it. A combination of this trick, a zee'd frame, a dropped axle, a chopped top and possibly a sectioned body would put you in the class*

RIGHT BELOW *DuVal and other makes of split-windscreens such as the one fitted to this replica of Neal East's famous Deuce hot rod were popular in the Fifties. So was the zee'd frame, filled and peaked grille shell and front nerf bar. Notice also the finned disc brakes*

Cadillac, Chrysler and Oldsmobile to the Ford transmission, and hot rodders were not slow to swap in their search for something special.

Other modifications favoured by the fifties rodder were the removal of the frame horns and the rolling of the rear pan. Petrol tanks were placed inside the trunk and the car took on a short,

LEFT The ugly bug ball culminated in the sixties when the show circuit awarded most points for most modifications. Taste lost. This was once a 1932 Roadster. It was Ray Farhner's decision to modify. The body was channelled a full 6 in., the top was chopped 3½ in. and most everything else was modified beyond recognition. The white undercarriage was complemented by white naugahyde upholstery everywhere, on the running boards and in the cab, pickup bed and engine compartment

LEFT BELOW A couple of years later Darryl Starbird of Wichita, Kansas, took an ordinary '32 Tudor, restyled it and called it Li'l Coffin. Starbird was at the time a design consultant for Monogram models – a plastic kit was sold. The full size creation was owned by Larry Farber and built by Stuckey Custom. With its radical body modificaions too numerous to mention and a multi-carburatted DeSoto engine it won Custom Rod of the Year at the 1963 Oakland Roadster Show.

I hate to admit I had a soft spot for this car when I was in my teens, I even bought the model. It's long lost now though

BELOW In 1967 it was Jess Leon's turn and he decided to use a three-window coupé as the basis for his ideas of what a '32 Ford should look like. Once again the bodywork almost defies description but its much sculptured curves were coloured in gold and pearl white as was the interior

bobbed appearance. Split, V-shaped boat-style windscreens made by Duval and Hallock were also favoured, but were rare because of the small numbers made.

The custom car scene had been gaining momentum throughout the fifties, and as hot rods became more radical there grew out of this a whole new area called show business. Of course there had been auto shows since 1948, but in the main the vehicles on display were competition orientated machines, but by 1960 guys had begun to build hot rods purely for show.

Initially this was seen as a good thing, it gave jobs to plenty of people, it put prize money into the pockets of rodders and it possibly put some interesting ideas into the minds of Detroit's designers. The development of the judging system, however, decreed that more modifications meant more points. So a situation developed where rodders were chopping cars about and adding bits purely to be more outrageous than the next guy. Many of the out-and-out show cars that were created in the sixties, many of them from '32 Fords, were downright ugly and were perhaps a worse fate for a Ford than being mashed up on an oval track.

The car which spread the hot rod craze throughout the world by means of the TV series 77 Sunset Strip *was this short-tailed T bucket built by Norm Grabowski. The car featured a multi-carbed Cadillac engine bolted to a '39 Ford transmission. Bodily it consisted of a '23 T tub, a shortened pickup bed and a chopped '32 Ford grille shell. The Californian fad T, as it became known, put the Deuce out of fashion for several years*

Another trend setter was Dick Scritchfield's Phaeton after its rebuild in the resto style. The car was imported by Scritch from Australia in the early-sixties. Its South Sea origins are discernable by the lack of beaded seams in the back panel. From the outside, apart from the fat wheels and low stance, the car looks original but mechanically it's all modern

The hi-tech hot rod trend originated on the milling machine of Li'l John Buttera who reputedly couldn't afford off-the-shelf parts so instead made his own out of aluminium. Independent suspensions, smooth lines and graffic stripes, as well as milled aluminium, are all trademarks of hot rods of the eighties

The show scene wasn't the only strange turn taken by the sport of hot rodding in the sixties. Drag racing was really big news and Detroit was finally, after 30 years, taking notice of the youth market. It was about to launch the muscle car, the factory hot rod that effectively put the home-built hot rod back in the yard – way back. Thankfully, hot rodders are hoarders and most of those old Fords were merely hidden away for another day.

What was happening on the street was influenced by a TV detective series called 77 Sunset Strip. In it a young car park attendant called Kookie, played by Ed Burns, drove an outrageous hot rod based on a Model T roadster pick-up. It was painted blue with red, white, yellow and orange flames. It had a Cadillac engine and a cut-down '32 grille shell and it started a worldwide craze for California-style T-buckets. Apart from its grille the Deuce was all but forgotten.

Obviously there were plenty of diehards who would keep the Ford flag flying, but the car was out of fashion until a most significant event in 1970.

A group of hot rodders under the new collective title of the National Street Rod Association were to hold their first national gathering in a farmer's field outside Peoria, Illinois. A few hundred cars, now noticeably called street rods rather than hot rods, turned up and more than a few were based on 1932 Fords. The NSRA and its calendar of events have grown steadily over the past years and the annual 'Street Rod Nats' now attracts approximately 6000 cars. Some journey from as far afield as Alaska, Hawaii, Europe and Australia, and a large percentage of them are Deuces.

The street rod scene was on the upturn, but many enthusiasts were into drag racing, muscle cars and various other motorized pastimes. But three years later they were to get another kick in the seat, this time the cinema seat, which would get them back behind the wheel of the forgotten Ford.

A young, almost unknown, American film director called George Lucas had made an autobiographical movie about one night in a small town in California in 1962. For most people the stars of the film were Richard Dreyfuss, Paul Le Mat and Harrison Ford. For car freaks the film had an entirely different line-up. The supporting cast were a '51 Mercury and two Chevys, a '55 and a '58, and the star was nothing other than a chopped and rodded 1932 Ford.

American Graffiti was a low-budget film which stirred more than one generation to not only go to the cinema but also get back to the garage and rediscover those long-forgotten Fords.

Strange really that this car should be a five-window, never one of the most popular body styles, but nevertheless it sparked off a worldwide resurgence of interest in hot rodding, similar to that generated with the 'Kookie' car from Sunset Strip.

This interest initially manifested itself in hundreds of look-alike Graffiti coupés. Pretty soon though the young guys began to realize that you didn't need a film car to have fun, any hot rod would do. The older generation perhaps recaptured some of their lost youth depicted in the film, but they too understood that you didn't necessarily need a canary yellow coupé to go cruising. Whatever their reasons or motives an awful lot of people around the world began to find themselves behind the wheel of an old car.

One hot rodder who had never actually got out of his Ford had, in the late sixties, contributed to another style. That man was Dick Scritchfield, the car he built was known as a resto rod and was based on a '32 Phaeton imported from Australia. Bodily the car looked original, even down to its side-mounted spare wheel, but mechanically the car was as rodded as they come.

These were therefore the two extremes of the sport. At one end of the spectrum the wild, chopped, hoodless, fenderless hot rod. At the other the smooth, sedate, silent resto rod. Between the two, just about every configuration you could imagine.

That was just about where the street rod sport was at until a chassis builder by the name of Li'l John Buttera gave us all something to think about. He took that tired, samey hot rod style, smoothed it out and took it into the eighties. Spun aluminium wheels replaced the five-spoke mags and gennie-look wires. Milled aluminium replaced blocks of chromed steel and graphic stripes replaced the lurid colours of murals and metalflake.

Now, in the mid-eighties this trend has also worked itself into a hole just like the show cars of the sixties. Hot rodders trying to outdo each other have modified their '32 Fords beyond recognition and some of them are just as ugly as their show circuit ancestors. Not at all as Henry intended. No doubt this over-exuberance will result in a decline in interest as hi-tech hot rods get too expensive and impractical for the average hot rodder. Who, after all, only wants to run his Ford a little bit faster than Henry intended.

The growth of street rodding has, however, benefited everybody, restorer and rodder alike. With such a huge worldwide demand for '32 Ford parts it was inevitable that manufacturers would tool up to reproduce almost everything for a Deuce from the frame up.

12 Hauls of fame

When one attempts to chronicle the history of the 1932 Ford one cannot ignore the fact that its existence may have, in some small way, affected the lives of people who are possibly not at all interested in cars, people whose main interest in life might be music or the cinema or even crime.

No doubt they will have hardly noticed the '32 Ford, it being merely a prop in the backdrop of life. Nevertheless it was there and it was a '32 Ford, not a '36, not a Chevrolet. For that reason we have included this chapter about three Deuces which, in my opinion, made some impact on lives in the twentieth century.

Bonnie & Clyde made history long before I was born, but I saw the film, which was a milestone in cinema history, if only for its violence. Little did I realize then that some years later I would be searching out the gruesome twosome's family snaps.

I've never actually owned a record player, but I remember the Beach Boys' Little Deuce Coupé album being given to my best friend's sister by her seaman boyfriend, who had brought it back from Hong Kong. I cannot remember now if it was the transparent red vinyl disc, something we'd never seen before, or the car on the jacket which attracted me most. Probably the car, because I was just about 15 then and buying my first plastic model kits, one of which was a drag racing Deuce Coupé.

As for the *American Graffiti* coupé, well, it probably made more impact on the hot rod world than anything before or since. For that reason one cannot ignore it.

Clyde 'Champion' Barrow poses with the tools of his trade, an arsenal of guns and a stolen Ford V8.

Bonnie & Clyde

According to the case file kept by Joplin, Missouri, Chief of Detectives Ed Portley (now deceased) in 1933, Bonnie Parker and Clyde 'Champion' Barrow, who were in their early twenties, aided by 17-year-old W. D. Jones, had already killed five men by the end of 1932. They were not then nationally known public enemies, but all that was to change when Texas Governor Miriam A. 'Ma' Ferguson issued a full pardon to Clyde's brother, Ivy 'Buck' Barrow, in March 1933.

Buck went home to his family in Dallas, Texas, on 22 March and was soon in contact with his brother, who was then living in Fort Smith, Arkansas. Having driven over in the 1930 Marmon his sister had given him, after trading in two Model As and $100 cash, the two brothers decided to move on to Joplin, Missouri, rent a place and have a vacation of sorts.

The Barrow gang left for Joplin in a three-car caravan; Bonnie and Clyde led in a stolen 1932 Convertible Sedan, Buck and his wife, Blanche, were in the Marmon and W. D. Jones drove a stolen V8 sedan.

Sometime on the trip up to Joplin, Blanche took these pictures with her Kodak camera.

Clyde found a perfect place for their vacation, an apartment above a double garage just off the main highway at 3347½ Oak Ridge, but the garage actually fronted on 34th Street. Posing as Mr Callahan, a Minnesota civil engineer, Clyde rented the apartment for $21 a month and paid $1 extra for the neighbourhood nightwatchman, Mack Parker.

The B-400 was parked in the garage below, alongside another tenant's car. Another lock-up garage was rented around the corner on Oak Ridge for the stolen sedan and sometime later yet another garage was rented for a '32 Roadster the gang later stole in Miami, Oklahoma.

For the next two weeks they played around and pulled a few robberies, well away from Joplin. The local police, however, were suspicious of their odd movements reported by local citizens.

Finally, on 13 April the Joplin Police Department issued a liquor search warrant for 3347½ Oak Ridge. Since Freeman Grove was outside city limits, part-time constable J. W. Harryman was asked to serve the warrant accompanied by two Joplin detectives and two Missouri Highway Patrolmen.

Around 4 pm two Joplin police cars, Harryman, Detective Tom DeGraff and Patrolman W. E. Grammer in one, Detective Harry McGinnis and Patrolman George B. Kahler in the other, pulled up outside the garage just as Clyde was closing its doors on the B-400.

DeGraff, seeing Clyde closing the doors, shouted to Harryman to 'Get in there quick, before they close it.' As Harryman ran for the door with the warrant in his hand Clyde pulled a sawn-off shotgun out of a special pocket in his trouser leg and fired it point-blank into Harryman's midsection, killing him instantly.

McGinnis was running from the other car when Clyde fatally wounded him.

Upstairs, Bonnie heard Clyde yell, 'It's the law.' She grabbed a rifle, smashed a window and began firing.

Those police officers still in action watched amazed as a terrified Blanche emerged from the apartment and ran off down 34th, a small dog at her heels.

Whilst Grammer ran to the corner house to telephone for help, DeGraff made for the windowless east side of the garage.

Kahler, noticing that his gun was almost empty, tried to retreat to a safer loading place when he tripped and fell. Thinking that he had shot him, Clyde emerged from the apartment, followed by W. D. Jones. Just then Kahler fired his last bullet, giving Jones a bloody but minor head wound.

As Clyde attempted to guide Jones, who was blinded by his own blood, back inside, DeGraff poked his gun around the corner and fired. The bullet ricocheted off the wall and hit Clyde in the chest.

Bonnie and Buck were already in the B-400 by the time Clyde had helped W. D. in and got behind the wheel. Bonnie, noticing Clyde had been hit, dug the bullet out with a hairpin.

Clyde then emerged from the garage to fire his automatic shotgun at DeGraff before Jones came out, carrying a mattress for protection, to move one of the police cars which was blocking the drive and their getaway. Someone else then ran out to move the two bodies. When their exit was clear the garage doors were flung open and the B-400 made off down 34th, pausing momentarily for Buck to grab both Blanche and the dog.

The whole episode had lasted less than ten minutes. By evening the garage was full of policemen and reporters, who found the four rolls of film from which these prints were made. The police also took away the Marmon and three stolen V8 Fords.

That night the gang escaped by driving more than 400 miles to Amarillo, Texas, but their reign as gangsters would not last for long. Buck was killed later in the year in another gun battle. Jones was captured in August. Bonnie and Clyde were killed on 23 May, 1934, in an ambush near Arcadia, Louisiana, incidentally, in a 1934 V8 Sedan.

LEFT *Looking rather sweet Bonnie Parker takes her turn in front of the stolen Convertible Sedan. The car was eventually abandoned in Vinita, Oklahoma*

RIGHT *This letter from Clyde Barrow to Henry Ford needs no explanation except to point out how close Clyde was to death when he wrote it. As you can see the letter was dated 10 April 1934. Bonnie and Clyde were ambushed and killed by lawmen on 23 May 1934*

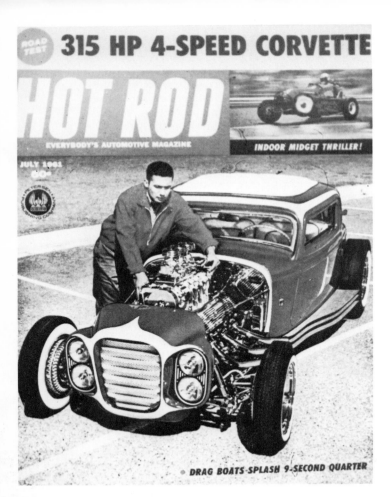

Little Deuce Coupé

To some of you this car may be an ugly travesty of a 1932 Ford, for that is what it is, but without a doubt it introduced two words, Deuce Coupé, to the world outside America, possibly even outside car circles and California.

Both the words and the car, the Silver Sapphire, featured on the cover of the Beach Boys' seventh LP, Little Deuce Coupé, which was released in 1965.

At the time the car was owned by Clarence 'Chili' Catallo, ironically from Dearborn, Michigan, and was in its fourth metamorphosis since leaving the factory, just a few miles up the road.

Clarence purchased the car in 1956 for $75 and fixed it up for street use in 1957. The following year he took it drag racing, but by 1959 it was appearing in auto shows. Continued alterations put the car on the show circuit and its fame culminated with an appearance on the July 1961 cover of Hot Rod magazine.

As you can see the car is hardly recognizable as a

LEFT *Its first claim to fame was an appearance on the front cover of* Hot Rod *magazine in July 1961*

LEFT *This Beach Boys LP cover was certainly my introduction to hot rods, the 1932 Ford and in particular the words* Deuce Coupé. *I suspect it was the same for many other people around the world*

RIGHT *The car in question, a radically modified De Luxe Coupé was owned by Clarence 'Chili' Catallo, ironically from Dearborn, Michigan. This chopped, channelled and sectioned rod was typical of show cars of the Sixties*

De Luxe Coupé. Clarence had the famed Alexander Brothers, Mike and Larry, who opened their Detroit body shop, Custom City, in 1956, perform most of the body work. They channelled the body a full six inches and then reworked the door until its bottom was once again in the same relative position as originally. The body was then sectioned six inches and one can see where the beading above the wheel now runs into the belt moulding.

The 'A' brothers also fabricated the distinctive grille shell and the curious aluminium fins that hide the frame rails. The cowl vent was filled and then the rear of the body was customized with a mouth-like rolled pan.

From there the car was taken out to George Barris in California, who sliced three inches out of the roof pillars and painted the whole creation in pearl white and translucent blue.

Most of the original mechanicals were junked to be replaced with a 1956 Oldsmobile 344 ci V8 fitted with a Clay Smith camshaft and Jahns pistons. Atop the gleaming engine sits a GMC 6-71 supercharger and three or sometimes six carburettors. Oldsmobile flywheel and clutch components were adapted to a 1937 La Salle transmission, which in turn drives a 1955 Olds rear axle.

The rear wheels were Olds centres grafted to Lincoln rims fitted with 8.2 × 15 in Inglewood slicks, while the fronts were Imperial centres fitted to reversed Mercury rims. Notice the front tyres had whitewalls on both sides.

In place of the original beam axle there is a 1937 tubular item fitted with stock Ford spindles, Kinmont finned disc brakes and Monroe shock absorbers.

For an interior Clarence had the Larsen upholstery shop stitch up deep-buttoned panels and seats in white Naugahyde. The steering wheel came from a 1959 Lincoln Continental and there were additional gauges both in the stock dash and in the header panel.

Like it or not the car claimed a lot of show trophies, ran a 12.9 quarter mile at 112 mph and perhaps helped spread the word about hot rods.

American Graffiti

My third and final star car is the American Graffiti coupé. The film it starred in was to be 28 years old George Lucas' first professional attempt at feature film direction. He had, however, made one other notable movie, whilst working with Francis Ford Coppola at American Zoetrope, a science fiction film called *THX 1138* and Lucas chose to plug it by using the letters THX 138 as the licence plate for the Graffiti coupé.

The car was actually picked by producer Gary Kurtz from half a dozen possibles because it already had a chopped top. The price paid? A mere $1300. At the time it was full fendered, with a black tuck and roll interior and under its hood was a small-block 283 cu. in. Chevy V8.

In typical tacky condition it was handed over to Henry Travers of Sonoma, California, a supplier of cars to Universal Studios. Henry passed it on to Johnny Franklin in Santa Rosa where the required modifications were made. First to go were the fenders, to be replaced with cycle guards on the front and bobbed rears in the back. The bonnet went too and the Chevy was given the glitter treatment by the addition of chrome headers, a Man-A-Free inlet manifold and four 2G Rochester carbs. The gearbox was also replaced with a T-10 four-speed manual which was much more suitable for the racing sequences. A sectioned grille shell and Canary yellow paint completed the make-up.

From the moment filming began Lucas had problems. He was on a tight schedule – 28 days and an even tighter budget – $750,000 which was less than he had had for *THX 1138*. Half of the first night shooting time was lost when it proved difficult to mount cameras to the cars. There were other complications unrelated to the automobiles but some nights later the coupé featured in another incident. Assistant cameraman Barney Coangelo slipped off the camera truck into the path of the coupé as it was being filmed and was run over.

Notwithstanding the difficulties Lucas got the film in on time. It did, however, go over budget by $25,000. It was released on 1 August 1973 and introduced to the world a hitherto unknown cast personally selected by Lucas: Richard Dreyfuss, Ron Howard, Paul LeMat, Charlie Martin Smith, Cindy Williams, Candy Clark, Mackenzie Phillips and perhaps the most famous of all, Harrison Ford. It was nominated for five Academy Awards; Best Picture, Direction, Original Screenplay, Supporting Actress (Candy Clark) and Film Editing. Unfortunately it won none but it was acclaimed the Best Screenplay Award by the New York Film Critics and national Society of Film Critics.

The film was re-released on 26 May 1978.

In financial terms the film saw more profit per dollar than Lucas blockbuster *Star Wars*. The direct cost of the film was the initial investment of $775,000, plus another half million dollars which was spent on advertising, and publicity.

In return Universal took $55,886,000 from the film rentals and that's only that portion of the ticket sales returned to the distributor. According to *Variety*'s list of all-time movie hits *American

Graffiti is listed as eighteenth having sold more than $117 million worth of tickets worldwide.

Fine, but what happened to the car? Well, it was offered for sale right after filming finished for just $1500. Nobody wanted it. So it sat in a shed at Universal until 1979 when it was dusted off to continue it's roll in *More American Graffiti*.

Lucas had little interest in this movie which was merely milking the original idea. Nevertheless he owed it to Universal and therefore acted as Executive Producer on this sad sequel which cost $6 million to make.

As far as we know the car is still sitting in Universal's back yard but, no, it isn't for sale!

ABOVE *The essential* American Graffiti *photograph. Ready to drag. On the left Bob Falfa, played by Harrison Ford, gets set in his '55 Chevy. This car, powered by a 454 ci Chevy V8 was the star in an earlier Kurtz road movie,* Two Lane Blacktop. *On the right Milner, played by Paul Le Mat, driving THX 138, a canary yellow coupé*

BELOW LEFT *The street drag racer's stance – arm on the door, cigarette dangling, tee-shirt. Paul Le Mat ready to make it run*

BELOW *Inside the Deuce Coupé was rough, at least during filming of* More American Graffiti *in 1979. The car could still be in this state today, but it's not for sale*

1 Specifications: V8 engine

Type	90° V
Cylinders	8
Material	Grey iron – 15% steel
Bore	3.0625 to 3.0635 in
Stroke	3.75 in (95.25 mm)
Cylinder numbers – from front of engine	Right side 1–2–3–4 Left side 5–6–7–8
Firing order	1–5–4–8–6–3–7–2
Offset of cylinders	
Offset of cylinder from crankshaft centre line	0.1875 in
Offset of crankshaft from engine centre line	0.265 in
Piston displacement	22.1 cu in (3622 cc)
Compression ratio	5.5 to 1
Compression pressure	105 to 114 ft.lb at 1000 rpm
Valve arrangement	L
Angle of mounting in frame	$2\frac{1}{2}°$
Weight complete with clutch and gearbox	615 lb
Horsepower rating (RAC and treasury) (UK)	S.A.E. 30
Horsepower developed	65 at 3400 rpm
Torque	126 ft.lb at 1000 rpm

CRANKSHAFT

Design	90° Fully counterbalanced
Type	Four throw
Material	Ford carbon manganese steel
Production	Forged
Length	24.47 in
Weight – finished	65.6 lb
Balance	Static and dynamic
Crank pin journal diameter	1.999 in
Crank pin journal length	1.937 in
Main bearing journal diameter	1.999 in
Main bearing journal length	
– front	1.801 in
– centre	1.737 in
– rear	2.253 to 2.255 in
End play	0.002 to 0.006 in
Main bearing surface area	36.5 sq in app
Connecting rod bearing surface area	48.75 sq in
Main bearing type	Babbitted in block
Number	3
Lubrication	Forced feed

CONNECTING RODS

Design	I-beam
Material	Heat-treated steel
Production	Forged
Length – centre to centre	7 in
Crankpin end bore	2.2197 to 2.2203 in
Width at crankpin end	0.8725 in
Weight	469 to 473 grams
Balance	Individually weighed and matched in sets

CONNECTING ROD INSERTS – BIG END BEARINGS

The fully floating big end bearings were a design unique to Ford, and although they argued that the load from each rod was spread over twice the bearing area, Laurence Sheldrick commented that they were difficult and expensive to make with no appreciable advantages.

CONNECTING ROD INSERTS: BIG-END

Type	Floating
Material	Babbitt coated steel
Design	Flanged
Number	4 – two rods on each insert 0.01 in clearance between rods
Length – overall	1.937 in
Diameter –inside	2 in
– outside	2.218 in
Clearance	0.003 in
End play	0.01 to 0.022 in
Lubriiation	Forced feed

SMALL END BEARING

Material	Bronze
Finish	Burnished
Bore	0.07502 in to 0.07505 in
Length	1.312 in
Lubrication	Spray and vapour

PISTONS

Aluminium alloy pistons were made for Ford by three companies: The Aluminum Company of America, Aluminum Industries and the Bohn Aluminum and Brass Company. According to the Service Bulletin, 'The skirt of the piston tapers approximately 0.001 in in its length, the large diameter being at the bottom of the piston, where it contributes to the wiping action of the piston. Pistons manufactured since approximately 1 June, 1931, have been cam ground to compensate for the expansion of the piston pin boss and supporting ribs. Since the piston skirt is neither straight nor round and the skirt is split it is impossible to check the piston size with micrometers. However, piston diameters are accurately held to a tolerance of plus or minus 0.0005 in.'

PISTONS

Type	Split skirt and cam ground
Material	Heat-treated aluminium
Design	Flat top
Weight – without rings or pin	287 to 291 g (10.5 oz)
Weight – with rings and pin	389.5 to 396.9 g

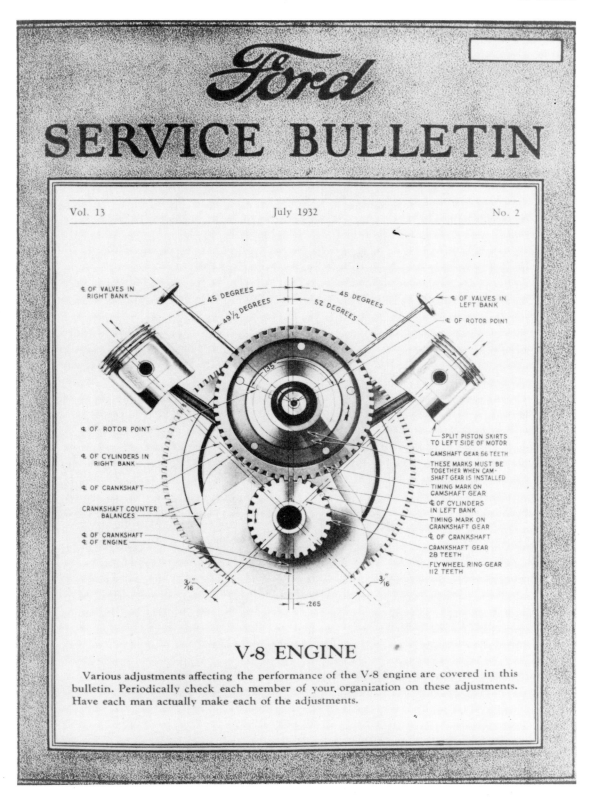

Ford

SERVICE BULLETIN

Vol. 13	July 1932	No. 2

¢ OF VALVES IN RIGHT BANK

45 DEGREES

45 DEGREES

49½ DEGREES

52 DEGREES

¢ OF VALVES IN LEFT BANK

¢ OF ROTOR POINT

135

¢ OF ROTOR POINT

¢ OF CYLINDERS IN RIGHT BANK

¢ OF CRANKSHAFT

CRANKSHAFT COUNTER BALANCES

¢ OF CRANKSHAFT
¢ OF ENGINE

SPLIT PISTON SKIRTS TO LEFT SIDE OF MOTOR

CAMSHAFT GEAR 56 TEETH

THESE MARKS MUST BE TOGETHER WHEN CAM-SHAFT GEAR IS INSTALLED

TIMING MARK ON CAMSHAFT GEAR

¢ OF CYLINDERS IN LEFT BANK

TIMING MARK ON CRANKSHAFT GEAR

¢ OF CRANKSHAFT

CRANKSHAFT GEAR 28 TEETH

FLYWHEEL RING GEAR 112 TEETH

3/16

3/16

.265

V-8 ENGINE

Various adjustments affecting the performance of the V-8 engine are covered in this bulletin. Periodically check each member of your organization on these adjustments. Have each man actually make each of the adjustments.

From the front page of Ford's Service Bulletin comes this interesting shot of the head-on profile of their V8 with numerous measurements

Length	2.97 in
Diameter	3.061 in to 3.062 in
Oil ring groove	
– width	0.156 to 0.157 in
– depth	0.154 to 0.159 in
Compression ring groove	
– width	0.0935 to 0.0945 in
– depth	0.154 to 0.159 in
Number of oil return holes in lower ring groove	7
Diameter	0.125 in on one side, channel on other
Balance	Individually weighed and matched in sets

PISTON PIN

Type	Floating
Material	Machined seamless steel tubing
Finish	Honed and polished.
Diameter	0.7501 to 0.7504 in
Length	2.77 in
Clearance in piston	0.0001 in tight to 0.0001 in loose
Clearance in rod	0.0002 in
Balance	Individually weighed and matched in sets
Lubrication	Spray and vapour

PISTON RINGS

Number – compression	2
– oil control	1
Width – compression	0.0915 to 0.092 in
– oil control	0.1545 to 0.155 in
Thickness – all	0.13 to 0.14 in
Gap – top	0.01 to 0.012 in
– centre	0.008 to 0.01 in
– oil control	0.005 to 0.008 in
Oil slot	0.07 to 0.075 in
Ring to wall pressure	6 to 9 lb

CAMSHAFT

According to Service Letter No. 68 of 7 July, 1932, a new-style camshaft, number 18-6250, was installed effective with motor number 18-33621 on 2 June. 'A spiral-cut oil groove has been added to the front and centre cam shaft bearings which will provide additional oil at these points.'

CAMSHAFT

Material	Ford carbon manganese steel
Production	Forged
Diameter – between cams	1 in
Bearings	3
Type	Babbitt backed in iron in cylinder block
Diameter	1.812 in
Length – front	1.656 in
– centre	1.375 in
– rear	2 in

Valve lift	0.295 in
Speed	half times crankshaft speed
Bearing lubrication	Forced feed
Cam lubrication	Spray and vapour

TIMING GEARS

Camshaft gear type	Spiral
Material	Bakelized fabric
Number of teeth	56
Fitting	Pressed
Crankshaft gear material	Steel
Number of teeth	28
Lubrication	Forced feed and splash

VALVES

Type	One-piece
Design	Mushroom stem
Material	Chromium, nickle-alloy steel
Production	Forged
Diameter of head	1.537 in
Diameter of stem	0.3105 to 0.3115 in
Diameter of stem end	0.55 in
Length of stem	4.75 to 4.751 in
Angle of valve seat	
– valve	44.5°
– block	45°
Stem to guide clearance	0.0015 to 0.0035 in
Valve lift	0.295 in
Valve clearance	0.0125 to 0.0135 in
Lubrication	Vapour from crankcase

VALVE TIMING

Intake opens	9.5° BTDC
Intake closes	54.5° ABDC
Exhaust opens	57.5° BBDC
Exhaust closes	6.5° ATDC

VALVE SPRINGS

Material	Oil-tempered steel
Free length	3.06 in
Test length	2.38 in
Pressure with valve closed	39 to 44 lb
Pressure with valve open	62 to 65 lb

VALVE GUIDES

Type	Two-piece (split)
Material	Cast iron

PUSH RODS

Type	Hollow
Design	Two-piece
Production	brazed
Material – body	Steel
– base	Hardened iron
Diameter – base	0.9992 to 0.9996 in
– top	0.5 in
Length	1.72 to 1.725 in
Lubrication	Spray and vapour

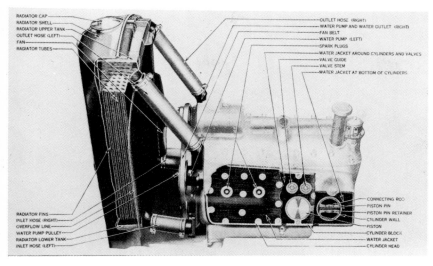

RADIATOR CAP
RADIATOR SHELL
RADIATOR UPPER TANK
OUTLET HOSE (LEFT)
FAN
RADIATOR TUBES

OUTLET HOSE (RIGHT)
WATER PUMP AND WATER OUTLET (RIGHT)
FAN BELT
WATER PUMP (LEFT)
SPARK PLUGS
WATER JACKET AROUND CYLINDERS AND VALVES
VALVE GUIDE
VALVE STEM
WATER JACKET AT BOTTOM OF CYLINDERS

CONNECTING ROD
PISTON PIN
PISTON PIN RETAINER
CYLINDER WALL
PISTON
CYLINDER BLOCK
WATER JACKET
CYLINDER HEAD

RADIATOR FINS
INLET HOSE (RIGHT)
OVERFLOW LINE
WATER PUMP PULLEY
RADIATOR LOWER TANK
INLET HOSE (LEFT)

The inter-relationship between V8 engine and its radiator and cooling system

LUBRICATION

Various minor changes were made to the lubrication system throughout 1932 and according to Service Letter No. 68 dated 7 July, 'Beginning May 13 with motor number 18-15164, a new style oil pan was released for V8 engine production.

'The oil level indicator which was located on the right side at the rear of the cylinder block has been relocated in the new oil pan on the left side of the engine.

'It is necessary to use the new style oil pump 18-6600, oil level indicator 18-6750-B and oil pan tray 18-6688 with the new style oil pan, as the oil sump is now located in the centre instead of the rear of the oil pan and the oil pump is equipped with a tube which obtains the oil from this point.'

These alterations were made to reduce oil surge, but more changes were to follow according to the Service Bulletin, 'Approximately June 25 the gear used for all production and service requirements in all oil pumps (V8 B and A) were changed from cast iron to steel, greatly increasing their strength.

'When replacing either oil pump gear in an oil pump equipped with cast iron gears with a steel gear, it will be necessary to replace both gears and install a cast iron cover.'

In September the oil pump tube was given a flared end to prevent any possibility of clogging.

LUBRICATION

Method	Forced feed, gravity and splash
Capacity	5 qts (US)
Oil pump type	Gear
Drive	Gear from camshaft
Capacity	1.88 gallons (US) per minute at 1000 rpm
Normal oil pressure	30 lb at 2000 rpm

WATER PUMPS

Initially the water pumps were designed in left- and right-hand versions. However, in October a universal pump with two grease fittings, one of which was blocked off, was released.

COOLING SYSTEM

Method	Dual pump and thermosyphon
Capacity	5.5 gallons (US) 4.5 gallons (Imp)
Pump type	Centrifugal 3-blade
Pump capacity	33 gallons (Imp) per minute at 3000 rpm
Location	1 in each cylinder head
Lubrication	Grease

RADIATORS

Radiators for the V8 were initially made by Ford, but by June these were supplemented by products from both McCord and Long. Dimensionally they were all the same, but core construction differed.

Later in the year McCord produced a special radiator for use at high altitudes and in hot climates.

RADIATOR

Type	Tube and fin
Cooling surface	374 sq in
Tube type	Oval
Rows – usually	3 or 4
Number of tubes – usually	136
Number of fins	132
Core size	$2.75 \times 17 \times 23\frac{3}{16}$ in

FAN

Initial type	2-blade
From May 1932	4-blade
Material	Steel
Diameter	15.5 in
Capacity	1650 cu ft at 1000 rpm
Speed	1.5 times engine
Drive	28° V belt
Length (approximately)	51.25 in
Width (maximum)	0.63 in

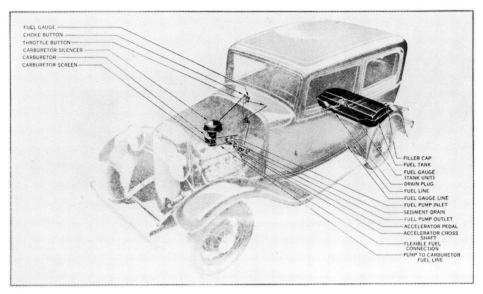

Another piece of Ford service bulletin, this time showing off the fuel system on the American V8

FUEL PUMP

Many changes were made to the V8 fuel pump during 1932 and Service Letter No. 67 dated 26 May requested, 'All fuel pump assemblies on the V8 display cars should be replaced with the new style fuel pump.'

This new fuel pump had a reduced diameter and unplated sleeve so as to prevent sticking.

According to Chassis Change Letter No. 29 of 6 October, an optional design 'Rocker Arm Type' fuel pump and push rod for use on the V8 units was released. Dealers were subsequently notified that, 'The present, or "sleeve" type pump cannot be used with the new style push rod, or vice versa.' In December Service Letter No. 84, dated 16 December instructed, 'Branches will immediately drill one $\frac{3}{4}$ in hole in each side of the fuel pump base, making these alterations on all branch and dealers' service stock and all production stock, including those in built-up cars. Also this change must be made in fuel pump bases 18-9375-B shipped with the 18-9385-B Lower Fuel Pump Bodies.

'Dealers should immediately be advised of this change and instructed to see that the fuel pumps on all V8 cars in their territory are removed and the drilled design installed.'

This change was made to prevent condensation and freezing in the fuel pump base.

FUEL SYSTEM

Type	Pump
Tank capacity	11 gallons (Imp)
	14 gallons (US)
Fuel pump type	Diaphragm
Make	A.C.
Drive	Eccentric on camshaft
Delivery pressure	1.5 to 2.75 lb per sq in
Fuel gauge type	Hydrostatic
Carburettor type	Downdraft with silencer
Make	Detroit lubricator and Ford
Size	1.25 in

IGNITION

The refinement of the ignition system was one of the major problems with the design of the V8 and after only 4250 cars a new distributor assembly was released. This new distributor had three, rather than four, mounting bolt holes, one of them being eliminated to facilitate the attachment of vacuum control by means of a tube from the inlet manifold.

Service Letter No. 74 of 12 August told of 'Improvements in the centrifugal governor have been incorporated in the 18-12000 distributor, smoothing out the spark advance at low engine speeds. The distributor with the improved governor can be identified by the gradation marks on the manual spark adjustment screw plate.'

Earlier in the year, in May, Ford had released an optional two-piece short coil held together by a metal strap. This was further developed and released for full production, without the metal strap, in November 1932.

IGNITION

Type	Coil and distributor
Make	Mallory
Control	Fully automatic-vacuum control
Initial advance	4°
Total advance	20°
Breaker gap	0.012 to 0.014 in
Coil resistance at 68°F	
– primary	0.505 to 0.535 ohms
– secondary	3350 to 3800 ohms
Condenser capacity	0.33 to 0.36 microfarads
Spark plugs:	
Type	C4X
	after October 1932 C4
	after December 1932 C7
Size – C4X and C4	7/8 in – 18TPI
– C7	18 mm
Gap	0.023 to 0.027 in

The 24 hp Model B engine as photographed on 29 January 1932 complete with an experimental vacuum clutch mechanism which never went into production. Notice the cast-iron water neck which also acts as a bracket

4-cylinder engines

GENERAL	B (24 hp)	BF (14.9 hp)
Type	In-line	—
Cylinders	4	—
Material	Grey iron – 15% steel	—
Bore	3.875 to 3.876 in	3.055 to 3.056 in
Stroke	4.25 in	—
Piston displacement	200.5 cu in (3285 cc)	124.6 cu in (2043 cc)
Compression ratio	4.6:1	5.2:1
Firing order	1–2–4–3	—
Maximum compression pressure	109.9 lb per sq in	100 lb per sq in
Pressure at cranking speed	85 lb per sq in	80 lb per sq in
Offset of cylinders	0.125 in	—
Valve arrangement	L	—
Angle of mounting in frame	$2\frac{1}{2}°$	—
Weight – complete with clutch and gearbox	*447 lb	466 lb
Horse-power rating	S.A.E. 24.03	S.A.E. 14.93
Horse-power developed	52 at 2600 rpm	42 at 3000 rpm
Torque	128.5 lb.ft at 1500 rpm	77 lb.ft at 2500 rpm

*This figure comes from a 1932 Ford Salesman's Reference Book, while Polyprints Restorers' Guide states 464 lb

CRANKSHAFT

Material	Ford carbon manganese steel
Production	Forged
Overall length	B–26.28 in BF–26.53 in
Weight (finished)	B–45 lb BF–38 lb
Balance	Static and dynamic

MAIN BEARING JOURNALS

Number	3
Diameter	1.998 to 1.999 in
Length – front	2.187 in
– centre	2.175 in
– rear	2.997 to 3.001 in
Surface area	approx 44 sq in
Bearing type	Babbitted in block
Lubrication	Forced feed and splash

CRANK PIN JOURNALS

Diameter	1.873 to 1.874 in
Length	B–1.623 in BF–1.625 in
Surface area	approx 38.25 in
Lubrication	Oil dippers and splash
Bearing finish	Honed and polished

CONNECTING RODS

Design	I-beam
Material	Steel
Production	Forged
Length (centre to centre)	7.5 in
Weight	B–750 g BF–735 g

BIG END BEARING

Type	Floating
Material	Babbitt coated steel
Finish	Burnished
Diameter (bore) inside	1.875 to 1.8755 in
Length	1.625 in
Lubrication	Oil dippers and splash

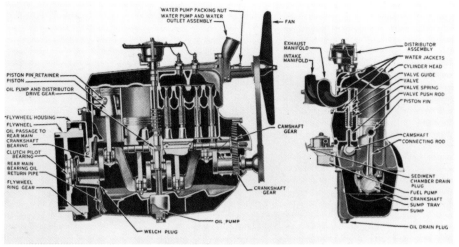

Sectional views of the four cylinder engine

SMALL END BEARINGS

Material	Bronze
Finish	Diamond bored
Diameter (bore)	1.0003 to 1.0006 in
Length	1.625 in
Lubrication	Splash

PISTONS

Type	Split skirt and cam ground
Material	B – heat-treated aluminium alloy or cast iron
	BF – heat-treated aluminium
Weight	B – aluminium 588 g
	– cast iron 1037 g
	BF – 321 g
Diameter	B – 3.8735 to 3.8745 in
	BF – 3.0535 to 3.0545 in
Width of ring groove	
– first compression	B – 0.125 to 0.126 in
	BF – 0.1245 to 0.1255 in
– second compression	B/BF – 0.1245 to 0.1255 in
– oil control	0.156 to 0.157 in
Piston pin bore	B – 0.9998 to 1.0001 in
	BF – 0.9995 to 1 in
Balance	Individually weighed and matched in sets
Oil return holes in lower ring groove	6 of 0.1 to 0.104 in dia.

PISTON PINS

Type	Fully floating
Material	Machined seamless steel tubing
Diameter	1.0001 to 1.0004 in
Length	B – centre retainer 3.546 in
	– end retainer 3.5385 in
	BF – 2.70 in

Finish	Honed and polished
Balance	Individually weighed and matched in sets
Lubrication	Splash and vapour

PISTON RINGS

Number – compression	2
– oil control	1
Width – compression	0.123 to 0.1235 in
– oil control	0.1545 to 0.155 in
Oil slot	0.075 in
Ring gaps	
– compression	*B – 0.01 to 0.015 in
	BF – 0.003 to 0.008 in
– oil control	*B – 0.005 to 0.013 in
	BF – 0.003 to 0.008 in
Ring to wall pressure	B – 8 to 11 lb
	BF – 4 to 7 lb

*These figures are from a Ford Motor Company Ltd Servicing and Repair Data book, whereas the Ford Service Bulletin for November 1932 states:

Top compression	0.012 to 0.015 in
Centre ring	0.01 to 0.012 in
Oil control	0.008 to 0.01 in

CAMSHAFT

Material	Ford carbon manganese steel
Diameter (between cams)	0.844 in
Drive	Gear
Bearings	3
Bearings (I.D.)	1.5615 to 1.5625 in
Type	Steel on cast iron
Journal diameter	1.559 to 1.56 in
Journal length	
– front	1.62 in
– centre	2 in
– rear	1.12 in
Maximum cam lift	B – inlet 0.334 in
	– exhaust 0.341 in
	BF – 0.338 in

Lubrication	Forced feed and splash
Cam lubrication	Splash and vapour
Camshaft speed	½ crankshaft speed
Camshaft to crankshaft centres	4.154 to 4.156 in

TIMING GEARS

Large gear:	
Mounting	Camshaft
Fit	Dowel and nut
Material	Bakelized fabric
Small gear:	
Mounting	Crankshaft
Material	Steel
Timing gear backlash	0.003 to 0.004 in
Lubrication	Forced feed and splash

VALVES

Type	One-piece
Design	Mushroom
Material	Chromium, nickle-alloy steel
Production	Forged
Clearance – inlet	0.013 to 0.015 in
– exhaust	B – 0.02 to 0.022 in
	BF – 0.015 to 0.017 in
Valve stem end diameter	0.498 to 0.51 in
Valve head diameter	1.537 in
Angle of valve seat	
– valve	44.5°
– cylinder block	45°
Valve stem diameter	0.3105 to 0.3115 in
Valve lift – inlet	B – 0.320 in
	BF – 0.324 in
– exhaust	B – 0.320 in
	BF – 0.322 in
Lubrication	Crankcase vapour

VALVE GUIDES

Type	Two-piece
Material	Die-cast iron
Inside diameter	0.313 to 0.314 in

VALVE SPRINGS

Material	Oil-tempered steel
Free length	2.938 in
Test length	2.5 in
Test pressure	34 to 40 lb

PUSH RODS

Type	
Design	
Material – body	
– base	
Length	B – 2.517 to 2.519 in
	BF – 2.485 to 2.487 in
Diameter – stem	0.5925 to 0.5935 in
– base	1.125 in
Lubrication	Splash and vapour

VALVE TIMING

B	
Inlet opens	8° BTDC
Inlet closes	56° ABDC
Exhaust opens	56° BBDC
Exhaust closes	8° ATDC
BF	
Inlet opens	30° BTDC
Inlet closes	78° ABDC
Exhaust opens	74° BBDC
Exhaust closes	26° ATDC

ENGINE LUBRICATION

Method	Forced feed, gravity and splash
Capacity	5 quarts (Imp)
Sump capacity	B – 7 pts (Imp)
	BF – 8 pts (Imp)
Oil pump type	Gear
Drive	Gear from camshaft
Capacity	1 Imperial gallon per minute at 1000 rpm
Oil pressure	5 to 7 lb per sq in

COOLING SYSTEM

Method	Pump and thermosyphon
Capacity	3 gallons (Imp)
Pump type	Centrifugal 3-blade
Location	Front of cylinder head
Lubrication	Grease

RADIATOR

Type	Tube and fin
Cooling surface area	374 sq in
Capacity	B–1⅞ gal BF–1½ gal
Tube type	Oval
Tube number	102
Rows	3
Number of fins	132
Core size	$23\frac{3}{16} \times 17 \times 2\frac{3}{32}$ in

FAN*

Type	2-blade
Material	Steel – pressed into form in two strips and welded together
Design	Aeroplane propeller type
Diameter	16 in
Capacity	855 cu ft at 1000 rpm
Speed	1½ times engine
Drive	5/8 in V-belt
Bearing	Roller

*Ford-America also fitted a Holley two-blade fan, again made in two pieces, but rather than being welded the blades were single thickness with part of each blade overlapping.

FUEL SYSTEM

Type	Pump
Fuel pump type	Diaphragm
Drive	Eccentric on camshaft
Delivery pressure	1.25 to 2 lb per sq in

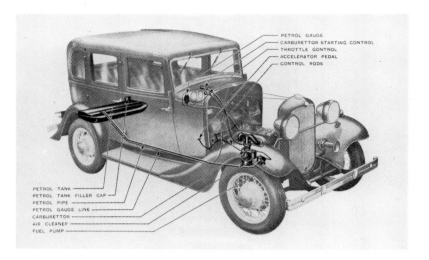

Four cylinder fuel system shown here on the 1933 Ford Fourteen

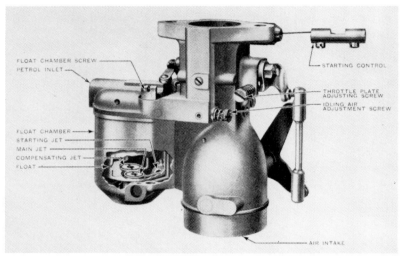

The updraught Zenith carburettor fitted to the 14.9 engine from 1933

Fuel gauge type	Hydrostatic	**FLYWHEEL**	
Carburettor type	Updraught	Material	Cast iron alloy
Make	Zenith with air cleaner	Weight (complete)	
BF (from 1933)	Zenith updraught	– V8	*32 lb 4 oz
		– B	†52 lb 2 oz
IGNITION		Ring gear material	Steel
Type	Coil and distributor	Ring gear mounting	0.01 in shrunk fit
Make		Balance – V8	Static and dynamic
Control	Fully automatic	– B/BF	Static
Initial advance	19.5°	Number of teeth	112
Total advance	33.5° movable cam	Ratio – starter to ring	11.2:1
	35.5° fixed cam	gear	
Breaker gap	0.018 to 0.022 in		
	movable cam.		
	0.01 to 0.15 in fixed cam.		
Coil resistance at 68°F			
– primary	1.52 to 1.58 ohms		
– secondary	4600 to 4800 ohms		
Condenser capacity	0.2 to 0.25 microfarads		
Spark plugs:			
Type	C5 or 3X		
Size	7/8 in – 18 TPI		
Gap	0.033 in		

*This figure is from a British 1932 Ford Salesman's Reference Book. The V8 Affair states 38.7 lb.
†This figure is from a British 1932 Ford Salesman's Reference Book.

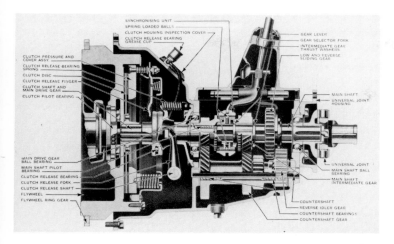

V8 and four cylinder gearbox

CLUTCH

Type	Dry – single plate
Number of driven plates	1
Clutch disc type	Dished
Material	Spring steel
Clutch disc lining	
– outside diameter	V8 – 9 in
	B/BF – 9.75 in
– inside diameter	V8 – 5.76 in
	B/BF – 5.5 in
– thickness	0.132 to 0.142 in
Material	Moulded asbestos composition
Number of springs in clutch disc hub	V8 – 12
	B/BF – none
Total acting surface of clutch facing	V8 – 75.8 sq in
	B/BF – 102.7 sq in
Pressure plate	
– diameter	V8 – 9.12 in
	B/BF – 10.125 in
– thickness	0.56 in
– pressure	V8 – 1555 lb at 4000 rpm
	B/BF 1440 to 1560 lb
Pedal pressure	30 lb
Clutch pedal free travel	V8 – 0.75 to 1 in
	B/BF – 1 to 1.5 in
Number of pressure springs	12
Release bearing	Heavy-duty ball bearing
Lubrication	Grease cup outside housing
Pilot bearing (in flywheel)	Large ball bearing
Lubrication	Pre-lube
Balance – clutch assembly	The out of balance must not exceed the effect of 0.2 oz hung 1 in from the centre of a perfectly balanced clutch.

GEARBOX

Type	Constant mesh, helical gear, silent second
Gear and shaft material	Carbon chromium steel
Helical gear finish	Burnished and matched in sets
Lubrication	Heavy semi-fluid oil (S.A.E. 90 EP)
Capacity	2.125 pints (Imp)
	2.5 pints (US)

Ratios

V8/B	– 1st	2.82:1
	– 2nd	1.604:1
	– 3rd	1:1
	– Reverse	3.383:1
BF	– 1st	3.115:1
	– 2nd	1.772:1
	– 3rd	1:1
	– Reverse	3.738:1

Chassis

GENERAL

Overall length	165.5 in
Wheelbase	106 in
Turning circle	39 ft
Track – front	55 in
– rear	$56\frac{9}{32}$ in
Road clearance	9 in

FRAME

Type	Double drop
Overall length	148.375 in
Width of flange	2 in
Depth (maximum)	6 in
Gauge	0.11 in

CROSS-MEMBERS

Length	
– front spreader bar	23.1875 in ($23\frac{3}{16}$)
– front	25.28125 in ($25\frac{9}{32}$)
– centre	36.125 in ($36\frac{1}{8}$)
– rear	40.25 in ($40\frac{1}{4}$)
– rear spreader bar	39.5625 in ($39\frac{9}{16}$)
Material	
– spreader bars	Tubular
– cross-members	Pressed steel
Thickness	0.11 in ($\frac{7}{64}$)

STEERING GEAR

Type	Worm and sector
Sector	3 tooth
Ratio	13:1 and 15:1
Steering wheel diameter	17 in
Worm bearings	2 tapered rollers
Worm end play adjustment	Shims
Sector shaft end play adjustment	Thrust screw
Backlash adjustment	Eccentric collet
Total play at steering wheel rim	1.5 in

FRONT AXLE

Type	I-beam
Material	Chrome alloy steel
Production	Forged
End type	Reverse Elliot
Tensile strength	*125,000 to 145,000 lb per sq in

*These figures come from a British 1932 Salesman's Reference Book, while Polyprints Restorer's Guide states 115,000 to 125,000 lb per sq in.

WHEEL ALIGNMENT

Caster – maximum	9°
– minimum	4.5°
Maximum variation between wheels	0.5°
Camber – maximum	V8 – 1° 10' B/BF – 0° 57'
– minimum	V8 – 1° B/BF – 0° 45'
Maximum variation between wheels	0.25°

Camber plus side inclination	
– maximum	V8 – 9° 10' B/BF 9° 12'
– minimum	V8 – 9° B/BF 8° 48'
Toe-in (in proportion to camber using a ratio of 10 to 1) 15° turn	V8 – $\frac{1}{16}$ in B/BF – $\frac{1}{32}$ to $\frac{3}{32}$ in 16.75°
Toe-out – 20° turn	23.5°
Tolerance	0.5°
King pin inclination	
– maximum	V8 – 8° B/BF – 8° 15'
– minimum	V8 – 8° B/BF – 8° 3'
King pin diameter	0.8115 to 0.8125 in

REAR AXLE

Type	$\frac{3}{4}$ floating
Ratios	3.78:1
	4.33:1
	4.11:1
	4.56:1
Type of final gearing	Spiral bevel
Finish	Hardened, matched and lapped in pairs
Number of teeth on driver gear	
3.78:1	34
4.11:1	37
4.33:1	39
4.56:1	41
Number of teeth on pinion – all	9
Tooth backlash	0.006 to 0.01 in
Pinion bearing adjustment	15 to 20 in lb

1932 Ford chassis plans

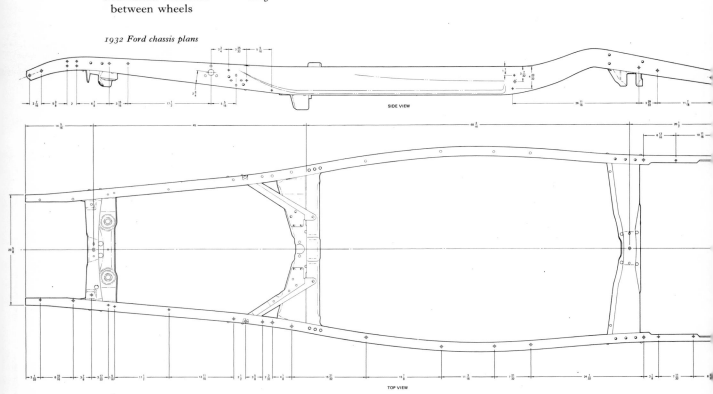

SIDE VIEW

TOP VIEW

Axle shaft diameter	1.13 in
Differential gears	Forged – integral with shaft
Differential pinions	3
Drive shaft	Tubular steel welded to forged ends
Diameter	1.75 in
Speedometer drive	Spiral gear mounted on front end of drive shaft
Universal joint	Special type with bushing
Lubrication	2 pint (Imp), 2.5 to 3 pints (US), S.A.E. 90 EP
Rear wheel	1 flexible roller each

OVERALL RATIOS — ENGINE TO REAR WHEELS

With 3.78:1 rear end	– high (third gear)	3.78:1
	– intermediate (second)	6.06:1
	– low (first)	10.66:1
	– reverse	12.79:1
With 4.11:1 rear end	– high	4.11:1
	– intermediate	6.59:1
	– low	11.59:1
	– reverse	13.89:1
With 4.33:1 rear end	– high	4.33:1
	– intermediate	6.94:1
	– low	12.2:1
	– reverse	14.65:1
With 4.56:1 rear end	– high	4.56:1
	– intermediate	7.29:1
	– low	12.85:1
	– reverse	15.4:1

SPRINGS

Spring base	113.5 in

FRONT SPRING

Type	Transverse
Number of leaves	12
Material	Chrome steel
Width	1.75 in
Free length	30.625 to 30.812 in
Loaded length	32.6 in
Free height	7.187 to 7.375 in
Loaded height	3.687 to 3.812 in
Compression rate of spring	392 lb per in of deflection
Lubrication	Graphite
Endurance tests	250,000 4 in strokes
Camber – free	4.94 in
– loaded	1.41 in
Average load rate	375 lb per sq in

SPRING SHACKLES — FRONT

Bushing	Rubber
Lubrication	Not required
Endurance tests	Over 1 million 4 in deflections of spring

REAR

Type	Transverse – Ford design

Number of leaves	*See below
Material	Cardon chromium manganese steel
Width	2.25 in
Free length	44.625 in
Loaded length	46 in (average)
Compression rate	230 lb per sq in of deflection
Lubrication	Graphite
Endurance tests	300,000 4 in strokes

BRITISH

Number of leaves	Variation in leaf Specifications	Load per 1″	Models Deflection
9 (Special)	2 different thicknesses	157 lb	Roadster (Std. and DeL.)
9 (Standard)	2 different thicknesses	180 lb	Phaeton (Std. and DeL.) All Coupé models Cabriolet
10	3 different thicknesses	205 lb	Tudor Victoria Convertible Sedan

V8 and four cylinder shock absorbers

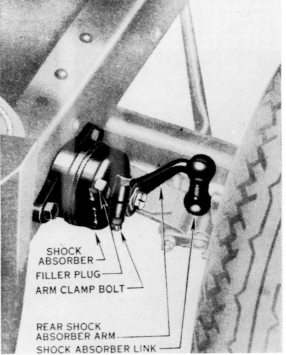

SHOCK ABSORBER
FILLER PLUG
ARM CLAMP BOLT

REAR SHOCK ABSORBER ARM
SHOCK ABSORBER LINK

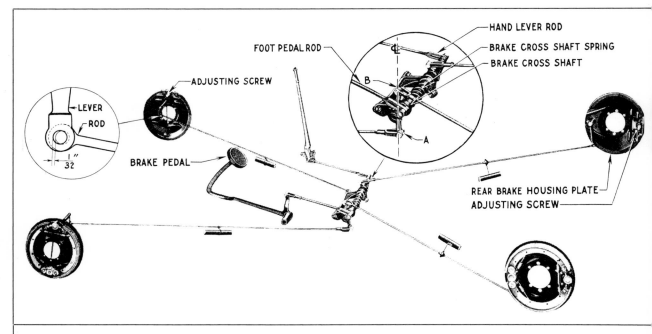

FOOT PEDAL ROD

HAND LEVER ROD
BRAKE CROSS SHAFT SPRING
BRAKE CROSS SHAFT

ADJUSTING SCREW

LEVER
ROD
1"
32

BRAKE PEDAL

B

A

REAR BRAKE HOUSING PLATE
ADJUSTING SCREW

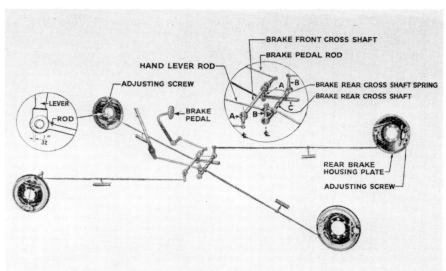

BRAKE FRONT CROSS SHAFT
BRAKE PEDAL ROD

HAND LEVER ROD

ADJUSTING SCREW

BRAKE REAR CROSS SHAFT SPRING
BRAKE REAR CROSS SHAFT

A B

A B

C

LEVER
ROD
1"
32

BRAKE PEDAL

REAR BRAKE
HOUSING PLATE

ADJUSTING SCREW

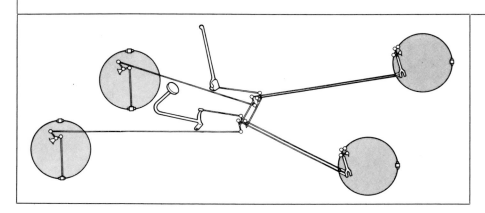

ABOVE *English brake system with two cross shafts and the handbrake working only the rear wheels*

TOP *American brake system with one cross shaft and the handbrake working all four wheels*

LEFT *German brake system with two cross shafts and the handbrake working the rear wheels only but with four brake rods*

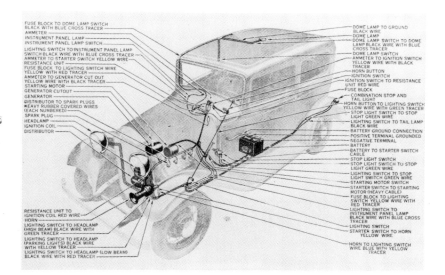

FUSE BLOCK TO DOME LAMP SWITCH
BLACK WITH BLUE CROSS TRACER
AMMETER
INSTRUMENT PANEL LAMP
INSTRUMENT PANEL LAMP SWITCH
LIGHTING SWITCH TO INSTRUMENT PANEL LAMP
SWITCH BLACK WIRE WITH BLUE CROSS TRACER
AMMETER TO STARTER SWITCH YELLOW WIRE
RESISTANCE UNIT
FUSE BLOCK TO LIGHTING SWITCH WIRE
YELLOW WIRE WITH RED TRACER
AMMETER TO GENERATOR CUT OUT
YELLOW WIRE WITH BLACK TRACER
STARTING MOTOR
GENERATOR CUTOUT
GENERATOR
DISTRIBUTOR TO SPARK PLUGS
HEAVY RUBBER COVERED WIRES
(EACH NUMBERED)
SPARK PLUG
HEADLAMP
IGNITION COIL
DISTRIBUTOR

DOME LAMP TO GROUND
BLACK WIRE
DOME LAMP
DOME LAMP SWITCH TO DOME
LAMP BLACK WIRE WITH BLUE
CROSS TRACER
DOME LAMP SWITCH
AMMETER TO IGNITION SWITCH
YELLOW WIRE WITH BLACK
TRACER
HORN BUTTON
IGNITION SWITCH TO RESISTANCE
UNIT RED WIRE
FUSE BLOCK
COMBINATION STOP AND
TAIL LIGHT
HORN BUTTON TO LIGHTING SWITCH
YELLOW WIRE WITH GREEN TRACER
STOP LIGHT SWITCH TO STOP
LIGHT GREEN WIRE
LIGHTING SWITCH TO TAIL LAMP
BLACK WIRE
BATTERY GROUND CONNECTION
POSITIVE TERMINAL GROUNDED
NEGATIVE TERMINAL
BATTERY
BATTERY TO STARTER SWITCH
CABLE
STOP LIGHT SWITCH
STOP LIGHT SWITCH TU STOP
LIGHT GREEN WIRE
LIGHTING SWITCH TO STOP
LIGHT SWITCH GREEN WIRE
STARTING MOTOR SWITCH
STARTER SWITCH TO STARTING
MOTOR (HEAVY CABLE)
FUSE BLOCK TO LIGHTING
SWITCH YELLOW WIRE WITH
RED TRACER
LIGHTING SWITCH TO
INSTRUMENT PANEL LAMP
BLACK WIRE WITH BLUE CROSS
TRACER
LIGHTING SWITCH
STARTER SWITCH TO HORN
YELLOW WIRE
HORN TO LIGHTING SWITCH
WIRE BLUE WITH YELLOW
TRACER

RESISTANCE UNIT TO
IGNITION COIL RED WIRE
HORN
LIGHTING SWITCH TO HEADLAMP
(HIGH BEAM) BLACK WIRE WITH
GREEN TRACER
LIGHTING SWITCH TO HEADLAMP
(PARKING LIGHTS) BLACK WIRE
WITH YELLOW TRACER
LIGHTING SWITCH TO HEADLAMP (LOW BEAM)
BLACK WIRE WITH RED TRACER

American V8 electrical system

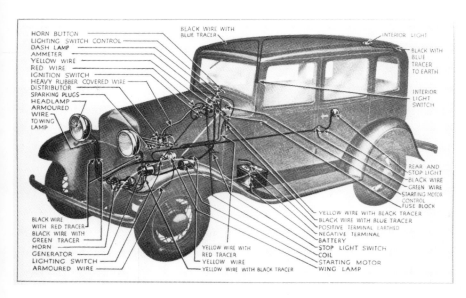

HORN BUTTON
LIGHTING SWITCH CONTROL
DASH LAMP
AMMETER
YELLOW WIRE
RED WIRE
IGNITION SWITCH
HEAVY RUBBER COVERED WIRE
DISTRIBUTOR
SPARKING PLUGS
HEADLAMP
ARMOURED
WIRE
TO WING
LAMP

BLACK WIRE WITH
BLUE TRACER

INTERIOR LIGHT

BLACK WITH
BLUE
TRACER
TO EARTH

INTERIOR
LIGHT
SWITCH

REAR AND
STOP LIGHT
BLACK WIRE
GREEN WIRE
STARTING MOTOR
CONTROL
FUSE BLOCK

BLACK WIRE
WITH RED TRACER
BLACK WIRE WITH
GREEN TRACER
HORN
GENERATOR
LIGHTING SWITCH
ARMOURED WIRE

YELLOW WIRE WITH
RED TRACER
YELLOW WIRE
YELLOW WIRE WITH BLACK TRACER

YELLOW WIRE WITH BLACK TRACER
BLACK WIRE WITH BLUE TRACER
POSITIVE TERMINAL EARTHED
NEGATIVE TERMINAL
BATTERY
STOP LIGHT SWITCH
COIL
STARTING MOTOR
WING LAMP

English four cylinder electrical system

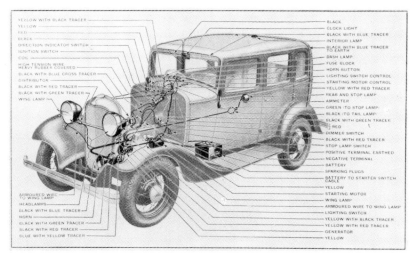

YELLOW WITH BLACK TRACER
YELLOW
RED
BLACK
DIRECTION INDICATOR SWITCH
IGNITION SWITCH
COIL
HIGH TENSION WIRE
HEAVY RUBBER COVERED
BLACK WITH BLUE CROSS TRACER
DISTRIBUTOR
BLACK WITH RED TRACER
BLACK WITH GREEN TRACER
WING LAMP

BLACK
CLOCK LIGHT
BLACK WITH BLUE TRACER
INTERIOR LAMP
BLACK WITH BLUE TRACER
TO EARTH
DASH LAMP
FUSE BLOCK
HORN BUTTON
LIGHTING SWITCH CONTROL
STARTING MOTOR CONTROL
YELLOW WITH RED TRACER
REAR AND STOP LAMP
AMMETER
GREEN (TO STOP LAMP)
BLACK (TO TAIL LAMP)
BLACK WITH GREEN TRACER
RED
DIMMER SWITCH
BLACK WITH RED TRACER
STOP LAMP SWITCH
POSITIVE TERMINAL EARTHED
NEGATIVE TERMINAL
BATTERY
SPARKING PLUGS
BATTERY TO STARTER SWITCH
CABLE
YELLOW
STARTING MOTOR
WING LAMP
ARMOURED WIRE TO WING LAMP
LIGHTING SWITCH
YELLOW WITH BLACK TRACER
YELLOW WITH RED TRACER
GENERATOR
YELLOW

ARMOURED WIRE
TO WING LAMP
HEADLAMPS
BLACK WITH BLUE TRACER
HORN
BLACK WITH GREEN TRACER
BLACK WITH RED TRACER
BLUE WITH YELLOW TRACER

English Fourteen electrical system

11	3 different thicknesses	232 lb	Fordor (Std. and DeL.)
12	3 different thicknesses	262 lb	Commercial Chassis Light Delivery

SHOCK ABSORBERS

Type	Houdaille — double acting
Adjustment — B — prior to April	Manual
— post April — all models	Automatic with thermostatic control

BRAKES

Type	Mechanical — internal expanding shoe
Control	
— foot pedal	Four wheels
— hand lever	
— US	Four wheels
— UK and German	Rear wheels
Adjustment — rods	Adjustable clevis
— shoe	External stud on each brake plate
Braking distribution	
— front	40%
— rear	60%
Brake drums:	
Material	Malleable iron alloy
Diameter	12 in
Brake Linings:	
Material	Woven asbestos
Length (per shoe) front and rear	13.45 in
Width — front and rear	1.73 in
Thickness — front and rear	0.185 in
Total area	186 sq in

WHEELS

Type	Welded steel spoke
Rim	Well base (drop centre)
Rim diameter	18 in
Rim width (inside)	3.25 in
Number of spokes	32 (16 inner and 16 outer)
Bolt pattern	5 stud
Diameter	5.25 in

TYRES

Size	5.25 × 18 in
Outside diameter of tyre (approximately)	28.5 in
Revolutions per mile (approximately)	729
Recommended tyre pressures	
— normal speeds	35 lb per sq in
— high speeds	40 lb per sq in

GENERATOR

Type	2 pole
Brushes	3
Regulation	3rd brush
Maximum output	
— B/BF	75 watts
— V8	189 watts
Maximum charging rate	
— B/BF	12 amps at 1000 rpm
— V8	27 amps at 1300 rpm
Normal charging rate	12 amps
Cut-in volts	6.7 to 7.5
Cut-in engine speed	500 rpm
Armature speed	$1\frac{1}{2}$ times engine speed
Drive	V-belt
Effective pulley diameter	
— engine	5 in
— generator	
— B/BF	3.06 in
— V8	3.85 in

STARTER MOTOR

Drive	Bendix
Number of teeth on pinion	10
Normal engine cranking speed	
— B/BF	150 rpm
— V8	100 rpm
Lock torque	V8 — 12 ft lb
	B/BF — 16 ft lb

Electrical System

BATTERY

Type	13 plate — 3 cell
Voltage	6
Earth	Positive
Height	$8\frac{11}{16}$ in
Width	$7\frac{1}{8}$ in
Length	$9\frac{3}{16}$ in

2 Body styles

Most historians of the 1932 Ford either ignore or simply do not know of the existence of models built outside the United States. This chapter therefore looks at models available worldwide and will hopefully put the record straight.

Major Ford plants in both America and Canada supplied body stampings and cars in knock-down (K.D.) form for assembly at both smaller domestic plants and at foreign plants. Body panels, knock-down assemblies and complete bodies were also supplied to Ford and its branches by Briggs and Murray.

Ford also produced dies for the two British sedan bodies. These were shipped to England, where Briggs produced stampings, knock-down assemblies and complete bodies, which were shipped to other plants for assembly. Unlike the American bodies most other foreign bodies were built on wooden frames. There are therefore slight structural differences between domestic and foreign sourced vehicles. In the main these differences are indiscernible from the outside, the exception being the Australian Phaeton, which does not have the two seams where the three rear panels are joined, as does the American version.

The only other area in which construction differed was on the Danish Cabriolet, which had its body riveted to the chassis.

Commercial vehicles differ greatly from country to country. Ford-America produced five variants on the 106 in wheelbase chassis. Most other countries were content to produce commercial chassis on which outside coachbuilders constructed a wide variety of bodies. Once again the Australians were the exception. They produced two versions of the open cab pick-up.

Many countries, but certainly Britain and Germany, had coachbuilding companies constructing special-bodied saloons and sports cars on both four-cylinder and V8 chassis, but as these were not factory backed, they are dealt with in chapter 11.

The following models are arranged in the order in which they appear in Ford Literature, except for the Imperial Limousine, which hardly appears at all in Ford literature and certainly is not listed in Dearborn Production Records.

The 123 in wheelbase chassis, complete with that distinctive side-rail pressing, was undoubtedly made by joining two frames together. It is unlikely that Ford envisaged large sales; it would therefore have been uneconomical to produce the huge dies necessary for rail stamping in order to manufacture only 60 frames.

Standard 1932-style cross-members were used, but an additional cross-member, not unlike a reversed gearbox cross-member, was mounted farther along the chassis.

Mechanically the Limousines were very similar to their predecessors, except for Canadian-made V8 engines with aluminium cylinder heads, a longer torque tube and Andrea Phillips hydraulic shock absorbers, which, according to the specification had a 'Thermostatic device to counteract variations in temperature and viscosity of shock-absorbing fluid, and automatic adjustment to compensate sudden, abnormal shocks.'

Twin gauges, mounted in the dashboard, monitored their operation. They could also be adjusted by means of firewall-mounted cylinders.

Bodily they were made up of bits and pieces. The grille, bonnet, splash apron, petrol tank and rear frame horn covers were standard '32 Ford parts. Even the peculiar English bonnet with its Model A-style raised louvre panel was retained. The front and rear wings were the new skirted types joined by extra long running boards. The body was an amalgamation of two- and four-door parts. The rear half was Fordor with elongated rear doors made in three parts, while the front half employed Tudor doors and the new curved-top windscreen with a chrome frame.

The door handles were American '32 style, which strangely had not been used on British-built cars in 1932.

Other small, external differences included the new acorn lights, straight headlight bar, with, in this case, a V8 emblem and Fourteen bumpers. Interestingly, and probably for reasons of economy, the rear lamps had flat glass rather than the 'blown-out' lenses usually found in 1932 Duolamps.

Internally the Limousine was very different from any other 1932-type Ford. The dashboard was the 1933 Model 40 type converted to right-hand-drive (for the UK) and fitted with both a glove box and the shock absorber gauges. Behind the front two seats there was a partition with a sliding glass screen that divided the driving compartment from the main passenger area. Into the bottom of this partition were fitted two folding, occasional seats. The rear seat was similar to those found in regular Fordors.

A few of these Limousines still exist, but the pair I was lucky enough to examine were sadly neglected. It could, however, be seen that they had once been quite luxurious motor cars with wooden cappings for the doors and partition and plusher than usual upholstery. Whether the Army originally ordered them and then cancelled (unlikely) or whether it was an attempt by Ford to break into a market it had little share of or whether it was merely an attempt to get rid of surplus parts, I don't know. I suspect it was a combination of the latter two, but whatever their reasons for going to all that trouble and expense to build just 60 cars the Imperial Limousine is an interesting variation on the '32 theme.

NOTE
Production figures are from Production Department records, but they do not include K.D. Exports from Canada and therefore cars assembled in Canada's natural market, the British Colonies, possessions and dependencies, plus any other markets it sold cars in.

Foreign production is for the plants listed and does not include complete cars delivered to dealers, American and Canadian exports are listed only as monthly model totals in Production Records. There was no breakdown as to which models went where. Cork production is not listed between February and September 1933.

Foreign plants included in foreign production totals:
Amsterdam, Holland
Antwerp, Belgium
Asnières, France
Barcelona, Spain
Buenos Aires, Argentina
Cologne, Germany
Copenhagen, Denmark
Cork, Ireland
Dagenham, England
Istanbul, Turkey
Mexico City, Mexico
Rotterdam, Holland
Santiago, Chile
São Paulo, Brazil
Yokohama, Japan

Phaeton

		V8	B
Body type	B-35		
Body type (Australia)	VP		
First unit	March 1932		
Location	Dearborn		
Last unit (Standard V8)	October 1933		
Location	Copenhagen, Denmark		

		V8	B
Total production			
– domestic	– standard	600	613
	– De Luxe	978	300
– K.D.	– standard	351	332
	– De Luxe	75	75
– Canada	– standard	369	305
	– De Luxe	336	54
– Foreign	– standard	305	463
	– De Luxe	118	39
Weight (lb)			
	– standard	2369	2238
	– De Luxe	2375	2268
Weight (body only) (lb)			
	– standard		554
	– De Luxe		579

Roadster

Body type	B-40
Body type (Australia)	VR
First unit	March 1932
Location	Dearborn
Last unit (Standard B)	May 1934
Location	Copenhagen, Denmark

		V8	B
Total production			
– domestic	– standard	568	984
	– De Luxe	7318	3727
– K.D.	– standard	78	63
	– De Luxe	184	316
– Canada	– standard	135	166
	– De Luxe	482	286
– Foreign	– standard	124	93
	– De Luxe	379	216
Weight (lb)			
	– standard	2242	2102
	– De Luxe	2308	2178
Weight (body only) (lb)			
	– standard	428	
	– De Luxe	487	

Standard Coupe

Body type	B-45
First unit	March 1932
Last unit (B)	January 1934
Location	Antwerp, Belgium

		V8	B
Total production	– domestic	31,112	20,692
	– K.D.	140	66
	– Canada	881	924
	– Foreign	97	195
Weight (lb)		2412	2261
Weight (body only) (lb)		551	

Sport Coupe

Body type	B-50
Body type (Australia)	VC
First unit	March 1932
Last unit (B)	May 1934
Location	Barcelona, Spain

		V8	B
Total production	– domestic	2169	742
	– K.D.	50	129
	– Canada	107	103
	– Foreign	133	157
Weight (lb)		2422	2286
Weight (body only) (lb)		557	

De Luxe Coupe

Body type	B-520
First unit	March 1932
Last unit (B)	January 1934
Location	Barcelona, Spain (2)
	Copenhagen, Denmark (1)

		V8	B
Total production	– domestic	21,175	970
	– K.D.	152	111
	– Canada	812	53
	– Foreign	277	124
Weight (lb)		2502	2364
Weight (body only) (lb)		631	

Victoria

Body type	B-190
First unit	March 1932
Last unit (B)	December 1933
Location	Antwerp, Holland

		V8	B
Total production	– domestic	8054	526
	– K.D.		107
	– Canada	527	66
	– Foreign	289	137
Weight (lb)		2488	2344
Weight (body only) (lb)		620	

Tudor Sedan

Body type	B-55
First unit	March 1932
Last unit (Standard B)	September 1935
Location	Dagenham, England

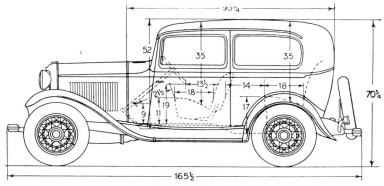

Tudor Saloon.

LEFT *Ford's contemporary drawing of the British Tudor Sedan which they lovingly called a saloon. It is interesting to note that the artist omitted the raised louvre panel found on the English sedans, whereas the drawings of American cars found in Ford-America literature have the raised louvre panel which of course was not fitted there*

BELOW *The photograph is dated 1933 and it's a British Police Car. Raining, as ever*

BOTTOM *Rare British 2 door Saloon owned by Jim Long and photographed at an English rally in the 1980s*

		V8	B
Total production			
– domestic	– standard	62,697	37,122
	– De Luxe	20,200	4082
– K.D.	– standard	4914	3497
	– De Luxe	1074	163
– Canada	– standard	2878	3152
	– De Luxe	696	290
– Foreign	– standard	2940	11,346
	– De Luxe	1216	1896
Weight (US cars) (lb)			
	– standard	2512	2378
	– De Luxe	2522	2398
Weight (US body only) (lb)			
	– standard	685	
	– De Luxe	703	

Fordor Sedan

Body type	B-160
Body type (Australia)	VS
First unit	March 1932
Last unit (De Luxe V8)	October 1934
Location	Copenhagen, Denmark
	Cork, Ireland

		V8	B
Total production			
– domestic	– standard	9984	4224
	– De Luxe	20,471	2684
– K.D.	– standard	1510	2073
	– De Luxe	1797	1697
– Canada	– standard	1264	839
	– De Luxe	1105	334
– Foreign	– standard	1243	3636
	– De Luxe	2594	5684
Weight (US cars) (lb)			
	– standard	2549	2413
	– De Luxe	2568	2432
Weight (US body only) (lb)			
	– standard	696	
	– De Luxe	720	

Convertible Sedan

Body type	B-400
First unit	March 1932
Last unit	August 1933
Location	Barcelona, Spain (1)
	Copenhagen, Denmark (1)

	V8	B
Total production – domestic	884	42
– K.D.	21	79
– Canada	103	47
– Foreign	155	65
Weight (lb)	2480	2349
Weight (booy only) (lb)	658	

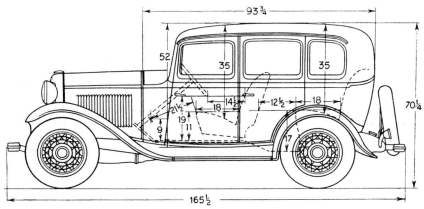

Fordor Saloon (Standard and De Luxe).

LEFT *The British Fordor – similar dimensions covered both the standard and De Luxe versions*

BELOW *Lovely promotion shot of the British Fordor from Ford of Britain archives. Notice that the door handles are nothing like the curvatious ones fitted to American cars*

LEFT *Another version of the British Fordor with the airbrush giving us more – note twin wipers, AA badge and spot/fog lamps*

RIGHT TOP *British commercial '32 Ford, with special bodywork. It's already wartime, hence headlamp blackout*

RIGHT BELOW *British coachbuilt 2 door with rear opening door. These are virtually unheard of today, but the modifications, performed by J. H. Jennings of Sandbach, cost at the time £14 10s.*

Cabriolet

		V8	B
Body type	B-68		
First unit	March 1932		
Last unit (B)	September 1934		
Location	Cork, Ireland		
Total production – domestic		5962	429
– K.D.		245	262
– Canada		690	60
– Foreign		411	316
Weight (lb)		2415	2295
Weight (body only) (lb)		555	

Station Wagon

		V8	B
Body type	B-150		
First unit	March 1932		
Last unit (V8)	December 1932		
Location	Chester (1)		
	Edgewater (19)		
	Somerville (2)		
(B)	Dallas (1)		
	Edgewater (29)		
	Long Beach (1)		
	Memphis (1)		
Total production – domestic		331	1052
– K.D.		0	0
– Canada		3	16
– Foreign			
(Mexico City)		0	4
Weight (lb)		2635	2505
Weight (body only) (lb)		850	

Panel Delivery

		V8	B
Body type	B-79		
First unit	May 1932		
Last unit (Standard B)	September 1933		
Location	Amsterdam, Holland		
Total production			
– domestic – standard		46	3457
– De Luxe		69	2550
– K.D. – standard		0	0
– De Luxe		0	0
– Canada – standard		3	68
– De Luxe		17	210
– Foreign – standard		0	58
– De Luxe		1	155
Weight (with front bumper only) (lb)			
– standard		2750	2620
– De Luxe		2780	2620
Weight (body only) (lb)			
– standard		938	
– De Luxe		981	

Sedan Delivery

Body type	B-410		
First unit	October 1932		
Last unit (V8)	January 1933		
Location	Cincinnati (1)		
	Norfolk (2)		
	Memphis (1)		

	V8	B
Total production – domestic	58	342
– K.D.	0	0
– Canada	0	3
– Foreign		
(Mexico City)	0	3
Weight (lb)	2592	2462
Weight (body only) (lb)	798	

Pick-up Closed Cab

		V8	B
Body type	B-82		
First unit	March 1932		
Last unit (standard)	March 1933		
Location	Istanbul, Turkey		
Weight (with front bumper only) (lb)		2496	2366
Weight (body only) (lb)		388	

Pick-up Open Cab

		V8	B
Body type	B-76		
Body type (Australia)	VL		
First unit	May 1932		
Weight (with front bumper only) (lb)		2387	2257
Weight (body only) (lb)		282	

ABOVE *British panel van with spare wheel mounted outside on the fender. Rare these are too*

LEFT *The Australian Type 304 Welltype Utility Car is extremely rare, probably less than 100 were built. Steve West, an American from Springfield, Ohio, found this one in Northern New South Wales and took it home with him. The car is still more or less as he found it and remains unrestored. Included in the original specifications were rubber floor mat, rear view mirror, cowl ventilator, fender well, electric windscreen wiper, grey fabri-cord upholstery and five tyres. Body dimensions were: Length 59 in.; width 48½ in. (extreme width 71 in.); height 15½ in. A feature of the model was its low loading height*

RIGHT ABOVE *This rare Imperial Limousine is part of a collection of 1930s Fords owned by Tony Moss of Wisbech, Cambridgeshire, England. Though somewhat neglected it is more or less original and almost all there. Tony found it after it had stood for nearly a decade after being discarded by its owners, a taxi company in the north of England.*

It can be seen that the grille shell and bonnet, with the raised louvre panel, are as per the British '32. However, the cowl and screen section plus the front doors from the 1933 Fourteen Tudor were utilized with a stretched door and rear section from a Fourteen Fordor. The wings are the skirted Fourteen types as is all of the brightwork with the exception of the wing mounted side lights which are not original. The 16 in. wheels are also not standard, the originals being 17 in.

CENTRE RIGHT *The dashboard was as fitted to the Fourteen except that it housed, in the centre between the cluster of switches, two Andre Phillips pressure gauges. Notice that the lighting switch is mounted in the centre of the wheel as per the Model 40 but that the wheel is still the two-piece English type from 1932*

BELOW RIGHT *The extra 17 in. in the wheelbase was used to accommodate two folding occasional seats which folded down into the partition between the passenger and drivers' compartments.*

ABOVE *The engine was the Canadian built, aluminium headed V8 though this may not be the original. Notice on the left, bolted to the firewall, the two reservoirs for the adjustable shock absorbers*

PLATE FAD

Believe it or not there are some people out there who just don't know what a 1932 Ford looks like or what the word Deuce means. To get the message across Ford owners the world over have attempted to arrange their licence plates so that there is absolutely no doubt as to what you see before you.

The Americans have a licensing system which allows them to choose their registration letters and this situation gives rise to all sorts of imaginative combinations. Most of the American plates you see here were photographed in just one day at the 1983 Western Street Rod Nationals in Merced, California, and were just a few of the personalized plates on display.

Britain, like the rest of the world, has no such system, but unlike most countries, which have to put up with what the government give them, the British can at least change plates from one car to another. Deuce owners have usually managed to find something suitable even if it has sometimes been a little obscure, like Kevin Pilling's Y BE 1. Even that is not so mystifying when you understand that the 1932 Ford was universally known in Britain as the Model B. The rest of the plates speak for themselves.

4 ReproDeuce

To produce anything for an automobile is expensive because of the development and tooling costs. However, to reproduce parts for a car which was not even in production for a full year is a very expensive and very risky business. For that reason both the restorer and rodder must agree that without each other it is possible that there would not be a sufficient market to make the wholesale reproduction of parts a viable proposition. With the combined numbers of the two groups, on the one hand restoring original cars, on the other rodding both original and completely new glassfibre-bodied cars, the equation becomes more balanced. A situation has therefore developed whereby one can almost build a wholly new '32 Ford using reproduction parts obtained from a mail order catalogue. Only the unavailability of steel bodies and some mechanical parts prevents the realization of what for many is a dream – a brand new thirty-two. Even that dream will possibly be fulfilled in the near future.

When Henry Ford predicted he would build $1\frac{1}{2}$ million cars in 1932 I doubt if he realized, when production stopped in February 1933 at around 300,000 units, that 50 years later that target might not seem so elusive. I doubt also that when they stopped pressing bodies in 1932 anybody in the Ford Motor Company could contemplate the fact that half a decade later someone would attempt to reproduce steel Roadster bodies. Nevertheless, that is what Californian Neil McNeil of A Ford has tried to do. Unfortunately, due to various problems, the project looks like being shelved. Thousands of dollars of investment capital would need to be tied up for years in order to produce the stampings and then any return would be a long, slow process. A sad fact of economics, especially when one understands that Neil has already managed to reproduce both right- and left-front fenders, the dashboard and the petrol tank – all in steel, all faithful copies of original sheet metal. Rear frame horn covers were under development, but the man making the dies unfortunately died and Neil now feels that the whole exercise may suffer a similar fate.

However, one American company is already manufacturing all-steel replicas of the Model A Roadster and it can't be long before somebody follows with a similar revival for the Deuce. Thankfully Neil is not the only man in the business of reproducing parts for 1932 Fords. he was, however, one of the few people contacted who bothered to reply to my enquiry about who was making what. The following list is therefore possibly not complete. It is hopefully accurate, but businesses come and go, products get deleted, stocks run out. Nevertheless, its size does indicate just how much interest there is in this ol' Ford.

This swap meet sight will be but a memory when Authentic American Reproduction come out with their repro firewall

Reproduction steel body parts

A Ford
612 30th Street
Paso Robles
CA 93446
USA
Tel. (805) 239-1041

All Ford Parts
701–18B Kings Row
San Jose
CA 95112
USA
Tel. (408) 998-8808
Frame horn covers and patch panels for cowl, quarter, rocker and door bottom

Authentic American Reproduction
12107-N Industrial
So. Gate
CA 90280
USA
Tel. (213) 531-8117
Rear fenders for Roadster, coupés and sedans in production. firewall, Roadster doors, sub-flooring and frame horn covers – coming soon

Hoosier Hoods and Accessories
2290 Salisbury Road South
Richmond
IN 47374
USA
Tel. (317) 962-7924

Rootlieb Inc.
815 S. Soderquist
Turlock
CA 95380
USA
Tel. (209) 632-2203
Bonnets

Race Rod Equipment
308 Longwood Road
Kennett Square
PA 19348
USA
Radiator shell – coming soon

Specialized Auto Parts
7130 Capitol
P.O. Box 9405
Houston
Texas 77261
USA
Tel. (713) 928-3707
Radiator splash shield

The 34 Store
34c Hanger Way
Watsonville
CA 95076
USA
Tel. (408) 722-1934

Unique Auto Parts
424 E. Front Street
Covina
CA 91723
USA
Tel. (213) 331-0323
Firewall – coming soon

Vintage Auto Parts Inc.
402 W. Chapman
Orange
CA 92666
USA
Tel. (714) 538-1130
Under seat floor pan – coupé and Roadster
trunk floor pan extension – Roadster
front seat frame – Roadster
front seat riser – Roadster
front seat adjuster – Roadster
package tray – Roadster
inner rear wing patch panels – 5-window Standard coupé, Cabriolet, Roadster and can be altered to fit Victoria
rear floor pan – Roadster and 5-window Standard coupé
rumble seat riser – Roadster and 5-window coupé
outer panel below deck boot lid – Roadster, 5-window coupé and 3-window coupé
outer panel above deck boot lid – Roadster
door bottom patch panels – Roadster, Tudor, 5-window and commercial
rear window drain assembly – 5-window, 3-window

Another great leap forward in the rebirth of the B came in the mid-seventies, when Californian Roy Fjastad decided that what hot rodders needed were brand new '32 frames. With this end in mind he launched the Deuce Factory and invested $45,000 and eighteen months to produce his first pair of new, thicker rails. The huge, thousand-ton presses of the McDonnell Douglas aircraft plant were used to form the sections and even then a great deal of reworking was needed to get them right. Further development and investment were necessary, but now these pressings are all but perfect and they are in fact 0.014 in thicker than the originals.

The availability of Deuce Factory chassis rails has probably had little effect on the restoration business, but it has revolutionized the rodding world. Roy has now sold over 1300 pairs of rails, which means that there are at least that many new Deuce street rods being built. It also means that there are a few more genuine chassis available to restorers.

Earlier and later Ford chassis are not as difficult to reproduce as the '32 because of its distinctive side pressing. The others are easily copied using box section, U-channel or even three separate pieces welded together, but one enterprising rodder in Sweden has managed to duplicate the Deuce side rail complete with the hiccup but without the expensive tooling used by the Deuce Factory. These frames are designed primarily for hot rods, but they are a viable alternative to Deuce Factory rails or scarce and possibly rusty originals.

Reproduction chassis parts

The Deuce Factory
424 W. Rowland Avenue
Santa Ana
CA 92707
USA
Tel. (714) 546-5596

Kugel Komponents
10821 Whittier Boulevard
Whittier
CA 90606
USA
Tel. (213) 695-6935
Frame repair parts

Speedway Motors Inc.
300 Van Dorn Road
PO Box 81906
Lincoln
NE 68501
USA
Tel. (402) 474-4411
Repro chassis rails

Eric Hanson
Rogstad
PO Box 6001
452 00 Stromstad
Sweden
Tel. (0526) 30016
Replica 1932 Ford hot rod chassis

With new chassis suddenly available it was not long before the demand for bodies, especially the Roadster, far outstripped the supply. To cash in on this market companies sprang up all over America producing glass-fibre replica bodies. Some of the products were good, some were bad and much depended upon the state of the original car from which the mould was taken. Many of the companies in the glass-fibre body business have disappeared, but hopefully those listed here are still operative. Unfortunately, we have no way of telling the

For the restorer or customizer switches and dashpanel parts are always difficult because they are easily destroyed. These new parts will help

good from the bad. All we can say is, practically all body styles with the exception of the Sport Coupé, Cabriolet, Sedans and commercials are available.

Glassfibre bodies and panels

American Street Rod Parts
2 London Road
Bedfont
Middlesex
England
Tel. Ashford (Middx.) 59784
Roadster and 3-window coupé

Art's Antique Bodies
7060 Hazard
Unit E
Westminster
CA 92683
USA
Tel. (714) 892-0093
Victoria

Downs Manufacturing
11830 Shaver Road
Schoolcraft
MI 49087
USA
Tel. (616) 679-5788
3-window coupé, Victoria

Gibbon Fiberglass Reproductions Inc.
PO Box 490
Gibbon
NE 68840
USA
Tel. (308) 468-6178
Roadster

Paul's Fibreglass & Antique Parts
RT.2 Box 250
Valmeyer
IL 62295
USA
Tel. (618) 935-2526
Roadster, Phaeton, Roadster pick-up and pick-up bed

Vintique Reproductions
9414½ S. Tacoma Way
Tacoma
WA 98499
USA
Tel. (206) 581-2316
Roadster, Phaeton and Victoria

VWT Corporation
413 Wolcott Road
PO Box 6164
Wolcott
CT 06716
USA
Tel. (203) 879-3437
3-window coupé

Southeastern Automotive
3070 NE 12th Terrace
Fort Lauderdale
FL 33334
USA
Tel. (305) 563-9522
3-window coupé

Speedway Motors Inc.
PO Box 81906
Lincoln
NE 68501
USA
Tel. (402) 474-4411
Roadster

Unique Auto
12675 Berwyn
Redford
MI 48239
USA
Tel. (313) 533-4457
Roadster, 3-window coupé, Victoria

Wessman Enterprises
1182 W-3050S
Ogden
UT 84401
USA
Tel. (801) 731-2622
3-window coupé

Wescott's Auto Restyling
19701 S. E. Highway 212
Boring
OR 97009
USA
Tel. (503) 658-3183
Roadster, Phaeton

Other glassfibre related parts

California Street Rods
17091 Palmdale
Huntington Beach
CA 92647
USA
Tel. (714) 847-4404
front floorpan for Roadster and Phaeton

Poli-Form Industries
334-A Ingalls Street
Santa Cruz
CA 95060
USA
Tel. (408) 427-0688
fenders, etc.

A body and chassis alone do not constitute a car; myriad parts are necessary for the construction of a complete automobile. There are therefore factories in countries as far apart as Taiwan and Sweden busy reproducing authentic parts. The list of products ranges from rubber grommets to complete interiors and there is hardly anything that somebody, somewhere does not produce.

Some of these people are manufacturers and some are merely distributors and it is often difficult to ascertain exactly who makes what and where. Hopefully, the following list is accurate. Nevertheless, most of the companies produce comprehensive catalogues that can be purchased for a few dollars. Those which specialize in certain components are noted for such below their address.

Al's Antique Auto Parts
9225 Gilardi Road
Newcastle
CA 95658
USA
Tel. (916) 663-2179
Lights

Autosport Enterprises
932 Marwood Trail
Indianapolis
IN 46340
USA
Tel.

American Antique Auto Parts
3612 W. LA State Drive
Kenner
LA 70065
USA
Tel. (504) 467-1614

Antique Auto Specialties Co
1425 42nd Street
Rock Island
IL 61201
USA
Tel. (309) 794-0168
Sedan top wood kits

Antique Ford Parts
9101-7 East Garvey Avenue
Rosemead
CA 91770
USA
Tel. (818) 288-3131

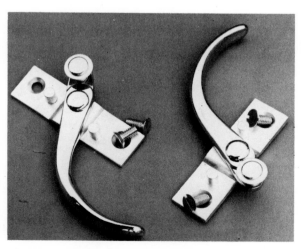

Beautiful chrome plated reproduction door handles are a sample of the huge range of repro parts now available for the Deuce

Dennis Carpenter Reproductions
PO Box 26398
Charlotte
NC 28213
USA
Tel. (704) 786-8139

Bob Drake Reproductions
1819 NW Washington Blvd.
Grants Pass
OR 97526
USA
Tel. (503) 474-0043
Rubber

Bowyer's Auto Service
936 E 2nd Street
Santa Ana
CA 92701
USA
Locking hub caps

Alan Darr Early Ford Parts
124 Canyon View Drive
Longview
WA 98632
USA
Tel. (206) 425-2463

Early Ford Reproductions
168 Western Avenue
Altamont
NY 12009
USA
Tel. (518) 861-5367

Ford Parts Obsolete, Inc.
1320 W. Willow
Long Beach
CA 90810
USA
Tel. (213) 426-9501

JF Firebird's Parts Mart, Inc
2750 S. 14th Street
Kansas City
KS 66103
USA

CL Gilbertson
916 West Mark Street
Winona
Minnesota 55987
USA
Tel. (507) 452-4863
Distributor body

Bill Hirsch
396 Littleton Avenue
Newark
New Jersey 07103
USA
Tel. (201) 642-2404

Joblot Automotive Inc.
98–11 211th Street
Queens Village
Long Island
NY 11429
USA
Tel. (212) 468-8585
Hard parts

LeBaron Bonney Co.
6 Chestnut Street
Amesbury
MA 01913
USA
Tel. (617) 388-3811
Upholstery

Larry's Glass House
5141 Paseo Rico
Yorba Linda
CA 92686
USA
Tel. (714) 779-5223
Glass

McDonald Ford Parts Co
RR3 Box 61
Rockport
IN 47635
USA
Tel. (812) 359-4965

Doug McRae
1922 Fairlawn Road
Topeka
KA 66604
USA
Tel. (913) 273-6581
Fuel pumps

M & S Hydraulics
18930 Couch Market Road
Bend
OR 97701
USA
Tel. (503) 388-4357
Shock absorbers

Mack Products
Box 278
Moberly
MO 65270
USA
Tel. (816) 263-7442
Pick-up bed hardwear

CW Moss
12911-A Malena Drive
Santa Ana
CA 92705
USA
Tel. (714) 771-3811

New Castle Battery Mfg. Co.
PO Box 5040-W
New Castle
PA 16105
USA
Tel. (412) 658-5501
Batteries

Newood Products
PO Box 128
1404 Broadway
Monett
MO 65708
USA
Tel. (417) 235-5872
Cabriolet top rear bow

Obsolete Ford Parts, Inc.
6601 S. Shields Boulevard
Oklahoma City
OK 73149
USA
Tel. (405) 631-3933

Oak Bows
122 Ramsey Avenue
Chambersberg
PA 17201
USA
Tel. (717) 264-2602
Topbows

Rubber Reproductions
9107-8 E. Garvey Avenue
Rosemead
CA 91770
USA
Transmission mounts

Rod Tin Interior Products
PO Box 1809
Chula Vista
CA 92010
USA
Tel. (619) 427-3249
Upholstery

Gene Reese
11111 Ables
Number 10
Dallas
TX 75229
USA
Stainless door latch parts

Rick's Antique Auto Parts
2754 Roe Lane
Kansas City
KS 66103
USA

Rock Valley Antique Auto Parts Ltd
Route 72 & Rothwell Road
Stillman Valley
IL 61084
USA
Tel. (815) 645-2271

Snyder's Antique Auto Parts, Inc.
12925 Woodworth Road
New Springfield
OH 44443
USA
Tel. (216) 549-5313

Standard Auto Parts
928 E. 12th Street
Oakland
CA 94606
USA
Rubber floor mats

Bill Sanders Reproductions
7215 Wheatland Road North
Salem
OR 97303
USA
Tel. (503) 393-1635
Glass

Sacramento Vintage Ford
1504 El Camino Avenue
Sacramento
CA 95815
USA
Tel. (916) 922-3444

The Early Ford Store
2141 W. Main Street
Springfield
OH 45504
USA
Tel. (513) 325-2408

The V8 Shop
21917 Aurora Road
Bedford Heights
Ohio 44146
USA
Tel. (216) 587-1664
Running boards

The Wood 'n' Car
2667 E. 28th Street
Signal Hill
CA 90806
USA
Tel. (213) 427-7388
replacement wood

Total Performance
406 S. Orchard Street Rt. 5
Wallingford
CT 06492
USA
Tel. (203) 265-5667

Vintique, Inc
402 W. Chapman
Orange
CA 92666
USA

Varco Manufacturing Co.
Route 9
Box 74
Midwest City
OK 73110
USA
Tel. (405) 732-1637
Trunks and luggage racks

Walker Radiator
694 Marshall Avenue
Memphis
TN 38103
USA
Tel. (901) 527-4605
Radiators

Wellbaum
1752 Mentone Blvd.
Mentone
CA 923594
USA
Tel. (714) 794-6000
Radiators

Roy Fjastad Jr of the Deuce Factory checks one of the rails which have undergone continuous development and refinement until they are near perfect. So far the Deuce Factory have sold at least 1300 sets

5 Where are they now?

Ford built less than 400,000 1932 Fords in the four years the model was in production. Some of them got crashed on the road; some of them got smashed on the race tracks; some of them disappeared in scrap metal drives; and some of them just plain rusted away, but some of them survive.

Considering the car was not a classic in its day, it was just another ol' Ford, surprisingly many of them survive. Even in Europe, where the rain and the rust rot everything except the stainless steel, there are new 'finds' almost weekly. Sadly, many of these cars are tucked away in the hands of keepers, people who will not sell on account of their value or the fact that one day they'll get around to restoring it. Well, they usually never do get around to it and before you know it the chickens are in, so are the mice, so are weeds and so's the rot.

Thankfully, Henry built 'em good 'n' strong back then and while lots are lost there are still some out there. From Arizona to Australia, from Scotland to the Canary Islands we've found evidence of their existence. Since the photographs were taken some of the cars have either been rodded or restored, but some of them, we know, are still right where we found them.

ABOVE *Racing at the dry lakes could be dangerous. Only the guy out front could see, everybody else was clouded in fine white alkali dust. However, the driver of this Roadster was killed at Muroc around 1940 when he collided with another car as they were warming up early in the morning. They shouldn't have been doing that*

BELOW *The hammer and torch happy hop-up, chop-up set probably went too far with their modifications. That is not the case with cars which were relegated to the jalopy and stock car races of the postwar period. Vic Ferriday wrecked this three-window coupé when he rolled it at a British stock car race in the late-fifties*

ABOVE AND RIGHT ABOVE *Photographer Mike Key pulled a 14.9 Tudor sedan out of ramshackle shed in Beccles, Norfolk, in 1972. Thankfully it was all there, almost, and not too far gone but the price was a little steep at £80.*

Key's B was to become one of England's first rodded Fords when Mike replaced the four-pot with a 327 ci Chevy and Turbo 350 gearbox. The leaf sprung live axle was replaced with Jaguar S type independent rear suspension and the original beam front axle was swapped for a dropped SuperBell. The old drum brakes were discarded in favour of Jaguar Mk 10 discs and the steering was swapped for a narrowed BMC 1800 rack and pinion unit.

The car has been on the road for over 10 years now and Mike continues to use it even though he has another street rod and two other projects

RIGHT *Call that a Deuce? It looks more like a wreck. This is in fact the rusted hulk of an English 1934 Fourteen Fordor which Mike Key has as his next project. Believe it or not he intends to convert what is left into a model that never was — an English Phaeton*

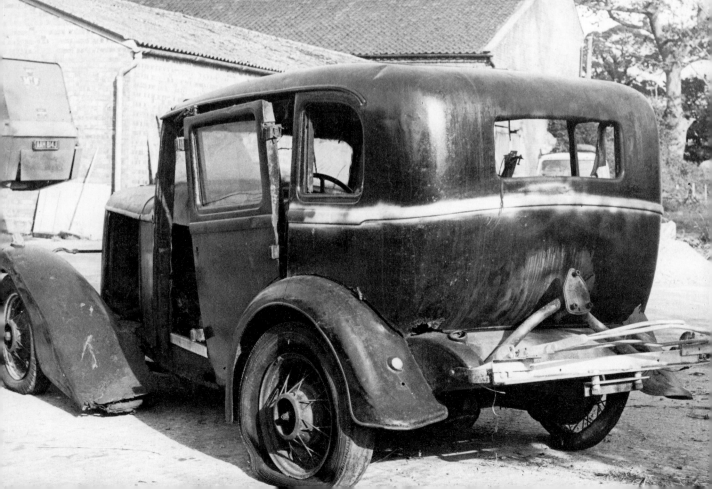

LEFT ABOVE *Though production was small, only around 2500 vehicles in total, the dry Australian outback has yielded many restorable relics like this Phaeton. Most of them were shipped to America in the early sixties as was this one purchased by Dick Scritchfield. Yes, it's the same car pictured on page 140 before Scritch rodded it. I don't think the cow came with it*

LEFT *Perhaps the most interesting find recently was this raggedy Cabriolet found on the island of Gran Canaria. As far as we know this Model B is still there as are the two Models Ys and the various other cars surrounding it*

ABOVE *Australian Phaetons like this fetched a $100 at most in the sixties and that was probably a good price then. However, seeing that hot rodded coupé in the background makes one wonder if this one ever made it back to the homeland. Incidentally, the engine damper on the firewall would indicate that this had been a four cylinder Model B*

These empty shells may look totally unrestorable to some of you but
the repro parts industry can virtually provide you with anything and
everything necessary to make a 'new' Deuce. In fact both the 3-window
above and the Vicky below are probably rebuilt by now

It's still possible to find old '32s in junk yards throughout the United States. Here are just four photographs to illustrate that fact. Pick carefully, though, for a lot of heartache and cash can flow before you would have any of these running, either as original or rodded cars

Several railroad companies, including one in Argentina, used Ford sedans fitted with special flanged rubber wheels to patrol their tracks. This fenderless Fordor was operated by the Detroit, Toledo & Ironton railroad which at one time was owned by Ford

Edsel Ford was, and is, a much maligned man. In 1919, aged 25, his father made him president of the Ford Motor Co. and then virtually ignored him and ran the company his way. Yet Edsel was responsible for many good things – he did all the essential things Henry refused to do amongst which were securing the strong future of Ford overseas and holding the company during several crisis periods in the 1930s. He also enjoyed his cars, something Henry didn't really.

Here's his '32 boat tail speedster, one of a line of hot rods he built, and not the first. It uses a V8, aluminium body and Model B grille. Not much more is known. Neat isn't it?

Index